F

I·

The Kennedy Restoration

by

T.P. O'Mahony

BLACKWATER PRESS

Editor: Rachel O'Connor

Design & Layout: Teresa Burke

© 1993 Blackwater Press, Airton Road, Tallaght, Dublin 24

Produced in Ireland by Blackwater Press

ISBN 0 86121 458 7

Contents

Acknowledgements

I am indebted to a lot of people for their help and encouragement in the writing of this book, beginning with Charles Daly, Director of the JFK Memorial Library in Boston.

My old friend, Father Joseph O'Hare, President of Fordham University, extended hospitality and facilities to me on two occasions. Ms Dorothy Marinucci and Mrs Lena Giordano of the President's Office were also very helpful, as was Mrs Theresa McGinn of Duane Library on the campus.

Jim Franklin of *The Boston Globe* and Ben Scott Jr in Washington, DC, did invaluable research for me.

Mr Theodore C. Sorensen was kind enough to allow me to interview him in New York, and Professors Arthur M. Schlesinger Jr and John Kenneth Galbraith were good enough to reply to my written quetions.

I had the pleasure of meeting Mr Benjamin C. Bradlee of *The Washington Post* in Dublin, and he was generous later in dealing with correspondence. So also was Mr Dave Powers, now with the JFK Memorial Library.

Ms Carol Leggett of *The Washington Post* also went to some considerable trouble to dig out some background material for me.

My deepest gratitude, however, is reserved for two of Robert F. Kennedy's daughters – Kathleen Townsend and Kerry Cuomo. Meeting them was the highlight of my visits to the USA. Had they not consented to my request for interviews, this book would not have been written.

Here at home, my thanks are also due to Nick Coffey of RTE and Michael Colley, both of whom put their impressive collections of works on the Kennedys at my disposal.

Mr John O'Connor of Blackwater Press was supportive from the outset, and Ms Rachel O'Connor was a diligent editor.

My wife, Elizabeth, once again coped with equanimity with the condition known as "author's tantrums".

The literature on the Kennedys since 1960 is vast. The publications I have found most useful and on which I have relied are listed in the Bibliography.

Preface

Like President William Jefferson Clinton, to me John Fitzgerald Kennedy has always been one of my heroes.

I saw JFK twice. This happened during his Irish visit in June 1963 – a visit which brought him to Cork city for a couple of hours. At the time I was 24 – and very much a Kennedy fan.

I had watched the swings and roundabouts of the 1960 campaign and I had greeted his victory over Richard Nixon with something approximate to rapture.

Lots of pride also – after all, wasn't there now a man in The White House who was both Irish and Catholic?

It didn't seem likely for a time. And in the end, it was so close. In fact, Kennedy's margin of victory was the smallest ever in a US Presidential contest.

More people voted in the 1960 election than in any before it, but it wasn't a Kennedy landslide – far from it. He won by the slimmest of margins – two-tenths of a per cent of the total.

Some say that didn't cramp his style. But it did impose real limits on what he could do.

As for style, he bounced into The White House with a verve and an energy the USA hadn't seen since Theodore Roosevelt, and a cultured outlook that rivalled Thomas Jefferson's.

He was the youngest President in American history, and young people responded to his enthusiasm and his wit. They felt inspired and challenged by him.

Life in Washington changed, and America's view of itself changed along with it.

And it wasn't just the young in America who shared in his vision. For all those of us throughout the West who were young then, it seemed that Kennedy opened up a new frontier, and gave hope a new meaning.

We thought Kennedy was special.

And now here he was in Ireland.

We were given time off from work – I was a textile fitter in Sunbeam – to see the motorcade as the President made his way from Collins Barracks to the City Hall.

There the Freedom of the City would be conferred on him.

I made my way in a state of some excitement to St Patrick's Bridge to await the motorcade.

As it passed, I was struck by how tanned President Kennedy looked, and how brightly white his teeth were.

He smiled and waved, and it was hard to imagine that one so youthful-looking could be President of the United States of America, remembering as I did the grey and avuncular Eisenhower years.

The streets were crowded, every vantage point occupied. The city was in festive mood, its people out to welcome home one of their own.

That's how JFK was perceived.

And we had just a fleeting moment of his presence, a quick glimpse, as he went past in an open limousine.

Months later when the awful news from Dallas came through, I would wonder if that was the same car as the one in Dealey Plaza.

All I knew was that the US Secret Service had flown the car into Ireland in advance of the Presidential visit. So perhaps it was the same car that Bill Greer drove along Houston Street and around the acute left-hand corner into Elm Street, passing in front of the Texas Book Depository.

That June day in Cork, however, JFK looked young and vibrant enough to live forever: nobody foresaw the horror that was just five months down the road.

When the motorcade crossed the bridge some of us elbowed our way through the crowd and ran down Merchant's Quay, taking a short-cut to the City Hall in order to get a second glimpse.

The motorcade had to proceed down through the crowds on Patrick Street, around into the Grand Parade, and down the South Mall before reaching the City Hall.

We had plenty of time to spare, but we finished up a good distance from the City Hall, the crowds being deeper now.

Inside, the Lord Mayor, Alderman Sean Casey, and the members of Cork Corporation were waiting in their scarlet robes to meet the President.

Kennedy was standing up in the limo as it came down the Mall, swung over Brian Boru Bridge and halted at the front steps of the City Hall.

For a brief moment he turned and waved – and then he was gone from view.

In making JFK a freeman of Cork, the Lord Mayor would say in tribute: "You stand for the weak against the strong, for right against might."

We thought that was appropriate. We thought that was fitting. We just thought it was right.

The next day in Shannon, before he departed on board Air Force One, he talked of coming back.

It was never to be.

The memories of that day in Cork – a dull June day – have lingered, poignancy sharpening their edges.

Back in 1960 we didn't think he could win the contest against Richard Nixon for The White House. The pundits said the "Catholic factor" would tell against him.

We all worried about that.

Ever since 1928 – when Alfred Smith, the first significant Irish Catholic candidate to run for The White House – it was deemed to be an insurmountable obstacle.

Smith was born and raised on New York's lower East Side by emigrant parents, and when he ran for President the issue had become not so much Irish as Catholic.

In a country where there was a clear separation between Church and State, the religious issue loomed large during his campaign, especially when the candidate was called upon to deal with wild rumours that Pope Pius XI had his bags packed and was ready to move to Washington.

Among other ridiculous rumours circulated – and apparently believed – was one suggesting that a special tunnel would be built from The White House to the Vatican. Not surprisingly, Smith's opponent Herbert Hoover won 40 States.

In 1960 the religious issue surfaced again, but JFK was ready for it.

His famous defence of his faith and of the separation of Church and State occurred on 12 September 1960, in Houston, Texas, during his campaign against Nixon.

And it happened in front of a largely unsympathetic and partly hostile audience.

Kennedy, alone on the rostrum (a master public relations stroke), fielded all the questions with masterful ease, and carried the day.

"I am not the Catholic candidate for President," he told a group of Protestant ministers. "I am the Democratic Party's candidate who happens to be Catholic. I do not speak for my Church on public matters and the Church does not speak for me."

With that performance, Kennedy laid to rest for ever the prejudice against Irish Catholics holding the highest office in the United States of America.

In my circle of friends, we all felt his Presidency marked a new beginning – though we had no idea where that might lead.

In the years from 1960 to 1963, we were reminded almost daily of the threatening presence of the Cold War.

It seemed to people like me, born in 1939, as a continuation of the struggle between the forces of darkness and light.

The defeat of the Nazis and the collapse in ruins of the Third Reich – and the subsequent emergence of Communist empires in the Soviet bloc and in China – had set the scene for my generation.

By the time of the Korean War (1950-53), I was at that impressionable age where the world is seen – like a John Wayne movie – as peopled by "good guys" and "bad guys".

We entertained few doubts about who was who in the Korean conflict.

When the Armistice came in July 1953, a name associated with the Cold War became emblazoned on my mind for ever – Panmunjom.

The Korean War was a significant event in the evolution of the Cold War, and in the USA it gave an impetus to the Red Scare and the rise of McCarthyism.

We saw it, as the Kennedy family did, along with thousands of other American Catholic families, in simple terms.

The Americans and their allies had won in Korea. Communist aggression and expansionism had been thwarted. And whatever was necessary to curb further Communist expansionist moves – whether of the Chinese or Soviet variety – was good.

So we cheered the election of the first Catholic President in 1960 – since to be Catholic, in our eyes, was to be anti-Communist.

This was very much the background against which we saw and evaluated the Bay of Pigs fiasco of April 1961, and the far more serious confrontation that has passed into the history books – the Cuban Missile Crisis.

I can still conjure up the tension and uncertainty of those dark days in October 1962 when the world seemed on the threshold of nuclear conflict.

Our hero, JFK, faced down the bad guy, Nikita Khrushchev – and the world was a safer place.

At the time of JFK's Irish visit, there was already talk of a second term in The White House.

Even as we watched him in Cork, those around Kennedy – men whose names (Sorensen, O'Brien, O'Donnell, Powers and Schlesinger) would become very well known to me – were already planning electoral strategies for 1964.

As he left our shores in June 1963 a blood-rimmed tragedy lay ahead: how horror-struck and unbelieving we would have been had we had some foreknowledge of it.

The thought that JFK would not see the year out would have left us dumbstruck.

Dark and demonic forces – active in the mind of one man or several – would bring down a bloody curtain on the JFK Presidency five months later in Texas.

November 22nd 1963 – the awful day – our hero, head shattered, lay dead under the clear, blue skies of the Lone Star State.

As he was shattered in body, so were we – psychologically.

Robert – who had revived our hopes and fashioned new promises – would be blown away in Los Angeles in 1968.

And Teddy – to whom the ideals of Camelot had passed – would self-destruct, electorally-speaking, on a small island called Chappaquiddick a year later.

The hope now rests with their children, and I believe it is not an ill-founded hope.

This book is about all of them – a book that looks forward as well as back, perhaps even more so.

"I hope this isn't another who-shot-Kennedy book," said my friend, Kevin Healy, Head of Radio Programming at RTE, when he learned I had embarked on a Kennedy project.

"No," I assured him. "It is not."

It is, of course, the story of a man who is to me – as he is to President Clinton – a hero.

But it is much more than that.

It is the story also of the younger Kennedys – of four in particular, from whose ranks may yet emerge the successor to William Jefferson Clinton.

Above all, it is a story of the politics of hope and the promise of renewal, the story – on-going – of the politics of Camelot.

T.P. O'Mahony
Cork, New York and Washington 1991-1993

1

An End and a Beginning

Was it three shots or four? Or, as some witnesses claimed, as many as six.

A President dies.

John Fitzgerald Kennedy. Aged 46.

That was Dallas, Texas, in November 1963.

Switch to Los Angeles in June 1968. The kitchens of the Ambassador Hotel to be precise.

A Presidential candidate is being ushered through – the hot favourite for The White House as the protest movement against the Vietnam War hots up.

Robert Francis Kennedy is on the glory trail.

More shots. Another shattered body. Blood on the floor.

One gun or two?

A second conspiracy?

It's the end of the RFK chapter.

The scene moves on a year, this time to an island off Cape Cod in Massachusetts. The island is called Chappaquiddick.

Sometime after midnight in July 1969 an Oldsmobile, driven by a US Senator, goes off a narrow wooden bridge into Dike Pond.

As the car sinks, the Senator manages to get out and swims to safety.

But a young girl, trapped inside the submerged vehicle, drowns.

Her name is Mary Jo Kopechne.

End of the Edward Moore Kennedy chapter.

Is this the end of the Kennedy dynasty as well, a dynasty wiped out by a triple disaster?

That question continues to shimmer and dance on the surface of American politics.

Or is there more to come? A new chapter in American political history?

Can another Kennedy pick up the torch first lit by JFK and carry it all the way back to The White House?

President William Jefferson Clinton is now blocking the way, and seems set to block it for another seven years.

He is only 44, the third youngest president ever, other than JFK – who was his hero.

Yet he has also opened the way, for the manner and style of his victory – like the manner and style of the man himself – is unmistakably Kennedyesque.

And that is no accident.

Two photographs testify to this is an especial way.

The first is that of a youth named Bill Clinton shaking hands with JFK in 1963. It is hugely symbolic.

The second, taken on 19 January 1993 – the eve of the Inauguration – shows President-elect Clinton placing a flower on the grave of JFK in Arlington Cemetery.

So Clinton is as much a conduit as an obstacle, a link as much as a loop – he represents a promise more than a threat of rupture or discontinuity. A Democrat is back in The White House, a Democratic President who even looks like, and reminds people of JFK.

And such is the Kennedyesque image and flavour of the Clinton Presidency, that new interest in what the Kennedys – and JFK in particular – stood for and hoped to achieve has been rekindled.

From the moment when the film commemorating the two slain Kennedy brothers was shown at the Democratic Convention in New York in 1992, the tone of the Clinton campaign and Presidency was set.

The torch symbolising commitment to certain ideals and to enlightened change had been picked up by the man from Arkansas, who as a youth idolised JFK.

Will it – via Clinton – be passed on to another Kennedy?

This much is certain: the Clinton victory and the hope it has engendered demonstrates the extent to which the Kennedy mystique endures.

What seemed impossible before November 1992 is now possible again – another Kennedy Presidency.

It may never happen, but the restoration to power of the Democrats, after 13 years in the wilderness, inevitably brings in its train the restoration of the Kennedy image and presence.

There is much in what I have just said that can – and will – be argued over. In the tumultuous, treacherous and sometimes violent world of American politics, attempting to predict who will be swearing the Oath of Office on the steps of the Capitol building on 20 January 2001 is a hazardous business indeed. A fool's game.

But one does not risk being consigned to the company of fools by acknowledging what is now there for all to see: the restoration of JFK's political reputation.

Here is how Ben Bradlee, Vice-President-at-large of *The Washington Post*, described it to me in December 1992: "Kennedy's reputation stands amazingly high today given all the unpleasant revelations about his private life. It's really quite amazing."

As for the prospect of another Kennedy making it to The White House, here is what Arthur Schlesinger Jr, former aide to JFK, told me: "If the rhythm of our politics holds, Bill Clinton's victory should usher in 15-20 years of progressive government in the United States. And the next generation of Kennedys includes some very promising young men and women."

It is a prospect that tantalises the imagination, all the more so now because of the changes in the political topography which the Clinton Presidency is forging.

Where those changes are leading is anyone's guess.

Perhaps even a return to Camelot – who knows?

2

America's Royal Family

In the eyes of the world, the Americans have everything – wealth, prosperity, natural resources in abundance, and endless opportunities for self-betterment.

America is also now, in the aftermath of the collapse of Soviet Communism, the only super-power on the planet.

But what the Americans do not have is a history – I mean, not a real history.

They have, in material terms, the most successful nation ever seen on the face of the earth.

They have the most technologically advanced industrial civilisation – a technology which enabled them to put a man on the Moon.

The United States is a technocracy which has bred seemingly endless success.

And millions of Irish people have shared in that success. In fact, of the 250 million Americans at present in 51 States of the Union, some 44 million claim Irish descent or Irish connections.

Even now, in the midst of a recession, America remains the mecca for emigrants not just from Ireland, but from dozens of other countries.

America is still the land of hopes and dreams, still the place where anything and everything is possible. It is still – at least in the popular imagination – the one place where anyone can go from rags to riches.

OK – things are not so hot there today. The economy, as Bill Clinton is finding out, is in trouble. The national debt is horrendous, and a lot of people are out of work.

Walking through sections of New York and other great cities on the American continent brings this home to you.

Shops and stores closed; "For Sale" or "To Let" signs everywhere. Out in the boondocks, things are even worse.

But side by side with this, the capacity for recovery and the potential for growth are enormous.

America is still a very rich place; Americans are still, in many ways, a very rich people.

But they lack a history. Or, in the words of Winston Churchill, Americans lack a sense of history.

The title of a fascinating 1972 book by William Irwin Thompson – *At The Edge of History* – is apposite.

It could serve in 1993 as a subtitle for AMERICA INC.

This lack of history shows. "Today," says historian Arthur Schlesinger, "for all the preservation of landmarks and the showbiz of bicentennials, we have become, so far as interest and knowledge are concerned, an essentially historyless people."

It shows in the awe which Americans display in cities like Athens, Rome, Istanbul and Jerusalem.

It even shows at places like Newgrange in County Meath.

These are all places where history reaches back to the beginnings of Western Civilisation, and even beyond that.

By contrast, the United States of America is a young nation – not much more than 200 years old.

If there is a native American history older than that, then it belongs to the true, native Americans, the dispossessed tribes of the Sioux, the Apache, the Cheyenne and the Cherokee – the "red Indians", as we used to call them in my school days.

The destruction of these Indian tribes, and the confiscation of their ancient lands, their hunting grounds, was the bloody prelude to the birth of the modern American nation, that and the successful War of Independence waged against the British.

Lacking a history has given the Americans an inordinate reverence for the past.

It has also created an inordinate veneration for the US Constitution – and a longing for king-like if not God-like leaders.

Hence the very special position today of the Presidency, and the unreal hopes and expectations vested in the holder of that most powerful of all secular offices.

The man – thus far it has always been a man – who is President becomes a repository for the hopes and dreams of a nation.

Such a man finds himself elevated to a status which is as close to monarchical as a Republic will allow.

To all intents and purposes, the President is a king and his family a royal family.

This is quintessentially so in the case of the Kennedys.

They, more than any other family associated with The White House, are America's Royal Family.

Wealth, glamour, success – and the capture of the ultimate prize, The White House itself – have all contributed to this.

Add in elements which find parallels in the Greek tragedies of Aeschylus, Sophocles and Euripides and you have a family of mythic proportions.

The Kennedys are central to the modern American myth; indeed, they have helped to shape and sustain that myth, particularly in the person of JFK.

Big, rich, good-looking families always beguile in the States; they are the embodiment of the American Dream.

And no family embodies it more totally and more romantically than the Kennedys.

The variety of their activities, the magnitude of their success, their sumptuous settings and lifestyles – it is the stuff of Hollywood.

At the head of the family was a tough, shrewd, outspoken father. Joseph Kennedy was nobody's fool. He wielded enormous power in financial and business circles, he had links with Hollywood and with some of its most glamourous ladies. And he had served in the Administration of Franklin Delano Roosevelt, most notably as Ambassador to Britain 1937-40.

The matriarch was Rose, a lovely woman, the daughter of a storied Mayor of Boston – stylish, deeply religious, and with a strong belief in committing her family to public service. She was, in many ways, the ideal mother.

The family she and Joseph bred and reared consisted of four boys and five girls who were soon to know all about the world of politics.

Politics and the power that came with it dominated everything.

Politics was both challenge and opportunity, and inevitably the Kennedy boys were drawn towards it, like needles to a magnet. Its pull proved irresistible. And early tragedies in the family – the death of Joe Jr and of Kathleen – were not allowed to deflect energies from the attainment of Joseph Kennedy's ultimate goal: the Presidency of the United States for one of his sons.

It might have been Joe Jr had he survived the war. But the prize was to fall to Jack.

And journalists who covered the 1960 campaign and the 1961–63 Presidency still insist there has been nothing quite like it since.

"It is hard today to conjure up the excitement that most journalists felt covering JFK," wrote Philip B. Kunhardt Jr, of *Life* magazine. "It was a different time then, with a seemingly naive set of rules."

Hugh Sidey, White House correspondent for *Time* magazine and considered Kennedy's favourite reporter, recalls what it was like: "There was the whiff of romance and adventure – James Bond come alive with lovely parties and beautiful women and men and laughter and naughtiness – and a cause that was as noble as any ever embraced by a politician.

"When covering Kennedy there was always the unexpected, the sudden surge of sheer joy at hearing his eloquence, the belly-laugh from his humour, the beauty of the settings that his family money could buy.

"He told me his favourite book was *Melbourne,* and the picture of young English royalty that emerges from those pages is the pattern for his life – honour and duty pursued with joy and indulgence."

Along with the constant intellectual ferment, Sidey found the Kennedy years filled with regal imagery and even yearnings.

"Kennedy wanted to ride with the gods, and I believe he did a bit."

Critics maintain this is part of the Kennedy myth, at the centre of which was the notion that the Kennedys were superior, the natural leaders of America, a dynasty born to rule.

But the problem is really an American myth, rooted in the Constitution and the public perception of the Presidency.

In short, Americans want their presidents to be kings.

But kings are expected to wield king-like powers. And that's where the problems really begin.

Playwright Arthur Miller, who understands the American psyche better than most, recognised this when he observed that: "The White House is our one approximation of a Royal Court."

So did the *Daily Mail's* Dermot Purgavie when he said: "The Americans want a big reassuring presence in The White House, an impossible symbol of America's Number One-ness."

As novelist and philosopher Umberto Eco put it: "Modern Americans like their reality to be larger-than-life or realer than real."

It's even worse than that, because the expectations associated with the Presidency are not confined to Americans.

It was the novelist and critic Anthony Burgess who once said that "the whole world has become Americanised". And to the extent that this is true beyond, say, the mere global availability of Coca-Cola, the rest of us share these unreal and unrealisable expectations.

But if The White House is the nearest America has come to having a royal court, then the Kennedys are its nearest approximation to a royal family.

That's why "Camelot" seemed so appropriate.

And it's also why America's fascination – if not love affair – with the Kennedys continues.

Some critics maintain that John Kennedy and his beautiful wife, Jacqueline, started it all off.

"Both Jack and Jackie had an enormous sense of their own presence," says historian Doris Kearns Goodwin. "It was almost as if they both created this image of this handsome couple."

That's only partly true, for the image was really America's creation.

The Kennedys fulfilled some psychic longing.

They were transformed into not just America's First Family, but into its Royal Family.

If, in the context of a Republic, there is a contradiction here, then its seeds lie in the American Constitution.

John Kennedy caught the imagination of the world more than any other modern leader.

The image of youthfulness, intelligence and energy – and the idealism and hope associated with the JFK Administration – conjured up a past age.

Camelot became the metaphor.

And, for good or ill, the metaphor endures.

Nothing can change the fact that those who hope for another Kennedy Presidency hope for a return to Camelot.

3

Camelot – Myth or Reality

Some say their youthfulness was the key. Others talk about the glamour, the excitement and the romance.

In any evocation of the Kennedy Years there has to be an acknowledgement that, for many, they meant a new beginning, a new age of hope and promise.

The poet Robert Frost (chosen by Kennedy to read a poem at the Inauguration) summed it up in two lines in a poem called "The Gift Outright" which he delivered that cold January day in 1961:

A golden age of poetry and power
Of which this noonday's the beginning hour.

In those early, heady days, as a new Administration took over in Washington, there was no talk of Camelot.

That came later, after one of America's darkest hours.

But it was there from the beginning, implicit in the style of the new Administration. And in its objectives as well.

The contrast with the drab, bleak Eisenhower Years could hardly have been more pronounced.

Camelot was a suitable metaphor for the Kennedy Years.

The very name conjures up visions of chivalry and magic, romance and courage, daring and adventure.

Back in the mists of time – halfway between history and myth – there came a man to lead his people to glory – King Arthur.

Under the guidance of Merlin, he drew the mighty sword Excalibur from a stone and won the Crown.

The magical Arthurian legend has gripped the imagination of successive generations.

In our Celtic lore (which Kennedy would have known) it is unmatched save for the legend of Cuchulainn. Such is the power of the legend.

It so happened – in one of those historical coincidences – that a few weeks before Robert Frost recited his poem at the Inauguration, Alan Jay Lerner's musical *Camelot*, starring Richard Burton and Julie Andrews, opened at the Majestic Theatre in New York.

Its recreation of the legendary court of King Arthur popularised the stirring tale among Americans, and it was perhaps just a matter of time before the myth-makers attached the name of Camelot to Washington and to the Kennedy White House in particular.

Jackie became Queen Guinevere, and the inner circle of decision-makers were likened to the Knights of the Round Table.

This inner circle, once described as "the best and the brightest" of their generation, were afterwards berated – especially for the tragedy of Vietnam.

But that was later.

1961, the advent of Kennedy to the Presidency, seemed to mark a break with the past.

Here he was at 43, the leader of the most powerful nation on earth. Elsewhere the world seemed to be in the hands of a gerontocracy.

Khrushchev held power in Moscow; Harold Macmillan was Prime Minister in London; Chairman Mao Tse-tung was in supreme control in Peking.

Then there was Nehru in India, Charles de Gaulle in France, Adenhauer in Germany, Franco in Spain, Salazer in Portugal and in Dublin, Eamon de Valera was President.

All of them had been born in the nineteenth century; all were children of the Victorian Age.

The contrast with the Kennedy Age could not have been sharper.

And age was the clue.

Among leaders who had known the Boer War, World War I, the Bolshevik Revolution, the Great Depression, and were old enough to have known Pope Leo XIII or Queen Victoria, he stood out because of his youthfulness. "Suddenly the world's most powerful country was being run by a young, good-looking man with a younger and very beautiful wife and two small children, a man who liked to go sailing and play touch football, a man who grinned a lot," wrote journalist John Graham.

"He seemed to be a new type of politician and he appealed to the new generations of Americans and Europeans who had emerged in the Fifties.

"While Kennedy plotted his path to The White House, economic recovery and prosperity throughout the western world had created the first teenagers. James Dean rose like a comet with *East of Eden*, *Rebel Without a Cause* and *Giant*. Elvis Presley and rock 'n' roll were outraging one generation and thrilling the next. Posters of Marilyn Monroe, Brigitte Bardot and Jayne Mansfield unashamedly adorned millions of bedroom walls.

"Youth was flexing the muscles of independence and terrorising its parents with the sound of motorbikes. Jack Kerouac, spokesman for the Beat Generation, wrote *On The Road*. Towards the end of the Kennedy Presidency even The Beatles had arrived . . . "

All of these stars represented a youthful world which Kennedy knew well, a world he could relate to.

It was a world that would soon thrill to the first of the James Bond movies – and Kennedy, like millions of others, was already a fan of Ian Fleming's rakish spy/playboy/hero.

Of Kennedy it could never be said, as it might have been of Eisenhower, that he had to grapple with a generation gap.

That gave him an immediate appeal, making it possible for young people to identify with him in a way that had never existed before in American politics.

With his Hollywood good looks and athleticism, he was the first movie-star President.

And that's why Kennedy was able to speak directly to youth, offering the rebels a cause.

"We stand today on the edge of a New Frontier . . . . I am asking each of you to be pioneers on that New Frontier."

He asked them to join him in a mighty task, no less than the "preservation of civilisation".

He amplified that task in his Inaugural Address, now regarded as the best this century and the one that President Clinton most wanted to match.

Its inspiring rhetoric has lost none of its force:

"Let the word go forth from this time and place, to friend and foe alike, that the torch has passed to a new generation of Americans – born in this century . . .

"Let every nation know, whether it wishes us well or ill, that we shall pay any price, bear any burden, meet any hardship, support any foe to assure the survival and the success of liberty . . .

"Let us never negotiate out of fear. But let us never fear to negotiate . . .

"And so, my fellow Americans: ask not what your country can do for you – ask what you can do for your country . . . "

Kennedy wanted a better, newer world; a world from which the common enemies of man – tyranny, poverty, disease and war – were banished.

Today it is fashionable in some quarters to accuse him and his brothers of hubris – or to say that Camelot was destroyed by vaunting ambition and an ill-founded notion of superiority.

He believed that under his guidance America and the world could enter a New Age.

Hugh Sidey was a man who knew him well, better than most commentators. Apart from the intellectual ferment, Sidey found the Kennedy Years filled with an aura of romance.

At the end, days after the shots in Dallas, Sidey framed the question that, like the shots, has echoed down the years: "What will the historians write of John F. Kennedy, President? Was his term of office too short for him ever to receive the mantle of greatness? I do not know. But it is my belief that when he is viewed from that distance which scholars deem appropriate, John F. Kennedy will be high on the horizon of history."

And so it has come to pass.

> *Grant to us Life that though the man be gone*
> *The promise of his spirit be fulfilled.*

These lines were penned by John Masefield, the British Poet Laureate. And the passage of time has not dimmed their relevance or distorted their force.

Promise was the key concept associated with the Camelot legend.

It remains the key concept of the Kennedy Presidency.

Kennedy was image conscious. No president before or since had shown such a keen interest in, or knowledge of, the workings of the news media.

And he understood the power of myth.

He was also ambitious – and even ruthless in his pursuit of power.

What can never be said against him is that he wanted power for his own sake. He wanted power so that he could change things, make the world a better, safer, more caring and humanising place. And that is no mean or petty agenda.

He had a vision that was noble – and that in itself justifies the Camelot imagery.

Adlai Stevenson, his one-time opponent, said it better than most: "John F. Kennedy was so contemporary a man – so involved in our world, so immersed in our times, so responsive to its challenges, so intense a participant in the great events and decisions of our day – that he seemed the very symbol of the vitality and exuberance that is the essence of life itself."

4

The Irish Connection

The two houses are worlds apart – in more senses than one. The first, a very small and humble place, stands in the countryside of County Wexford in the south-east of Ireland.

The other stands in splendour on Pennsylvania Avenue in Washington DC.

The single-storey house in Wexford is located on the side of a narrow, winding road (little more than a boreen) about four miles outside New Ross.

It is tiny by today's standards – it would fit comfortably into the living-room of a modest semi-detached. These days the roof is almost entirely covered in ivy. And bushes all but obscure the small sign which is meant to identify the location of the house for the visitor.

The Kennedy ancestral homestead at Dunganstown is not easy to find. And, once found, it is not much to look at. But then for a Wexford family like the Kennedys in the mid-nineteenth century there was not going to be much more.

Presumably that's why Patrick Joseph Kennedy left New Ross in October 1848 for the hazardous crossing to Boston on board the *Washington Irving*, a journey that took 40 days.

A record of the ship's manifest is stored with thousands of others in The Kennedy Centre at North Quay in New Ross.

In September 1992, the centre – supported by The Kennedy Trust whose directors include Mary Ann Ryan, a cousin of the late President – was formally opened by President Mary Robinson.

To her fell the honour of keying in the details of Kennedy's departure on the computer data base at the centre.

There is a certain irony here which would not be lost on JFK. All the ships' manifests now stored in New Ross, were rescued from the US Government's Archives – just as they were about to be shredded to make way for the papers of former President Richard Nixon.

They were retrieved by genealogist, Dr Ira Glazier of Philadelphia, who holds a doctorate from Harvard University. In time it will be possible to access this data through a sophisticated computer system at Ellis Island.

The beginnings of the American dimension of the Kennedy story lay in this data.

But what of the Irish dimension?

What did Ireland contribute to the formation of the Kennedys, particularly the formation of Jack and Bobby?

The Kennedys were very proud of their origins, very proud of their Irishness.

This was demonstrated in no uncertain terms in 1963 when President Kennedy paid a three-day visit to the country of his ancestors.

And again later when other family members came to the green shores of Erin.

On 2 March 1970, Senator Edward Kennedy paid a visit to New Ross, to visit the ancestral home and the John F. Kennedy Arboretum, which covers 252 hectares on the southern slopes of Slieve Coilte.

Journalist Des Nix, now with *The Sunday Press*, remembers the visit for two reasons.

"Ted Kennedy's helicopter landed in a field on the outskirts of the town and, on the way, the car in which he was travelling struck a metal fitting protruding from the ground in the centre of the gateway with such force that the boot of the car flew open with a loud bang.

"It sounded like a gunshot and the Senator went white. He got the fright of his life . . . "

Later, at the end of his visit, the Senator greeted a crowd which had gathered in the centre of New Ross.

Possibly with the negative fall-out from Chappaquiddick – which had happened less than a year before – on his mind, he hollered: "Do you still love the Kennedys?"

The headline in *The Irish Press* the following morning carried the reply – NEW ROSS STILL LOVES THE KENNEDYS.

No story better illustrates the affection which the Irish feel for the Kennedys than the one about The Dubliners.

It happened in Boston, a couple of years after the death of President Kennedy.

The Dubliners were doing an American tour and at a reception before a concert in Boston, they were introduced to Senator Robert Kennedy and members of his entourage.

When it came to Barney McKenna's turn, the bearded and genial musician shook the former Attorney General's hand, and simply said: "Very sorry about the brother."

It was all there: concern, sympathy, empathy, warmth and fellow-feeling.

This was also demonstrated in June 1976, when the widow of the murdered President came to Ireland for a holiday, with her two children, John Jr and Caroline.

Jackie Kennedy received a tremendous welcome.

"I am just happy to be here in this land my husband loved so much, with his children. For them I think it is a little bit like coming home," she told the crowd of well-wishers at Shannon Airport.

John Kennedy himself, of course, had experienced at first hand the esteem in which he was held during his three-day visit to Ireland in June 1963.

On the flight from Berlin to Dublin he recalled his previous visit to Ireland in 1947 when he stayed with his sister Kathleen in Lismore Castle, the palatial home of her in-laws, the Duke and Duchess of Devonshire.

His friend, Dave Powers, who now works at the JFK Memorial Library in Boston, takes up the story: "One day he borrowed one of the Castle's station wagons and drove to Dunganstown, near New Ross, looking for the home that his great-grandfather, Patrick Kennedy, had left during the potato famine in 1848 to emigrate to Boston.

"He took with him, for company, an English lady who was also staying at the Castle. They found the Kennedy farm and visited his father's second cousins.

"When they were driving back to Lismore, the English lady said, 'That was like Tobacco Road'. The President said to us, recalling the scene on the plane in Dublin sixteen years later, 'I felt like kicking her out of the car. For me, the visit to that cottage was filled with magic sentiment' . . . "

Later, when the Presidential party was being driven to Dunganstown, JFK remembered that when he was making his way to his ancestral home in 1947, he had asked a man named Robert Burrell for directions.

"Ask somebody on a road in Ireland for directions," he told Powers, "and you get a more entertaining performance than you'll get at a Broadway show."

At the little house, Kennedy asked Powers to see if he could locate Burrell in the crowd.

A Secret Service agent located him and said: "Would you like to meet President Kennedy?"

Burrell glanced at the agent, unimpressed, and replied: "I met him sixteen years ago."

Burrell might not have been overly impressed during the three days of the President's visit – but thousands upon thousands were, as the joyous scenes in Dublin, New Ross, Cork and Shannon demonstrated.

"Those were the three happiest days of my life," he was to say later.

At Shannon, before boarding Air Force One, he spoke to the assembled throng: "This is not the land of my birth, but it is the land for which I have the greatest affection – and I will certainly come back."

Dave Powers remembers one very poignant moment.

"We drove across the airfield to Air Force One, where the girls from Bunratty Castle in their medieval dresses gave him one last chorus of 'Danny Boy' before he waved and went inside the plane.

"While the girls were singing, I saw somebody in the crowd holding up a sign, scrawled with the title of another old song popular in Ireland, a sad ballad about a young man who left his girl to go off to fight and die in a war against the British.

"Five months later, when we were bringing President Kennedy's body back from Dallas, I thought of that sign at Shannon Airport and I think of it often now. It said, 'Johnny, I Hardly Knew Ye'."

There was one other moment of great poignancy – outside Ireland but with Irish ramifications.

This is Dave Powers' account of it.

"After the President's plane left Ireland, it made an unscheduled and unpublicized stop at Waddington Royal Air Force Base in England. There he was met by the Duke and Duchess of Devonshire, who flew with him, and his sister Jean and Lee Radziwill, in a helicopter to their estate at Chatsworth to visit the grave of his sister Kathleen, who was married to the Duke's older brother, the Marquess of Hartington, for four months before he died in action in Normandy during World War II.

"Kathleen, or 'Kick' as the President called her, remained in England after her husband's death, and was buried at Chatsworth after she was killed in a plane crash in France in 1948.

"This was the President's first and only visit to Kathleen's grave. He knelt and prayed, and watched Jean place a bouquet of red and white roses, picked in Ireland that morning, beside the headstone, which was inscribed with the words, 'Joy she gave – Joy she has found'."

JFK also gave much joy in his lifetime, not least to Ireland and the Irish.

But what did Ireland contribute to him, to Kennedy the man, the politician, and the statesman?

Faith, a religious view of life, and a strong and abiding sense of patriotism.

The latter was most notably reflected in the famous passage from his Inaugural Address in January 1961: "Ask not what your country can do for you – ask what you can do for your country."

Religion inculcated into the Kennedy family a firm and fixed sense of public service which is summed up in one of Mrs Rose Kennedy's favourite Biblical passages (Luke 12:48): "For unto whomsoever much is given, of him shall much be required.'

It has been asserted more than once that JFK was not a very religious man, though he was a regular Mass attender.

It has been asserted that his Catholicism never meant much to him.

But it was part of the very texture of his being, like his Irishness.

It is often forgotten that the members of this extremely wealthy family could have opted for *la dolce vita*.

With Joe Kennedy's millions behind them, they could have swanned around the world, living in the lap of luxury and lapping up the multifarious pleasures that await the idle rich.

A sybaritic lifestyle could have been theirs for the asking.

Instead, it is clear that the family, by and large (certainly its most prominent members) has been motivated by a high-minded sense of public service.

And it is worth bearing in mind that this happened and continues to happen in the aftermath of two tragedies which could have provided an ample and understandable excuse for the younger Kennedys to opt out of public life.

Staying in public life undoubtedly carries with it, to this day, an element of risk – even if one regards Teddy Kennedy's verdict (after Chappaquiddick) that the family is "cursed" as an aberrant comment made at a moment of extreme stress.

Being a Kennedy in the world of the 1990s is to lead a double-edged existence; it carries with it instant celebrity-status, but also the threat of being zapped by some psychopath.

The scene in Robert Altman's 1975 film *Nashville*, in which a Kennedy-like political candidate is assassinated, has a deadly relevance for the real-life Kennedys.

Celebrity attracts obsessively – and for some it is the gateway to glory or notoriety, the ticket to instant stardom.

When Mark Chapman gunned down ex-Beatle John Lennon he knew one thing for sure – his name would be remembered.

That's the reason why show-biz stars go to enormous and expensive lengths these days to protect themselves, not just against over-zealous fans, but against the lurking gunman who thinks life and the world and recognition has passed him by.

Don't talk to the Kennedys about that. And yet they refuse to be deterred by it.

I walked down a Manhattan street with one of Bobby Kennedy's daughters, Kerry Cuomo, and remarked how easy it would be for someone to blow her away.

She shrugged: "You can't let that kind of thing stop you."

Call it fatalist. Call it faith. Call it a belief in providence.

Ireland gave the Kennedys their faith, their religion – and one can find therein some clues as to their characters.

"Oh, God," read a tiny plaque on the President's desk, "thy sea is great and my boat is so small."

Religion accounts in part for the Kennedy commitment to public service, for Christianity carries with it a social, some would even say a political, component.

The seed of this socio-political component is to be found in the injunction to "love thy neighbour as thyself".

Theologians have argued that this must translate into communal responsibility and communal action.

As was noted earlier, some of the Kennedys – JFK in particular – were not particularly religious.

Yet the link between religion and social action and social responsibility was instinctively understood, especially by JFK.

Fed by his Irish and Catholic roots, Kennedy saw the world as tragic and comic. He could laugh at the folly of men, and cry over their wickedness.

And he quite demonstrably brought a moral sensibility to bear on public affairs.

When Kennedy learned of a new willingness by the Kremlin to reach agreement on a nuclear Test Ban Treaty, his response was wholly positive.

This was for moral reasons, even though he knew such a treaty would be fiercely resisted by the military-industrial establishment at home and the American Right.

He made it clear he would fight to win approval for such a treaty, however politically difficult.

"It may sound corny," the President remarked, "but I am thinking not so much of our world but of the world that Caroline will live in."

That is moral sensibility in action.

Even if one drifts into wayward behaviour – as JFK undoubtedly did – that sensibility and its core values can and do remain.

In this sense, the Kennedys, even the most wayward of them, could be said to be religious beings – or, in more secular terminology, moral beings.

JFK certainly suffered at the hands of those who have a tendency to see morality in exclusively sexual terms, and to judge a person's moral behaviour solely in terms of how he or she behaves in a sexual sphere.

According to this restricted and indeed distorted concept of morality, some of the Kennedys were flawed people.

JFK's reputation, in particular, has suffered because of this.

His reputation as a satyr, the picture of him as a high-profile figure in the grip of satyriasis, flows in part from this lop-sided concept of morality, and in part from pure mischievousness.

But a person's moral standing or moral worth isn't just something that can be assessed on the basis of what happens in bedrooms.

In this regard, I'm reminded of the comment made by one Kennedy insider that if JFK was involved with even a fraction of the women he is reputed to have been involved with, he would have had little time for anything else.

The Irish connection contributed to the pronounced sense among the Kennedys of public duty and public service.

"For unto whomsoever much is given . . . "

And their Irish background – I'm thinking now of the nineteenth century origins of the family – also gave the Kennedys an innate sympathy for and empathy with the underdog, the underprivileged and the outsider.

This, when the scene shifted to the United States, made them natural Democrats.

And it is reflected today in the on-going commitment to and championing of justice, peace, equality and human rights by the younger Kennedys.

It's another manifestation of the Irish connection.

5

New Light on the Cuban Missile Crisis

They were tense days that October, days of foreboding when we wondered if we would see a tomorrow.

Some of us joked about it, talking with false glibness about a shoot-out at the OK Corral.

The joke would have been lost on Burt Lancaster and Kirk Douglas – and on another man interested in Hollywood and in movies – John Kennedy.

Thirty years would pass before the detailed and chance-ridden nature of the crisis emerged – a crisis that brought the world to the brink of nuclear catastrophe.

In an editorial on 14 October 1992 entitled "The Most Dangerous Days", *The New York Times* summed it up thus: "It was a narrow squeak, narrower perhaps than a scared world guessed.

"Just 30 years ago today, a U-2 spy plane returned with photographic evidence that the Soviet Union had secretly deployed two dozen nuclear missiles in Cuba. A week later President Kennedy exposed the Soviet stealth, he circled warships around Cuba and made a televised ultimatum demanding removal of the missiles. The next 96 hours had the smell of Armageddon. In Argentina the Rev. Billy Graham preached on 'The End of the World'. In Washington, high officials were issued coded ID passes, their pictures laced with gold wire, to a bomb-proof hideaway in a Virginia mountain. The renowned nuclear scientist Leo Szilard, certain of catastrophe, fled to Switzerland."

A classic confrontation of nuclear superpowers was taking place. And the world held its breath.

The real history of the missile crisis has been coming out bit by bit for years, partly from Soviet and Cuban sources, and partly from secret US documents released by the CIA.

It ranks as the climactic moment of the Cold War; indeed, it has been described as a superpower morality play – but morality had very little to do with it, and no play ever posed such a threat to its audience.

The script involved the most lethal weapons of mass destruction known to mankind – and all of mankind constituted the audience.

The drama was played out in full view of millions upon millions of ordinary citizens the world over.

That is what the newsreel version of the crisis conveyed, but it was an oversimplified version of a whole complex episode which has come to be regarded as a textbook case of leadership in a time of acute international tension.

We now know it was a textbook case with a secret subtext.

The world had been led to believe that President Kennedy went eyeball-to-eyeball with Nikita Khrushchev, and the Soviet leader blinked and removed his missiles from Cuba.

Thirty-one years on, the story of the crisis is not so simple: there was more to it than one leader-gunfighter facing down another leader-gunfighter. The "gunfight at the OK Corral" imagery is not helpful.

Ironically, the man who mainly contributed to this imagery – the then Secretary of State, Dean Rusk – was also the man who revealed the big secret, 25 years later.

At a crucial stage during the 13 days of the crisis, it was Rusk who said: "We're eyeball to eyeball, and I think the other fellow just blinked."

It wasn't until March 1987, however, that Rusk revealed details of a secret deal between Kennedy and Khrushchev which finally defused the crisis.

It began on 14 October 1962 with the return of the U-2 spy plane carrying photographic evidence of the secret deployment by the Soviet Union of nuclear missiles in Cuba.

On 22 October Kennedy went on television and made a sombre speech to the nation and to the world.

"We will not prematurely or unnecessarily risk the costs of world-wide nuclear war in which even the fruits of victory would be ashes in our mouth, but neither will we shrink from that risk at any time it must be faced . . . "

Kennedy, having told the world that he knew what the Soviets were up to, rejected advice from the Pentagon for a military strike against the bases, established a naval blockade, and delivered an ultimatum demanding removal of the missiles which were just 90 miles from the US coast.

Two days later, on 24 October, news came through to the Situation Room in The White House basement that Soviet ships approaching the US Navy's mid-Atlantic line had stopped dead in the water.

On 25 October Ambassador Adlai Stevenson made a dramatic presentation of U-2 photographs at the United Nations, showing the missiles themselves in Cuba.

He challenged Soviet Ambassador Valerian Zorin to deny their presence, and when the latter hesitated, Stevenson proclaimed: "I am willing to wait until hell freezes over for your answer."

The chanciest day, as *The New York Times* acknowledged in 1992, was 27 October, when a surface-to-air missile brought down a U-2 plane over Cuba, killing Major Rudolf Anderson – the sole fatality in the crisis.

When US Air Force Chief, General Curtis LeMay, learned about the shooting down of the spy plane, he acted on standing orders calling for a massive reprisal strike.

Pilots were being briefed, planes poised for take-off, when a White House official frantically told the General not to launch an attack until he received direct orders from the President.

"He chickened out again," fumed General LeMay, as quoted by Dino Brugioni, then a top CIA photo-analyst, in a 1992 book entitled *Eyeball to Eyeball.*

Finally, on 28 October, Radio Moscow made an announcement that Cuba had ordered the missiles removed from Cuba. The crisis was over. Those of us who had watched, helplessly, from the sidelines knew at least there would be a tomorrow.

To mark the 30th anniversary of this crisis, a lot of commemorative material appeared in magazines, newspapers and on television.

Much of this material was an attempt to look afresh at the crisis, its origins and its outcome and long-term consequences.

The faded black-and-white photographs and film from the archives are a grim reminder that the world came closer to destruction than at any time before or since.

But just how close has not been fully appreciated until now.

With the imposition of a quarantine, the stage was set for military conflict. As *The New York Times* commented: "The next 96 hours had the smell of Armageddon."

The awful irony, as former Defence Secretary Robert McNamara acknowledged decades later, was that "no one intended to create such risk", though Khrushchev was a believer in atomic diplomacy, and was obsessed by the Soviet Union's strategic inferiority.

Today nobody believes the Soviet leader had nuclear war in mind, but, with willing support from the Castro regime, he was prepared to take a gamble with Cuba, seeing the installation of missiles there as a quick and easy way to redress the nuclear balance.

It was a gamble which could have had the most horrendous consequences.

"The missile crisis had its origins in the Bay of Pigs invasion and the superpower arms race," according to journalist Tom Morganthau.

"The Bay of Pigs debacle, 20 months earlier, convinced Khrushchev that Kennedy would buckle under pressure, and it may have led him to believe Cuba needed Soviet protection against another US invasion. But his essential motive for the missile gambit was strategic."

In a long essay in *Newsweek* in October 1992, Morganthau makes an essential point:

"Despite Khrushchev's bluster, both sides knew the Soviet Union was far behind the United States in missiles, bombers and deliverable nuclear warheads."

The key to the de-escalating of the crisis was in the secret negotiations between the two superpowers.

The question has always been: "Who blinked first – Kennedy or Khrushchev?"

But the real question is: "Did it have to happen?"

On Thursday, 5 March 1987, survivors of the missile crisis came to Hawk's Cay, a luxury resort in Florida – barely 130 miles north-east of Havana – to relive two of the most momentous weeks of their lives, and to seek an answer to that question.

These veterans of the Kennedy administration were: former Secretary of Defense, Robert McNamara, former Secretary of the Treasury, Douglas Dillon, former Under-Secretary of State, George Ball, former Presidential aides, Theodore C. Sorensen and Arthur M. Schlesinger Jr, and former National Security Adviser, McGeorge Bundy.

Former Secretary of State, Dean Rusk, and General Maxwell Taylor, the man who was chairman of the Joint Chiefs of Staff during the missile crisis, were unable to attend because of illness. Rusk did, however, make a very important contribution by letter.

Taylor, four years earlier, at the age of 81, did say in a taped interview that there were essentially three choices for getting the missiles out of Cuba: "talk them out", "squeeze them out", or "shoot them out".

He made it clear that, like his Joint Chiefs of Staff colleagues in the Pentagon, he never wavered in his advocacy of shooting them out, "until my Commander-in-Chief took another decision".

He said in retrospect he was very glad – "because it proved to be enough".

Why had it proved to be enough, and what might have happened if the Joint Chiefs got their way?

That's what the Kennedy aides, along with a dozen or so scholars of that era, gathered to consider during a four-day conference.

It was during this conference that the startling revelation was made that a deal had been made, and that the Russian leader agreed to withdraw Soviet missiles from Cuba in exchange for an American pledge to withdraw Jupiter missiles from Turkey.

We now know that the last thing the two leaders desired was direct confrontation.

We also know that Kennedy was prepared to go much further in the search for compromises than he and his aides ever let on in 1962.

The first real evidence of this came in Robert F. Kennedy's book *Thirteen Days – A Memoir of the Cuban Missile Crisis*. This book was written, according to Theodore Sorensen, in the summer and autumn of 1967, and it was based on Bobby Kennedy's personal diaries and recollections.

"It was Senator Kennedy's intention to add a discussion of the basic ethical questions involved: what, if any, circumstances or justification gives this government or any government the moral right to bring its people and possibly all people under shadow of nuclear destruction?"

Sorensen tells us that RFK wanted to rewrite or complete the book, but he never had the opportunity.

Even as it stands, it provides a unique, first-hand account of the drama as seen from the very top echelon of the Washington power structure.

But it was only in 1987 that an account of the full extent to which Kennedy was prepared to go in search of compromise became available.

And it makes a nonsense of claims that Kennedy's politics were "confrontational", and that he was an old-fashioned Cold War warrior.

On 27 October, the grimmest of all evenings during the crisis, shortly after Robert Kennedy was despatched to put the United States "ultimatum" to Soviet Ambassador Dobrynin, Dean Rusk and the President discussed what they would do if Khrushchev refused to go along.

What, in particular, would they do if the Soviets refused to accept the ambiguously phrased "deal" over the Jupiters in Turkey, a deal that the United States would disown if the Kremlin ever mentioned it publicly?

Would the world be plunged into war over missiles the United States didn't even want or need anymore?

That was the fear in The White House, so Kennedy decided to move to avert this frightening possibility.

In his letter Rusk wrote: "There is a postscript which only I can furnish. It was clear to me that President Kennedy would not let the Jupiters in Europe become an obstacle to the removal of the missile sites in Cuba because the Jupiters were coming out in any event.

"He instructed me to telephone the late Andrew Cordier, then at Columbia University, and dictate to him a statement which would be made by U Thant, the Secretary General of the United Nations, proposing the removal of both the Jupiters and the missiles in Cuba.

"Mr Cordier was to put that statement in the hands of U Thant only after a further signal from us. That step was never taken and the statement I furnished to Mr Cordier has never seen the light of day. So far as I know, President Kennedy, Andrew Cordier and I were the only ones who knew of this particular step." Rusk kept secret for 25 years the details of the deal that was done.

Soviet missiles out of Cuba, and US missiles out of Turkey – that was the deal.

And in 1963 Jupiter missiles were removed not just from Turkey, but from Britain and Italy as well.

The precise details of the deal were kept secret from the US public, and all but a handful of people around Kennedy.

Rusk's letter was a genuinely important revelation.

It showed that the President ordered his Secretary of State to lay the ground for a previously unknown concession to Moscow.

The President enjoined him to tell only one person, who, on further instructions, was to transmit the concession to U Thant, the Secretary General of the United Nations.

This secret move by Kennedy indicated, as McGeorge Bundy has pointed out, that JFK was "prepared to go the extra mile to avoid a conflict, and to absorb whatever political costs that may have entailed".

It is certain there would have been some political damage had details of an explicit trade of American and Soviet missiles leaked out.

Hence the great secrecy . . .

On Saturday, 26 October 1962, with the crisis as yet unresolved, the President made this comment to his brother: "If anybody is around to write after this, they are going to understand that we made every effort to find peace and every effort to give our adversary room to move. I am not going to push the Russians an inch beyond what is necessary."

Later, in Ireland in July 1963, JFK offered an explanation of his stance during the 1962 crisis to the Taoiseach (Irish Prime Minister), Sean Lemass.

He told Lemass that "the giving of nuclear weapons to Germany would produce an emotional, if not a very logical, reaction.

"It was the same for the US in reaction to Cuba. There was no difference in the danger to the US between missiles in Cuba and missiles in submarines in the Caribbean Sea, but the emotional reaction of America was very definite, nevertheless."

Robert S. McNamara, Secretary of Defence in the Kennedy Administration at the time, wrote an article for *The New York Times* in October 1992 under the heading "One Minute to Doomsday", which sought to draw key lessons.

Describing the missile crisis as a case of "blind versus blind", McNamara revealed what had been learned from a series of top level meetings in Florida, Havana and Moscow since 1987.

These meeting were attended by surviving officials of the Kennedy, Khrushchev and Castro administrations, as well as historians and other scholars.

Speaking of the fifth such meeting, held in Havana in January 1992, McNamara says the danger of a doomsday situation had been greatly underestimated.

"The Russians told us the Soviet forces in Cuba possessed 36 nuclear warheads for the 24 intermediate-range missiles targeted on US cities. At the time, the CIA stated it did not believe there were any nuclear warheads there."

In fact, in an intelligence report prepared for Kennedy on 1 August 1962, the CIA maintained that the Soviet build-up in Cuba would almost certainly be limited to defensive weapons.

Amazingly, that judgement – which was way off – was reaffirmed in a second report on 19 September 1962 – the day after the CIA received a top secret document from an agent inside Cuba giving precise locations for bases under construction for Soviet SS-4 ballistic missiles – missiles which would target East Coast cities such as Miami, New York, Boston, Philadelphia and Washington DC.

That document, written in invisible ink, has since been released by the CIA.

Little wonder that McNamara could write: "The missile crisis is replete with examples of misinformation, misjudgment, miscalculation. Such errors are costly in convention war. When they affect decisions relating to nuclear forces, they can result in the destruction of nations.

"This must lead to the conclusion that, insofar as it is achievable, we must seek to return to a non-nuclear world," says McNamara.

President Kennedy regarded the avoidance of nuclear conflict over the missiles as one of his greatest achievements.

Some scholars have insisted that once the crisis of 1962 was resolved, it was unlikely the superpowers would ever come so close to disaster again.

On the American side, it is pointed out that at the height of the crisis, Kennedy admitted to looking over the precipice and contemplating the horrible reality that, in a nuclear conflagration, human beings had the power to end civilisation.

It also made Kennedy more determined than ever to bring about a nuclear Test Ban Treaty.

The outstanding lesson for JFK, if nuclear catastrophe was to be averted in the future, was to make crisis avoidance rather than crisis management the over-riding consideration.

He said as much to the Taoiseach, Sean Lemass, when they met in private at the American Embassy in Dublin.

Hitherto classified documents in the National Archives in Dublin show that during his 1963 visit, Kennedy expressed his hopes and fears about Khrushchev's reaction to a Test Ban Treaty.

He thought the main stumbling block would, in fact, be the possibility of the Chinese testing a bomb the following year, and this could disrupt any agreement "in circumstances embarrassing to the Russians".

He feared that the Chinese would become a nuclear power, and with their "enormous population and Stalinist doctrines, they will, by then, be the major problem for the world, which our successors will have to face".

There was, moreover, a threat of unlimited nuclear proliferation.

He was worried that "if China develops its weapons, India will want hers also. The dangers in Israel and the United Arab Republics are obvious".

We also know now that there was an Irish dimension to the Cuban Missile Crisis.

The Irish Government, at the behest of Kennedy, played a secret and crucial role.

This only came to light in January 1993, with the release of Cabinet papers under the 30-year rule.

As part of the diplomatic approaches to accompany the blocade, Kennedy wrote to Lemass asking Ireland's support at the UN, for the American resolution calling for the removal of missiles from Cuba under the supervision of UN observers.

He also requested and received Irish co-operation in the mounting of "an immediate nuclear quarantine" which, he explained, was necessary to prevent the construction of further offensive missile installations by the Soviet in Cuba.

Papers made public in the National Archives in January 1993 show that Lemass instructed his Minister for External Affairs, Frank Aiken, to pledge our support for the US stand on Cuba.

But Kennedy's real worry was Shannon Airport. The American Government believed that some material for the Soviet nuclear bases in Cuba was getting in via Shannon.

A top official at the US Embassy, acting on JFK's instructions, told the Taoiseach's Department that Washington was "worried" about the extent to which traffic through Shannon might have helped in the build-up in Cuba.

A document in the State files shows that the official admitted to the Taoiseach that "Washington has been somewhat puzzled about how warheads have got into Cuba".

Kennedy told Lemass he wanted two things – (a) details of all overflights of Irish territory by Cubana Airlines and CSA (Czechoslovak Airlines), and (b) searches by the Irish authorities of all Cuban-bound planes passing through Shannon.

The Americans asked, on the highest authority – Kennedy himself – for "manifest data" in respect of flights through Shannon.

Lemass responded by arranging to supply all details of overflights to the US authorities.

In addition, he ordered Army munitions experts to search all Cuban and Czech planes travelling to Cuba for war material.

To facilitate this, the Minister for Transport and Power invoked new powers under Article 35 of the International Convention on Civil Aviation.

State papers reveal that the Taoiseach phoned the American Ambassador and informed him that "we will in future have CSA/Cubana aircraft searched".

In addition, the Irish Government declared that "if we find that they are carrying war-like material we would consider refusing them rights of transit".

Both airlines had been regularly using Shannon as a refuelling stop-over for flights between Moscow and Havana and back.

After the defusing of the crisis, Lemass wrote a private letter to Kennedy in which he praised the latter for the "wisdom and restraint" with which he handled "this very delicate and vital matter".

The letter continued:

"We sincerely believe that this result is a positive achievement of great significance for the reduction of world tension, and promises world peace and security through the elimination of serious causes of friction and the elaboration of a code of international conduct inspired by the principles of the UN Charter," he wrote.

But even Lemass didn't know of the top-secret deal between Kennedy and Khrushchev.

As for Kennedy, even he didn't know that the stakes were higher than they appeared to be on the table.

Nearly three decades later, his Defence Secretary, Bob McNamara, was able to reveal that six tactical nuclear weapons for use against American invasion forces were actually on Cuba, assembled and ready for use.

"We didn't know," says McNamara. "Kennedy stopped nuclear war without knowing it."

It was the most dangerous crisis of the Cold War era. And also, in the opinion of Richard Goodwin, a Kennedy speech writer, the turning point of Kennedy's Presidency.

The impact of the Cuban Missile Crisis on him profoundly changed the way he handled the Cold War.

His handling of the crisis – as we can now appreciate – also gives the lie to the idea that his was a politics of confrontation, that he thrived on challenge and crisis, and was a politician-as-gunslinger, an existential politician defining himself by activity.

JFK was much more complex than that. He was a complex political leader in a complex political situation. He had one foot in the Cold War and one foot in a new world he saw coming.

"Contrary to revisionist myth," historian Arthur Schlesinger Jr tells us, "Kennedy did not relish confrontation."

According to Schlesinger, the distinctive note of his justly-famous Inaugural Address expressed a different concern.

"Let us never negotiate out of fear," Kennedy said, "but let us never fear to negotiate."

On his handling of the crisis, Theodore Sorensen, who was there, had this to say: "Kennedy in fact relied not on force and threats alone but on a carefully balanced and precisely measured combination of defence, diplomacy and dialogue."

And Sorensen insists Dean Rusk was wrong when he said Khrushchev blinked at the time of the Cuban Crisis.

"It was indeed eyeball to eyeball, and fortunately both men blinked.

"Otherwise," Sorensen adds soberly, "this planet might now be in ashes."

One wonders what Kennedy would have thought if he could have envisaged the collapse of the Soviet Communist system.

His concern in 1963 – in the aftermath of the Cuban Crisis – was to prevent the dangerous development of nuclear proliferation.

To achieve this, the US wanted nuclear weapons kept to the "club of four" – USA, USSR, Britain and France.

In fact, five weeks later JFK achieved his greatest triumph in foreign affairs with the signing by the Soviet Union, the US and Britain of the Test Ban Treaty prohibiting the testing of nuclear weapons in the atmosphere.

France and China refused to sign, but Kennedy had made a crucial breakthrough.

In doing so, he greatly reduced the risk of a nuclear holocaust.

The lessons of Cuba had been taken to heart.

6

Dirty Tricks

Tall, quiet-spoken, fastidious, Theodore C. Sorensen is as I expected him to be. A clean-cut Kennedy intellectual. A man for whom displays of emotion are rare.

A thoughtful man, a scholar, he served in The White House as special assistant to the President, and he has even been called JFK's alter ego.

His book was the second I ever read on John F. Kennedy. The first was Hugh Sidey's 1965 *Portrait of a President*, a book I read and re-read.

"It's a good book," commented Sorensen when I told him.

We met in his office in a large complex on the Avenue of the Americas in Manhattan.

Clinton had just been elected and we talked about that for a few minutes.

With a new team preparing to settle into The White House, his thoughts must have been transported back to the final weeks of 1959 and the forming of the New Frontier.

This is where Sidey's book starts.

The search for talent was on.

And Sorensen was a key player.

I tried to draw him on this, to get him to reminisce. But he skirted round it. It was a very special part of his life, but it is over now.

I wanted to talk a bit about the uses of presidential power and about the relationship between morality and power.

I was mindful of an analysis made by George Keenan, former US Ambassador to Moscow, in the course of which he argued that when it comes to the use of power, presidents should not be "unduly legalistic and moralistic".

In the context of the Kennedy Presidency, it seemed to me that these issues were crystalised in two areas – what became known to the world as Operation Mongoose, and the *coup d'état* which toppled President Diem in Vietnam late in 1963.

Years before, again in New York, I had been invited to a lecture given by William Colby, former head of the CIA.

It was about the changing nature of intelligence gathering, with satellites taking over from spooks.

Colby knows a lot about both, especially about spooks.

He also knows a lot about the kind of "dirty tricks" covered by Operation Mongoose.

It started after the Bay of Pigs fiasco in April 1961, a humiliating set-back for Kennedy and the Americans.

In truth, it had started in January 1959 when Fidel Castro and his Marxist revolutionaries ousted the American-backed dictator, Batista.

The new Cuban regime led by Castro was anathema in Washington. And Kennedy, like many Americans, was affronted by what they took to be a Soviet satellite in America's backyard.

The CIA plan, which led to the ill-fated Bay of Pigs invasion, was hatched during the days of the Eisenhower Administration.

The plan entailed the training of anti-Castro Cubans who were to spearhead an invasion with the ultimate aim of overthrowing Castro.

During the transition period Eisenhower told Kennedy about it, and recommended that the incoming President should give it his support.

In what was to prove to be the first major mistake of his term of office, Kennedy, albeit with misgivings, agreed to go ahead with plans for the invasion.

It turned out to be a fiasco.

One result of the postmortem carried out in The White House was the strengthening of Kennedy's resolve to remove Castro.

This plan, again masterminded by the CIA, was given the code name Operation Mongoose.

Certain aspects of it were bizarre in the extreme, involving collusion between the intelligence services of the USA and Mafia bosses.

The latter were only too willing to participate in the plotting to destroy Castro because he had closed down the lucrative gambling clubs, strip-joints and prostitution rings which had been run by the Mafia in Havana during the Batista years.

Even today it is not clear just how much Kennedy knew about the unholy alliance of the CIA and the Mafia.

That aside, there is no doubt that there was a Kennedy vendetta against Castro.

Whether the President actually sanctioned murder plots against the Cuban leader is another matter.

Professor James N. Giglio, historian, from Southwest Missouri State University says Kennedy approved of Mongoose.

This was true in principle.

Did he know of the CIA-Mafia links?

Sorensen doubts this.

"I don't think Kennedy knew of the details of Operation Mongoose," he told me.

It was like something straight out of a James Bond novel, with various plans to poison Castro or to bribe some of the officers around him to assassinate him by any means they could.

The covert operations were called off after the Cuban Missile Crisis in October 1962, when Kennedy gave Khrushchev an assurance that the United States would not invade Cuba.

Operation Mongoose may never have been under the direct control of The White House.

Was the same true of what has been called one of the strangest episodes in the annals of American foreign policy and practice?

I refer to the *coup d'état* which led to the fall – and death – of Diem in Saigon in November 1963.

It has been termed "strange" – and rightly so.

And again, even now, we don't know the full extent of JFK's knowledge of, or involvement in, this episode.

Ngo Dinh Diem, the President of South Vietnam, was overthrown and murdered by his own officers on 1 November 1963 – just three weeks before Kennedy's assassination in Dallas.

"The Pentagon's secret study of the Vietnam War discloses that President Kennedy knew and approved of plans for the military *coup d'état* that overthrew President Ngo Dinh Diem in 1963 . . . "

This is a passage from The Pentagon Papers as published by *The New York Times.*

Is it true?

On a cold Thursday in November 1992, I sat in Mulligan's Bar in New York and pondered that question as I prepared for my interview with Sorensen.

In front of me I had notes on the coup which I had worked on in the library at Fordham University over the previous few days.

Did Kennedy know?

In a fascinating political thriller called *The Tears of Autumn*, Charles McCarry even goes so far as to suggest that not only did he know, but that it was the Vietnamese – specifically, members of Diem's extended family – who orchestrated the assassination in Dallas.

They hired Oswald to revenge Diem's death.

Although McCarry lays it all out as part of a work of fiction, he does put together a very credible plot.

And it is worth remembering that McCarry was once an intelligence officer with the CIA.

A much more senior figure came to the same conclusion. A few months after the Dallas assassination, President Lyndon Johnson told a friend that President Kennedy's assassination was punishment for Diem's assassination.

Just as he was blamed for the failure of the Bay of Pigs invasion, Kennedy was also blamed not just for the coup that toppled Diem, but also for his murder and that of his brother, Nhu, who acted as his secret police chief.

Sorensen totally rejects these allegations.

"I can assure you that Kennedy never wished for, let alone authorised, Diem's death."

According to Sorensen, he may not even have known the details of the plot to stage a coup.

"Historians will have to sort it all out. My own hunch is that military and intelligence agencies gave the green light for a military coup. And Kennedy may not have known about it. Some people in the State Department may have known about it."

We know that they did.

General Maxwell Taylor was in the room when the news of Diem's death was conveyed to Kennedy.

"The President who was obviously shaken, sprang to his feet and walked out of the room saying nothing to anybody – and stayed out of the room for some minutes."

In *Backfire*, his book on the Vietnam War, Loren Baritz, who was chairman of the History Department of the University of Rochester, makes a telling point: "Many members of Camelot's inner circle rightly insisted that the Administration had not initiated the coup against Diem."

Operation Mongoose and the Diem coup remain among the most unsavoury features of Kennedy's one thousand days in The White House.

They were part of the much larger tragedy of Vietnam.

Professor Schlesinger agrees that Vietnam presented the most troubling case of national-liberation war for the Kennedy administration.

If national-liberation wars were to be the great new Soviet weapon, ways had to be found to check such wars.

"This led Kennedy for a season into the fantasy of counter-insurgency – a mode of warfare for which Americans were ill-adapted – which nourished an American belief in the capacity and right to intervene in foreign lands and which was both corrupting in method and futile in effect."

Vietnam was to become the great problem, but so for a time was Cuba, and it became a particular target for covert action.

"All this gave special power to the CIA who carried its dark deeds further, judging by available evidence, than Kennedy knew."

The plot, or plots, to assassinate Castro originated with the Eisenhower administration. Even then the CIA was recruiting Mafia hitmen to do the job.

The plotting continued into and throughout the Kennedy administration and even into the Johnson Presidency.

The assumption underlying many of the claims about Kennedy (and applying also to Eisenhower and Johnson) is that he knew at all times what the CIA was up to.

This is dismissed by Schlesinger: "There is no evidence that any of the three Presidents authorised or knew about – except as something over and done with – the CIA's assassination policy."

Even after Kennedy had altered his policy towards Castro and was attempting to normalise relations with Cuba, the CIA's plotting continued.

Schlesinger recalls that even while Kennedy was in Dallas on 22 November 1963, a CIA officer provided a Cuban defector with murder weapons for use against Castro.

Vietnam provided even greater scope for covert action by the CIA, as we know from the horrible details of the Phoenix programme in particular.

"Kennedy accepted the line drawn by the previous administration and on occasion even endorsed Eisenhower's 'domino theory'," admits Schlesinger.

"He increased the number of American military advisers to more than 16,000, 73 of whom were killed in combat. But he steadily opposed Pentagon recommendations for the despatch of American military units, and steadily pressed the authoritarian Ngo Dinh Diem to broaden his base through political and economic reform.

"Diem disdained such advice, and his brutal repressions led his generals to plot his overthrow. A message from Washington, later characterised by Kennedy as a 'major mistake', informed the generals that the United States would recognise a successor regime. Nine weeks later the generals deposed and – despite American plans to fly him out of the country – murdered him."

In his 1971 memoirs, LBJ would write that the Saigon coup was a "serious blunder", and would charge that Kennedy aides had been responsible for it.

However, as William Manchester has pointed out in *One Brief Shining Moment*, Diem's overthrow was inevitable.

Manchester contends that if any American was involved, it was Henry Cabot Lodge, the US Ambassador in Saigon, who simply told the generals that if they moved against Diem the United States would remain neutral.

"His end, after eight years in office, came amid a tangle of intrigue and violence as improbable as the most imaginative of melodramas," says Stanley Karnow in his bestselling history of the Vietnam War.

"His collapse would have been impossible without American complicity."

That much is true, but the complicity was in Saigon rather than Washington.

7
JFK and Vietnam

One of the darkest and most disturbing chapters in American history came to an ignominious end in Saigon on 30 April 1975.

Shortly after dawn the last US helicopter lifted off from the roof of the abandoned US Embassy in the centre of the city.

As its whirling blades carried the final group of embassy and military personnel to waiting ships in the South China Sea, the helicopter departure signalled the end of a dreadful and senseless war.

It was a war that was to cost the lives of 58,000 American servicemen and over two million Vietnamese.

And it has left a dark shadow over the Kennedy Presidency.

The war destroyed many lives, but it caused other damage as well, not least to American faith in government and authority.

Some would say it cost America its innocence, and it still haunts its conscience.

In the 15 years since its publication, Michael Herr's *Dispatches* has become the standard bible of the Vietnam War memorial industry.

Of that war, Herr says: "It's part of the American psyche and to this day we still haven't found a language to discuss it."

It was America's longest war and the only one to end in defeat.

It was not just a conflict waged in south-east Asia.

It was also a struggle fought in America, in American institutions, in the American streets and, above all, in the American conscience.

And today the key question remains – was it fought for the right reasons?

And what responsibility does Kennedy bear for it?

Some, even now, believe it was fought for the right reasons.

Peggy Noonan, who was a speechwriter for President Reagan, has well summed up the thinking of those who feel this way: "I still think that America's desire to help another people in a country far away to resist a Communist takeover was not proof of America's cynicism but an illustration of that peculiar American mix, one part idealism and one part strategic calculation, which may have been wrong but which at least had a point."

In the end, answering the question – was it fought for the right reasons? – comes down to issues of morality and power.

You can tease out the issues, and then say yes or no.

Getting at Kennedy's motives and intentions is another matter.

What did he really intend? Would he have kept American forces in Vietnam if he had survived? Would he have escalated the war the way his successor, LBJ, did?

Or would he – as many of his inner circle contend – have withdrawn?

In any reappraisal of the Kennedy Presidency these are core questions.

On them depend to a large degree the restoration of his political reputation.

So what way is the evidence pointing, how is it stacking up 30 years after his death?

Should we continue to see him as a quintessential Cold War warrior – or as a leader trapped in circumstances not of his own making, but determined to unmake them or to free himself from them?

There is no doubt that Kennedy felt an obligation to intervene in Vietnam.

As journalist Neil Sheehan has written: "[by December 1961].... President John Kennedy had committed the arms of the United States to the task of suppressing a Communist-led rebellion and preserving South Vietnam as a separate State governed by an American sponsored-regime in Saigon."

There is no doubt that Kennedy subscribed to the "domino theory" first formulated during the Eisenhower administration.

Nor is there any doubt that he viewed South Vietnam as a threatened outpost of the American Empire, the greatest ever created in the aftermath of World War II.

But the key decision which changed the nature and scale of the war didn't come until almost a year after his death.

It was the infamous Tonkin Gulf incident in August 1964 which dramatically altered American involvement in south-east Asia.

On foot of that incident, President Johnson asked for and received approval from Congress to take "all necessary action" against the Communist regime in North Vietnam.

That resolution – passed nine months after Kennedy was killed – allowed LBJ to commit 500,000 American troops to Vietnam.

It Americanised the conflict in south-east Asia in a way that Kennedy never envisaged and could never have endorsed or permitted.

Wasn't it Kennedy, after all, who, back in September 1963, made the following comment: "In the final analysis it is their war. . . . We can help them . . . but they have to win it, the people of Vietnam, against the Communists. "

That came during an interview with Walter Cronkite of CBS News.

And the Tonkin Gulf incident itself was an invented pretext.

Robert Scheer, former editor of *Ramparts*, takes up the story: "We didn't know until some 20 years later, again when the documents were finally forced out of the government, that the Gulf of Tonkin attack by North Vietnamese PT boats on American ships on August 4, 1964, was a fabrication. Captain John J. Heurals, the hapless commander of the destroyer *Maddox*, told me in 1985 that his crew had misidentified the signals of a newly installed sonar system bouncing off his ship's zigzagging rudder and said they were being attacked by enemy torpedoes.

"He figured out his mistake and alerted headquarters, but Johnson wouldn't wait for clarification and rushed instead to get on television before America went to bed to announce that American ships had been attacked.

"Details of that nefarious 'attack' were broadcast widely by the American media, and provided Lyndon Johnson with the pretext and congressional resolution to escalate the Vietnam War."

In many ways the most damning evidence against Kennedy is to be found in David Halberstam's book *The Best and the Brightest.*

" . . . the Kennedy intellectuals had been praised as the best and the brightest men of a generation and yet they were the architects of a war which I and many others thought the worst tragedy to befall this country since the Civil War."

Halberstam saw Kennedy very much as a prisoner of the Cold War mentality. "He had come in at the latter part of the Cold War; at the beginning he had not challenged it, though he had, in the last part of his Administration, begun to temper it. On Vietnam his record was more than cloudy. More than any other member of his Administration, he knew the dangers of a deep US involvement, the limits of what Caucasian troops could achieve on Vietnamese soil, and yet he had significantly deepened that involvement . . . "

If Kennedy inherited the "domino theory" as part of the rationale of the Cold War, as his critics insist, he also took on board the doctrine of "limited war" outlined by General Maxwell Taylor in his 1959 book *The Uncertain Trumpet.*

Even as late as the 20 November 1963 – two days before his assassination – Kennedy sent McNamara to a top-level conference in Honolulu where the thinking on the American side continued to be governed by the presumption that the war in South Vietnam could be controlled – kept as a "limited war" – by exerting military and economic pressure on North Vietnam.

Two days after the November Honolulu conference, John Kennedy was shot in Dallas.

At that stage, as Sheehan and others have acknowledged, the war in Vietnam which Kennedy's successor, Lyndon Johnson, inherited was not much of an American war by comparison with what was to follow.

Sheehan, who worked as a correspondent in Vietnam, tells us: "There were 17,000 US servicemen in the South. Less than 120 had been killed, and the number of men wounded seriously enough to require hospitalization had not yet reached 250."

Four days after Kennedy's death something happens which alters the nature of the American commitment, and rules out any turning back.

President Johnson draws up a top-secret National Security Action Memorandum (NSAM), overturning plans by Kennedy to pull 1,000 Americans out of Vietnam by Christmas.

The order to withdraw was contained in National Security Action Memorandum-263.

This was to be part of a phased withdrawal.

Johnson and the men in the Pentagon would have none of it.

America was now in Vietnam to stay – and to win, irrespective of the cost.

NSAM-263 is probably the single most important document on Vietnam of the entire Kennedy Presidency. No scholar has paid more attention to it than historian, John M. Newman of the University of Maryland.

The fruits of his painstaking research became public in 1992 with the publication of his book *JFK and Vietnam.*

That volume removes all but the most niggling of doubts about Kennedy's intentions in South East Asia.

"At 12.30 p.m. on November 22, the shots rang out in Dealey Plaza that took the President's life. His Vietnam policy died with him.

"On the surface, the shift in the war effort seemed gradual: it was 15 months before the first American Marines waded ashore at Da

Nang, South Vietnam. Some aspects of the reversal, however, were more sudden – almost instantaneous.

"The underlying reason why the larger change took as long as it did was that Johnson faced the same problem Kennedy had: the 1964 Presidential election.

"The key to understanding how this campaign problem differed for these two men is this: Kennedy had to disguise a withdrawal; Johnson had to disguise intervention."

Newman presses home the argument that Kennedy was misled from the beginning about the situation in south-east Asia. When he became aware of the true nature of the conflict there, he made secret plans to withdraw.

"There seems little doubt that Kennedy was headed for a total withdrawal – come what may – from Vietnam when he left for Texas . . .

"The tragedy in Texas, in the end, brought about the outcome that Kennedy had opposed throughout his Presidency: full-scale American intervention in Vietnam," concludes Newman.

Sheehan, whose 1988 book *A Bright Shining Lie* is regarded by no less a person than John Le Carré, as the best single volume on Vietnam, tells us of the belief of Marine General Victor Krulak, whom Kennedy admired.

"If John Kennedy had lived, Krulak thought the war might have gone differently. Kennedy's fascination with counter-insurgency and the lessons he would have learned by 1965 would have enabled him to grasp the importance of what Krulak was saying when Krulak had gone to the Oval Office with his strategy paper in hand. The President would have forced the Army generals to fight the war intelligently.

"If Krulak was right about Kennedy, if there was any substance to his musing, it was another of the many might-have-beens of Vietnam . . . "

This is backed up by Stanley Karnow, author of *Vietnam: A History.*

"Kennedy was not quite prepared to pay any price or bear any burden to protect South Vietnam."

The suspicion remains that JFK was holding on in Vietnam because he was afraid of losing the 1964 election. There is evidence, direct and indirect, that he had to resort to subterfuge. He had to appear to be doing one thing, while planning the opposite.

There is evidence also that, both in terms of his rhetoric and his understanding of the Cold War, and the limits of US power, Kennedy did a 180-degree turn between his inaugural address, and his speech to the American University in 1963.

On the 29th anniversary of Dallas, I asked JFK's former White House aide, Dave Powers, a blunt question: "Are you convinced JFK would have ordered a withdrawal from Vietnam in a second term?"

His answer was as brief as it was unequivocal: "Yes."

Ben Bradlee, former Editor and now Vice-President-At-Large of *The Washington Post,* is not so sure.

This is what he told me in December 1992, in reply to the same question I had put to Powers: "There is no strong evidence that JFK was planning a withdrawal from Vietnam. There is some anecdotal evidence and there is the feeling among some of us – including me – that he was instinctively responsive to liberal critics. He knew he couldn't appeal to the extreme conservatives, especially the non-intellectuals, but he felt a kinship for most of the intellectual – and non-crazy – Left."

Mike McGinn, who served in the Carter White House, and who now lives in a splendid old castle in Mallow in County Cork, made another point to me: "You mustn't forget that Bobby Kennedy continued to support the war up until 1968."

One wonders, though, how much of that was due to political considerations.

Bobby Kennedy wanted to be President, and he may well have calculated that the tide of popular feeling against Vietnam didn't begin to swing decisively until then.

By 1966 Bobby Kennedy knew what the war was doing to the country – it was causing real divisions.

He could feel the dissent growing, sense the widening disaffection.

But President Johnson was fully committed to the war, and was not slow to say that he was following through on a policy initiated by his predecessor.

This may have left Bobby Kennedy with a difficulty.

In addition, we must not forget that Richard Nixon could ignore the mounting anti-war sentiment up to 1968, the year of the My Lai massacre.

If RFK's calculations had an element of *realpolitik* about them, then so be it.

Nobody ever said the Kennedy brothers were blind to *realpolitik*.

Nevertheless, both JFK and RFK would have faced a very different situation if the former had gone on to a second term.

And the electoral omens were good.

Kennedy's defeat of Nixon had been extremely close in 1960, so close that he knew he had to operate within very real constraints.

But by 1963 he was a popular President.

"The common assumption was that he would easily win a second term," is Neil Sheehan's verdict.

Such a win would have created a whole new ball game.

Lyndon Johnson, a most hard-headed politician, knew this as well.

When he took over the Oval Office, he told the generals in the Pentagon: "Wait until I am elected, and then you can have your war."

The difference is that Kennedy was going to take the war away from them.

And that, as Oliver Stone argues in his movie *JFK*, may well have contributed to his death in Dallas.

You don't have to go along with the Stone thesis. But I believe we have to accept the evidence that Kennedy was planning a U-turn on Vietnam.

To me, that evidence is compelling.

The truth is that JFK was growing and learning all the time.

It is much easier to make speeches than it is, finally, to make the judgements, he commented ruefully in 1963 as he contemplated the quagmire of Vietnam.

"He would not stand for long the sight of pine coffins coming back from a futile battle," columnist Mary McGrory, of *The Washington Post* who knew him well, once said.

I think she was right. Dead right.

Professor James N. Giglio, in an otherwise excellent history of the Kennedy Presidency, contends that "Kennedy's Vietnam policy was in a shambles at the time of his death".

On the contrary, by November 1963 Kennedy had concluded – as he told his aide Kenny O'Donnell – that the war was getting out of hand.

It was time to end it.

And that was the plan.

He would have to get re-elected first; he knew that.

Then he would withdraw, even at the risk of being "damned everywhere as a Communist appeaser".

It never came to that.

The shots in Dealey Plaza changed everything.

8

Space: The Last Frontier

"If John Kennedy hadn't been there, the Apollo programme probably would not have happened – and we'd have had to wait until the next century to go to the Moon."

This is the verdict – delivered in 1993 – of Arthur C. Clarke, the distinguished science fiction writer whose best known work is *2001 – A Space Odyssey.*

Kennedy did not live to see that momentous day in July 1969 when man first set foot on the Moon.

But he, more than anyone, made it possible, and that must be seen as part of his legacy.

And Neil Armstrong, as he stepped onto the lunar surface, could have been speaking for Kennedy when he said: "One small step for man; one giant leap for mankind."

That was part of the Kennedy vision, that's how he saw Space. And it is fitting that the Space Centre at Cape Canaveral is named in his honour.

As Arthur Clarke has said, the Apollo and Saturn programmes located there stand as a monument to the President's dream of conquering space for peaceful purposes.

It may not have started that way. In fact, it didn't.

Most experts agree that The Space Age began in Peenemünde in Germany in the 1940s where a team of rocket experts under Werner von Braun assembled, under instructions from Hitler, to construct what became known as the V-2 rocket.

This ballistic missile was conceived from the outset as a weapon of war.

But when World War II ended, Dr von Braun and his team (some were taken to the USA, others to the Soviet Union) provided the nuclei of the rocket, missile and space programmes of the two superpowers.

With the sundering of the unity of the Allies after 1945, and the emergence of the Cold War, a race began for military supremacy – a race which was to provide political and financial justification for space weaponry.

The Americans, though ahead in nuclear technology, were smug on other fronts – and under Eisenhower were caught napping.

The nation suffered a severe shock to its national pride when, in the early hours of 4 October 1957, the roar of a three-stage rocket broke the silence in Soviet Central Asia.

As the last engine in stage three cut out, the protective nose-cone opened to reveal Sputnik-1, a 23-inch, 184-pound satellite – the world's first artificial satellite.

In just 96 minutes, the "bleeping" satellite, which many of us saw in the skies over Ireland, had completed its first orbit of the Earth – and in doing so had opened the way for "Space".

It is doubtful if even those involved in space technology in 1957 would have predicted the tremendous and far-reaching developments that would follow during the next 25 years.

Even as renowned a visionary as Clarke (who, like other science fiction writers, were light-years ahead of the scientists in their imaginings) said he did not believe in his wildest dreams that man would reach the Moon in his lifetime.

John F. Kennedy changed all of that.

He provided the crucial leadership and inspiration which ultimately transformed the space fiction of writers like Clarke into reality.

The excitement in the Soviet Union at the launch of Sputnik was matched by disbelief in the United States.

The launch of Sputnik-1 was a stunning blow to the Americans.

On 3 November 1957, the Soviets followed with the launch of Sputnik-2, containing the dog Laika, the first living creature to orbit in space.

The effect on the US was dramatic, not least because the US scientists knew something their Soviet counterparts did not.

Since 1948, the scientific community had been debating whether a nuclear warhead could be put on a missile. At that stage nuclear warheads were so huge that many experts declared it would be impossible in the foreseeable future to develop warhead-equipped missiles which could span continents.

Yet within a few years, after a series of spectacular breakthroughs in nuclear weaponry, US scientists found out how to package a nuclear bomb a fraction of its former size.

The age of the Inter-Continental Ballistic Missiles (ICBMs) was upon us.

But the knowledge which the Americans had gained worked against their rocket programme. With smaller nuclear missiles there was no need any longer for monstrous rockets.

The Soviets were in a different situation; their atomic art lagged behind that of the Americans – so they went on building huge booster rockets.

Yet this was to give them an edge when it came to manned exploration of Space.

Sputnik showed this in dramatic fashion.

On 12 April 1961 the Russians again enhanced their lead by sending Yuri Gagarin into orbit around the Earth.

"Let the capitalist countries try to catch us," taunted Khrushchev.

The US response came of 21 May 1961 when President Kennedy decided to commit massive resources in an all-out effort to overtake the USSR in the space race. In effect, he was taking a gamble, but it paid off.

Going on national television, he committed the US to "landing a man on the Moon and returning him safely to Earth before the end of the decade".

The crash programme which followed paid off.

On 20 July 1969, Apollo II landed on the Moon, and millions of people all over the world saw on their television men walking on the Moon.

Within an hour Neil Armstrong and Buzz Aldrin talked to President Richard Nixon and gave him the chance to say something that was, for once, incontestable.

"Neil and Buzz," he said, "I am talking to you from the Oval Office at The White House and this certainly has to be the most historic telephone call ever made."

He also said something that a lot of people at the time felt was true.

"For one priceless moment in the whole history of man," he said, "all the people of this Earth are truly one. One in their pride at what you have done, and one in our prayers that you will safely return to Earth."

That night, someone placed a note on the grave of President John Kennedy at Arlington,Virginia. It simply said: "Mr President, the Eagle has landed."

This was a most poignant acknowledgement that it was Kennedy who, after the Russian triumphs of Sputnik 1 in 1957 and the flight of Yuri Gagarin in 1961, gave the signal for the race to the Moon.

Much more was to follow – the Soyuz spacecraft from the USSR in October, 1968; the Salyut orbital station in April 1971, and in May 1973, Skylab, the first US orbital station.

The Soviets continued with the development of space station technology, while the Americans concentrated on the development of the space shuttle, with Columbia in 1981 becoming the first re-usable spaceship.

The space race undoubtedly began primarily for military purposes: it was a race for military supremacy.

All of that was to change, and even in the sixties Kennedy was not alone in seeing Space as a means of promoting and securing universal peace.

The seeds of his vision are discernible in the speech he made at the American University in Washington on 10 June 1963.

From the outset he committed himself to an enduring peace – "not a Pax Americana enforced on the world by American weapons of war . . . not merely a peace for Americans, but a peace for all men; not merely peace in our time but peace for all time . . . "

Knowing that demonisation was going on on both sides, Kennedy urged a mutual re-examination of attitudes.

"If we cannot now end our differences, at least we can help make the world safe for diversity.

"For, in the final analysis, our most common basic link is the fact that we all inhabit this planet. We all breathe the same air. We all cherish our children's future. And we are all mortal . . . "

Already Kennedy was planning a limited Test Ban Treaty between the superpowers; now he was preparing the ground.

"We do not want a war. We do not expect a war. This generation of Americans has already had enough – more than enough – of war and hate and oppression . . .

"We shall be alert to try to stop it. But we shall also do our part to build a world of peace where the weak are safe and the strong are just. We are not helpless before that task or hopeless of its success. Confident and unafraid, we labour – not toward a strategy of annihilation – but toward a strategy of peace."

The speech was almost ignored by the American media. Yet the *Guardian* in England described it as "one of the greatest State papers of American history". And in the USSR, both *Izvestia* and *Pravda* – on Khrushchev's instructions – printed the full text.

More than any other words uttered by him, it showed how far the young American President was prepared to travel to secure a lasting peace.

Kennedy wanted to avoid both a monopoly of Outer Space by one of the superpowers, and the militarisation of Space.

In an address to the UN General Assembly on 20 September 1963, he called for increased US-Soviet space co-operation, including, specifically, a joint expedition to the Moon.

It was too early for the latter, but both superpowers did foreswear any territorial rights in Outer Space.

A foundation was emerging which would have implications within three decades which Kennedy could not have foreseen.

With the 21st century looming up, the exploration and commercialisation of Space could yet be the saving of mankind.

From a 1960s perspective such a claim might have seemed far-fetched. Not in the 1990s.

Since the demise of Soviet Communism and the break-up of the Soviet bloc, several co-operative programmes have been formulated.

With the Cold War over, superpower rivalry or the quest for military supremacy are no longer the driving forces behind the space programmes.

And given the huge costs involved in space exploration, international co-operation makes sense.

The Russians and the Americans are already co-operating at the highest levels.

Both sides have much to learn from each other. The Americans are ahead in some sectors of the space programme; they have better rocket, computer and communications technology.

They also have the space shuttle.

The Russians have led the way in other sectors. They have a space station in orbit. And they have successfully kept an astronaut in space for over a year – amassing an incredible amount of information which will prove crucial to future space missions.

The European Space Agency – which is already a model of what co-operative effort can achieve – also has a vital role to play.

The benefits to mankind of space colonisation could be immense.

At least as significant are the insights we will gain about the origins of the Earth, our Solar System and, ultimately, the Universe itself.

As this story unfolds, we will see that it is also our story – the story of mankind.

Inherent in that story are powerful unifying forces.

Space brings home to us the essential oneness of mankind.

Viewed from the perspective of the Moon, the regional conflicts currently reshaping the map of Europe and parts of the old Soviet Union – to say nothing of our own local conflict in Northern Ireland – appear trivial.

Nowhere does the concept of the Earth as a "global village" come into sharper focus than from outside the Earth.

The journey through Space is a journey into self-meaning. Kennedy understood that: it was part of his Catholic inheritance.

No one has expressed it better than the poet, T.S. Eliot:

> *We shall not cease from exploration*
> *And the end of all our exploring*
> *Will be to arrive where we started*
> *And know the place for the first time.*

To be in awe of all of this is an understandable human response. Yet if our growing understanding and perception of the earth, of Space and of Earth's place in the Universe inspires awe, it also inspires new visions of human endeavour, action and initiative.

Questions about man's place and destiny in the universal scheme of things may provide us in tomorrow's world with the basis for a new and enriched insight into what it is to be human.

Arthur C. Clarke is right. This is also part of the Kennedy legacy.

It was acknowledged in a book published in May 1993 entitled *The 100: A Ranking of the Most Influential Persons in History*, in which author Michael H. Hart places JFK at 81 because of his institution of the Apollo Space Programme.

If JFK was President of the New Frontier, he also deserves to be remembered as President of the Last Frontier.

9

A Phallic Presidency?

If a Martian landed in Lafayette Square in Washington DC and, sitting amid the trees and the squirrels, perused some of the books written about JFK over the past decade, he, she (or it) might be forgiven for thinking that prior to 1961 there had never been illicit sex in The White House.

Gazing across at the imposing structure (based, incidentally, on a design by an Irishman), the Martian might conclude that purity, moral probity and marital fidelity were indispensable characteristics of all of the 34 previous occupants.

Was there no licentiousness, no hanky-panky, until Kennedy moved in?

One might think so given some of the literature.

Kennedy as Presidential rake is a theme common to much of this literature.

We are given a portrait of a President with little else on his mind except fornicating.

And he is reputed to have done so much of it, in so many places with so many different women, that it is amazing he ever found time to put his signature to a single piece of legislation.

Kennedy may have given a new currency to the notion of a phallic presidency, but he definitely didn't invent that notion.

He was not the first president to play around.

Yes, he was a womaniser. There isn't much doubt about that now. In fact, there isn't any.

And at least one of his liaisons was potentially very dangerous.

But he did not introduce bedroom frolics to The White House. Nor did he have anything like the number of affairs he is alleged to have had. Indeed, the comment once made by Frank Sinatra would have been most apposite in JFK's case.

Replying to questions once about his love life, Ol' Blue Eyes quipped: "If I slept with all the women I am supposed to have slept with, I would now be in a glass jar in the Harvard Medical School!"

It is easy to imagine Kennedy, with his sense of humour, replying in a somewhat similar fashion, while flashing that boyish smile of his.

Were someone ever to write a book called *All The Presidents' Women*, JFK would, of course, figure prominently.

Not alone, however. No way.

Tales of extramarital sex have a long tradition among incumbents in The White House.

For one thing, unhappy marriages have not been unusual among the high-powered people who make it to the Presidency, and adulterous affairs have often remained secret for years – though most eventually come to light.

Kennedy was by no means alone; the list is impressive. Warren G. Harding (1921-23), generally considered one of the worst presidents, conceived an illegitimate child with mistress Nan Britton on a couch in his Senate office while a Senator in 1919. She was 30 years younger than Harding.

Continuing the affair after he became President, the pair would sometimes have sex in a large closet near his office in The White House.

Britton recounted the affair in painstaking detail in a sensational 1927 book, *The President's Daughter*, dedicated to unwed mothers.

It is part of the historical record that Franklin D. Roosevelt (1933-45) had a long extramarital affair with Lucy Page Mercer, after his wife Eleanor hired her as her social secretary.

Once Eleanor found out about it, Franklin promised to end it, but the affair later resumed and Mercer was with him when he died in 1945.

Grover Cleveland (1885-1889 & 1893-1897) is alleged to have fathered a lovechild in Buffalo, New York, before becoming President.

The 49-year-old Cleveland managed to survive the scandal and get to The White House, where he stirred further controversy by marrying a 21-year-old woman.

The third President of the United States, Thomas Jefferson (1801–1809), the man who drafted the Declaration of Independence, fathered several children by a black slave.

The two Presidents who preceded and succeeded Kennedy – Dwight D. Eisenhower (1953-61) and Lyndon B. Johnson (1963-69) – also had affairs.

Eisenhower had a notorious wartime affair with his Irish-born driver, Kay Summersby; and Johnson continued a long-term relationship with the beautiful Alice Glass, a reddish-blonde who was also the mistress of Charles E. Marsh, a wealthy Texas publisher.

Kennedy, as some of those close to him have testified, had a devastating effect on women.

His effect on them was electric. You only have to look at photographs of him campaigning, first for the House of Representatives and the Senate, and later in 1960 for the Presidency, to realise this.

Gloria Steinem may be exaggerating, though not greatly, when she called JFK the first sexually viable President.

Women loved him, great numbers of them. They adored him, wanted to be near him, to touch him, to hug him, to kiss him.

It is all there in the photographs.

His movie-star good looks and his charm made him irresistible to the opposite sex.

Women had never before seen a candidate like him. He contradicted their common image of politicians.

Instead of Edward G. Robinson, they were looking at Tyrone Power or Gary Cooper.

A later generation would look upon him as a cross between Robert Redford and Paul Newman.

His Hollywood good looks certainly turned their heads and captured their attention.

He was sexy – and inspired sexy thoughts.

I have no doubt that the character played by Robert Redford in the 1972 movie, *The Candidate*, was in part inspired by the peekaboo or keyhole version of the Kennedy legend.

That legend is inextricably bound up with women.

Sex and politics are the legend's two main ingredients.

It is a potent mix – as Henry Kissinger acknowledged when he made his now famous remark that "power is the greatest of all aphrodisiacs".

He knew what he was talking about.

Kennedy's sex appeal was unmistakable, and helped to put him into The White House.

Later on, it would also work – electorally speaking – for his two brothers, Bobby and Teddy.

And currently it works for his son, John F. Kennedy Junior.

That appeal has been testified to by many, including the actress Theresa Russell.

In *Insignificance*, the 1986 movie, the Marilyn Monroe-like character played so convincingly by Ms Russell made a list of the ten men in the world she most wanted to sleep with – Albert Einstein was her first choice.

Then in "20 Questions" in *Playboy* in June 1988 Theresa Russell herself gets asked the question.

John Kennedy and Robert Kennedy feature on her list.

The Kennedy aura intrigued many, many women – some of them very famous.

And it continues to do so.

There were reminders of this throughout 1992 when Bill Clinton was running for President.

Rumours about his sexual infidelity flourished for a time, threatening to derail his campaign.

It was a campaign noteworthy for being Kennedyesque in more ways than one.

The sexual overtones – and undertones – were obvious.

The biggest and most threatening undertone came in the shapely form of Gennifer Flowers, a woman from Clinton's home State of Arkansas, who claimed she had had an affair with the then Governor.

Clinton and his aides denied this.

The man from Arkansas survived – and went on to take The White House away from George Bush.

It wasn't that easy.

In order to survive, Clinton, with his wife Hillary by his side, had to submit to a televised discussion of his private life.

This happened on 26 January 1992, a date to remember, for it signified a new maturity, a new tolerance on the part of the American electorate.

John F. Kennedy would have approved.

I suspect he would also have had a good laugh.

At the time Gennifer Flowers was described by one English newspaper as "the most dangerous woman in America" because of her involvement with the then Presidential candidate, Bill Clinton.

"Sex is one thing, and history tells us lots of presidents apparently enjoyed it illicitly and still governed well, so does it really matter?"

Art Harris of *Penthouse* magazine, in asking the question – does it really matter? – was pointing to a sea-change in American attitudes.

It has long been a peculiar paradox of American life that the greater the relaxation of standards in the private lives of voters, the greater the demands made for politicians to be above reproach.

That paradox – as Clinton's election showed – may finally be breaking down.

"The importance of great men in history has nothing to do with their sex lives," declared Charles Spalding, who knew JFK and was a friend of the Kennedy family.

In a comment on the latter's sexual escapades, the actress Shirley MacLaine spoke for many when she said: "I would rather have a president who does it to a woman than a president who does it to a country."

Kennedy's sex life, of course, was not as chequered as some authors and gossip-mongers have alleged.

Attempts were even made to link Kennedy with the Profumo scandal which rocked Britain in mid-1963.

In June of that year John Profumo, Secretary of State for War in Harold Macmillan's Government, resigned because of his relationship with Christine Keeler, who was having an affair with Yevgeny Ivanov, a Soviet naval attaché, at the same time.

A subsequent inquiry failed to establish that Profumo had divulged classified information, but he resigned from the Government and from Parliament in disgrace.

Shortly afterwards, a story appeared seeking to link "one of the biggest names in American politics" with the Profumo scandal.

The anti-Kennedy and conservative *New York Journal American* alleged that in 1960/61, JFK had had an affair in New York with Marie Novotny, a 19-year-old call-girl from London who was a friend of Keeler.

The latter visited America in 1962, but an FBI investigation established that Kennedy was not involved with her.

Claims of a tangential linkage to "Operation Bow Tie", the FBI code name for the Profumo affair, have never been substantiated.

The suspicion persists that this was part of a "dirty tricks" campaign by FBI chief, J. Edgar Hoover, to smear Kennedy.

Other stories, somewhat less lurid, of sexual escapades have remained in circulation.

"We live in an age obsessed with sex," says Arthur Schlesinger. "This obsession had bred the National Enquirer school of biographers to collect unsubstantiated and unattributable rumours, treat them as if they were undisputed facts, and use them as the basis for a highly speculative character analysis."

Mindful of the long list of women with whom JFK is supposed to have slept – from Hollywood sex sirens like Marilyn Monroe and Jane Mansfield to anonymous White House secretaries – Schlesinger dismisses the image of Kennedy as an insatiable womaniser.

John Kenneth Galbraith was one of Kennedy's close advisers. Asked whether the allegations of womanising affected Kennedy's effectiveness as President, he replied: "I have never paid any attention to such matters. They were clearly unimportant. I concern myself only with civilised questions of some significance. Those matters are brought up by people who are not intelligent enough to talk about anything else."

Hugh Sidey, who was a correspondent in Washington during the Kennedy years, says simply that, "We never had irrefutable evidence of the women".

There were some, of course.

Including famous names – as we shall see.

10

White House Ladies

They were big names, actresses, Hollywood stars. They came into JFK's life before the biggest star of all – Marilyn Monroe.

Some of the names associated with JFK were Gene Tierney, Angie Dickinson, Sophia Loren and Jean Simmons.

Of these four, Gene Tierney is the only one who has admitted to a relationship with Kennedy, and that was before he became president. Angie Dickinson, while never admitting that much, has coyly hinted at an affair. And there is some circumstantial evidence in support of this.

Sophia Loren came to Kennedy's attention at a party. The statuesque Italian actress, who broke many a heart, caused Kennedy's to flutter.

Considered one of the most beautiful women to have graced the screen, Loren was approached by JFK at a reception.

At the time the Naples-born actress was working in Hollywood in roles that brought her an international audience (her first American film, *The Pride and the Passion,* was made in 1957).

She was also married to producer Carlo Ponti.

The Kennedy charm hit her at full wattage, but her resolve didn't crumble, and she rebuffed his advances.

A different story is told about Jean Simmons, who married the actor Stewart Grainger in 1950 and divorced him in 1960. Later that year she married the director Richard Brooks.

Born in London in 1929, Simmons became an American citizen in 1956. Her 1960 role as Sister Sharon in *Elmer Gantry,* the screen version of the Sinclair Lewis novel (for which her co-star, Burt Lancaster, won an Oscar) is the highlight of her cinematic career.

After meeting Kennedy, she was clearly wooed.

It was said that she never forgave her press agent for persuading her not to spend a weekend with him.

JFK also showed more than a passing interest in Kim Novak and Janet Leigh, both of whom he knew through his connections with Frank Sinatra.

With the ravishing Gene Tierney he had a full-blown affair.

They first started dating during his Navy days. But it was when they met in Los Angeles in 1946 – when she was still married to fashion designer Oleg Cassini – that the affair began in earnest.

A woman of whom it was said that nothing in her films equalled the drama of her life, Tierney divorced her husband in 1952.

Sometime afterwards she began an affair with Aly Khan, who had just divorced Rita Hayworth.

Eight years later, the aristocratic Cassini was chosen by Jackie Kennedy to design her inaugural wardrobe. The star of such movies as Otto Preminger's gripping murder mystery *Laura* (1944), and the romantic drama *Leave Her To Heaven* (1945), Gene Tierney's exquisitely modelled features graced 30 feature films over a period of 25 years.

Her feline appearance, high cheek bones and heart-shaped face made her one of the beauties of the cinema in the forties and fifties.

During JFK's Presidency, she played a Washington matron in *Advise and Consent*, one of the best films ever made about American politics.

That was in 1962 and it reunited her with Otto Preminger, for whom she did her best work.

In her 1974 book, *Self-Portrait*, she talked openly about her affair with Kennedy, and how they kept up the acquaintanceship.

"He had the most beautiful eyes," she said. "He gave you his time, his interest. And he knew the strength of the phrase, 'What do you think?' He made you feel very secure."

Tierney, who died in November 1991, was upfront about her involvement.

Others were more circumspect.

The stories about Angie Dickinson are intriguing.

She has never denied having a "close relationship" with JFK, and there is a giveaway film clip on file which shows her waiting in line to greet him at a White House reception.

One of Hollywood's most beautiful actresses, Angie Dickinson was born in Kulm, North Dakota, and was married twice – first to Gene Dickinson (divorced in 1959), and then to composer Burt Bacharach.

She married the latter in 1965 and they were divorced in1980.

For the period of Kennedy's Presidency, therefore, she was unwed.

Famous most of all perhaps for her role as "Feathers" opposite John Wayne in Howard Hawks' 1959 Western *Rio Bravo*, she also won critical acclaim for her role as the promiscuous Kate Miller in Brian De Palma's 1980 psychological thriller *Dressed To Kill*.

In 1960 she campaigned for JFK, and it is easy to understand why JFK should have been attracted to her.

A captivating blonde and very sexy, with legs voted "the best in the world", she even charmed John Kenneth Galbraith when he was Kennedy's Ambassador to India.

In his marvellous *Ambassador's Journal*, published in 1969, he describes how he met her in Washington in November 1961.

By coincidence, she was leaving for Los Angeles at the same time as he was, and they travelled together.

"By halfway to Los Angeles, I was deeply in love. She has fair, pure skin, blonde to vaguely reddish hair, merry eyes and a neat, unstarved body. She also has a bubbling sense of humour and a quick interest in life. I never had a lovelier companion and the trip went in a minute . . . "

Angie Dickinson was also moving in the Frank Sinatra circle when Kennedy was campaigning for the Presidency, and in 1960 she starred along with Sinatra and Kennedy's brother-in-law, Peter Lawford, in *Ocean's Eleven.*

Now 60 – and still looking remarkably well – Dickinson is said to be working on her memoirs in which, she says, she will reveal all.

If she does indeed "reveal all", it should re-open the debate about Kennedy's womanising.

Although she denies that her relationship with JFK was anything more than "just good friends", she has said of him that he was "the sexiest politician that I ever met. He was the killer type, a devastatingly handsome, charming man".

Her home in LA's Coldwater Canyon is a shrine of JFK memorabilia, adding weight to the controversial rumour – that they had a sizzling affair when he was President.

On the night of his inauguration, JFK slipped away from Jackie to make an appearance at a private party hosted by Frank Sinatra at the Statler-Hilton Hotel.

Among the guests were Kim Novak and Janet Leigh, with whom the new President chatted and joked.

Hollywood, and gossip about it and its star inhabitants, had a particular fascination for him.

Pierre Salinger, who was Kennedy's Press Secretary, explained in an interview in January 1993 why he stayed out of the stories about Kennedy's love life.

"One journalist came to me and said he had a hot story about Kennedy's mistresses. I said, 'Look, this guy is President. He works 14, 15 hours a day in the world's most gruelling job. If he has time and energy for mistresses after that, good luck to him.' That was the end of it."

But it wasn't really. Far from it.

The illicit sex mightn't have mattered. And Salinger had a point about the time and energy bit.

But Kennedy had three liaisons which were downright dangerous; liaisons which exposed him to very great risk – the risk of compromise, of blackmail, perhaps even worse.

One of those liaisons occurred before he assumed the Presidency, but it too left him exposed.

The three women with whom he was dangerously involved were Mary Pinchot Meyer, Judith Campbell Exner and – most famous of all – Marilyn Monroe.

It is to this trio of lovelies and JFK's entanglements with them that we must now turn.

11

Murder in Georgetown

In 1986 the daughter of an American President, Margaret Truman, wrote a mystery novel entitled *Murder in Georgetown*. It was a tale of political intrigue, passion and skullduggery set in and around the classy and expensive suburb of Washington DC where many of the politicians and lobbyists reside. As a place to live, it is an address with a high price-tag.

John and Jackie Kennedy had a house there during JFK's time in the Senate.

So had an extraordinarily beautiful woman. A blonde. An artist.

And the title of Ms Truman's novel serves as an apt heading for an episode which links all three – an episode with a bloody ending. Today a file bearing the name of the beautiful blonde is stored in a cabinet in Police Headquarters in Washington.

The name on the file is Mary Pinchot Meyer.

On Monday, 12 October 1964 – nearly eleven months after Dallas – she was murdered.

At 12.45 on the afternoon of that day she was shot in the head while out walking.

The paint was still damp on Mary Meyer's final canvas when she pulled on a sweatshirt and a blue hooded sweater and left her studio to go for a walk.

The studio was only a short distance away from the homes of some of her closest friends. Her sister, Toni, and Toni's husband at the time, Ben Bradlee of *The Washington Post*, lived at one end of the row of townhouses; Mr and Mrs John Kennedy lived at the other end until they moved to The White House.

Occasionally Mary Meyer would take walks with Jackie along the towpath paralleling the old Chesapeake and Ohio barge canal.

That's where she headed, having left her studio – left on 34th Street, down to the footbridge that leads across the canal and onto the towpath between the canal and the wooded embankment that descends to the Potomac.

She reached the towpath about noon that day. Mary Meyer was two days away from her 44th birthday.

That same day around noon an Air Force Lieutenant left the Pentagon Athletic Centre on the Virginia side of the Potomac, crossed over the Key Bridge and began his regular run two miles west along the towpath to a fishing spot on the river called Fletcher's Landing and back again.

His name was William Mitchell.

He passed three people on his way west – a middle-aged couple and a young white man in Bermuda shorts.

On his way back east to Key Bridge he passed two more people. First the woman in the blue sweater, and then, 200 yards further east, a black man wearing a light coloured windcheater and walking in the same direction as the woman.

A man called Henry Wiggins heard the screams. He had come with his truck from an Esso petrol station on M Street to Canal Street where a car with a dead battery was stranded.

He had just raised the bonnet of the car when a woman screamed from the vicinity of the canal.

"Someone help me!" she cried.

Then there was a gunshot.

Wiggins ran across the road to the stone wall above the canal.

As he ran a second shot rang out.

When he looked over the wall he saw a black man in a light jacket standing over the body of a white woman in a blue sweater. The black man put a dark object into the pocket of his windcheater, and then ran off down the far side of the towpath, into a wooded area.

James Angleton got the call from his wife, Cecily, while he was in the middle of a conference at CIA headquarters at Langley.

At the time he was chief of counter intelligence, and Cecily interrupted the meeting to tell him that according to a radio bulletin an unidentified woman had been killed on the towpath that afternoon. Cecily was fearful the victim was their close friend, Mary Meyer. She had often warned Mary not to go on the towpath alone.

Angleton dismissed his wife's fears. That evening they had plans to drive Mary Meyer to a poetry evening, and he saw no reason to change anything.

When they arrived at Mary's home that night, her car was in the driveway yet the lights were out inside.

No one answered the bell.

They soon learned that Mary had been murdered.

The Angletons hurried to the Bradlees' home where they helped make funeral arrangements.

It was a short time later that the CIA chief learned about the diary. He was told that Mary Meyer kept a secret diary and that it contained details about an affair – a very special affair.

After the call from Henry Wiggins, the police hunt began immediately. The five exits from the towpath across the canal to the streets of Georgetown were sealed.

When Detective Bernard Crooke arrived at the scene he was struck immediately by how beautiful the murdered woman was.

"I've seen a lot of dead women," he said, "but none who looked beautiful when dead. She even looked beautiful with a bullet in her head."

Minutes earlier another detective who had gone east along the towpath came across a black man named Raymond Crump. When he was brought before Henry Wiggins, the latter said: "That's him."

But things weren't that simple.

The police started to build a file on Mary Meyer and her friends, and they learned very quickly of a CIA connection.

In the spring of 1945 Mary Eno Pinchot married Cord Meyer Jr in New York. They were both rich and talented. She was the most beautiful girl in Vassar's class of '42, and came from one of America's most prominent families – the Pinchots of Pennsylvania. Her uncle, Gifford Pinchot, had served two terms as Governor of his home State in the twenties and thirties, and had been mentioned as a "dark horse" for the Republican Presidential nomination.

Cord Meyer's father was a diplomat. At the time of the marriage Cord himself was serving as a military aide and had fought the Japanese in Guam during World War II.

In 1947 he was named one of the ten outstanding young men in the United States by one Chamber of Commerce.

At the urging of the boss of the CIA, Allen Dulles, Cord Meyer joined the Agency in 1951 and eventually became assistant deputy director of plans, better known as the dirty tricks department.

By 1956, after 11 years of marriage, Mary, then 36, could no longer tolerate living with Cord and the CIA, which she hated.

They divorced and she moved across the Potomac from McLean, Virginia, where Bobby Kennedy had been her next-door neighbour and friend.

She took up residence in a townhouse in Georgetown, around the corner from her sister and Ben Bradlee and their mutual friends, Senator John Kennedy and Jackie.

In time she was to become the secret Lady Ottoline of Camelot.

She had actually met John Kennedy while at Vassar. His Harvard class of '40 dated several members of Mary's class.

But in Georgetown a much more serious relationship between them developed, a relationship that continued during Kennedy's White House years.

She regularly attended functions in The White House in the company of her sister, Toni, and Ben Bradlee.

And according to the *National Enquirer*, a sexual relationship between Mary and JFK began in January 1962.

After her divorce, Mary started painting and, ironically, her first exhibition opened in Washington's Jefferson Place Gallery in the awful month of November 1963.

Apart from tributes to her beauty, the words most commonly used by her friends to describe her were warmth, vibrancy, loyalty, mystery and strength.

Sometime before she was killed, Mary Meyer confided to her friends James and Ann Truitt the fact of her affair with JFK and the existence of a secret diary recounting their times together.

The precise contents have never been disclosed. And never will be, because the diary was destroyed by the CIA.

The Truitts were in Tokyo when Mary Meyer was murdered; James Truitt was serving there as the *Newsweek* bureau chief. When word reached them of the towpath killing, they told their mutual friend, James Angleton, about the existence of the diary.

Angleton organised an immediate search of Mary Meyer's home. He had been told she kept the diary in a bookcase in her bedroom, along with clippings of the JFK assassination.

It was not there after her death.

The following day it was discovered in her studio in a locked steel box filled with hundreds of letters.

When Raymond Crump went on trial for the murder of Mary Meyer on 19 July 1965, neither the police nor the court was made aware of the diary or the letters.

On 30 July, after being out for 11 hours, the jury returned a verdict. They found Crump not guilty.

His acquittal left the murder of Mary Meyer officially unsolved. And the Washington police never re-opened the case. They closed the towpath murder file after the trial.

Fourteen years after the murder the *National Enquirer* broke the story of the JFK-Meyer affair.

Its front-page headline on 2 March 1976 read: JFK 2 YR WHITE HOUSE ROMANCE – Socialite then Murdered and Diary Burned by CIA.

According to the story, JFK first asked Mary Meyer to go to bed with him in The White House in December 1961.

A current involvement with an artist caused her to reject his proposal. But from January on they began an affair which lasted until his assassination.

The Enquirer also disclosed that Mary's personal diary containing references to JFK, and several love letters from him, were discovered and handed over to the CIA.

The Enquirer account raised the question of an official CIA connection to the death. The tabloid called the murder "unsolved" and suggestively characterised the official view of the case as "a lone gunman" theory.

Immediately after the acquittal of Ray Crump, there was talk in Georgetown circles of the possibility of a conspiracy in Mary Meyer's death.

The real questions relate to Mary's diary – what was in it, and who read it?

Did it not only reveal details of the nature of their relationship, but also details of JFK's plans and policies garnered in pillow talk?

Ms Dovey Roundtree, one of the best homicide lawyers in Washington, who defended Crump, only found out years later that Mary Meyer had a high White House clearance and that her diary was burned before the trial.

"I thought the government had something to do with the whole case," she said afterwards.

She is not alone in this.

Key questions remain unanswered.

Was there a CIA link to the killing?

If so – why?

What was being covered up?

The murder of Mary Meyer was never solved – and it triggered an unsettling series of events involving some of the most powerful figures in Washington.

"I was stunned by news of the affair," said Ben Bradlee, who was in Dublin in 1992 to give a lecture at Trinity College, where I met him. "Not quite as stunned as my wife. I think it was a real blow to her."

And 29 years on, it remains as a tragic and bizarre aftermath to one of the strangest episodes in the life of a president, a life which had its share of strange episodes.

Mary Meyer was 43 when she was murdered, and she had powerful connections.

This bloody incident, which occurred almost a year after the assassination of JFK in Dallas, has left a string of unanswered questions. The fall-out from these can still cause ripples in the American political, intelligence, military and media establishments.

Kennedy's affair with Meyer was his last, and it went on from January 1962 to November 1963.

But speculation continues that she may have known more about Kennedy's political plans and intentions than anyone realised at the time of her murder.

Since then the accumulation of evidence pointing to CIA and Pentagon complicity in the assassination of Kennedy has fuelled suspicions that what happened in Dealey Plaza was part of a carefully worked-out plot.

And the purpose of this plot was to ensure that a presidential decision to end the US involvement in Vietnam would never be implemented.

This is, of course, the central thesis of the Oliver Stone movie.

In it she revealed details not just of her love affair with Sinatra, and the glitzy lifestyle to which he introduced her, but also something far more sensational.

She told the world of two other affairs – one involving Mafia boss Giancana, and the other involving the President of the United States.

To many members of the public, this did not come as something terribly new and shocking. In 1975 some investigative work was done by sections of the media, and both *Time* magazine and *Newsweek* carried stories in December of that year.

What the liaison eventually led to was a frightening allegation – that FBI boss, J. Edgar Hoover had blackmailed the President with information gained from wiretaps that linked Kennedy to a girlfriend of a Mafia chieftain.

Is it conceivable that Kennedy would compromise himself in such a manner with the Mafia – or at least leave himself open to the possibility of such a compromise?

Anthony Summers, author of *The Kennedy Conspiracy*, is one who thinks so.

"A connection between Kennedy, the privileged Easterner, and Giancana, the Mafia graduate of a Chicago street gang, is not as improbable as it might seem. They shared a number of mutual friends, including Frank Sinatra . . . "

It was Sinatra, in fact, who introduced Kennedy to Exner in Dean Martin's hotel suite in Las Vegas.

In her book, *My Story*, Exner describes this meeting.

"Although it began as a typical Las Vegas weekend it ended, for me at least, quite differently, for this was the weekend I met Jack Kennedy.

"The first time I saw him was at ten o'clock Sunday evening, February 7 1960. He and Teddy were at Frank's table in the Sands lounge. He looked so handsome in his pin-striped suit. Those strong white teeth and smiling Irish eyes. The introduction, as all introductions in that group, was so perfunctory that it took me a moment to realise this was actually Pat Lawford's brother. But of course the moment he opened his mouth there was no mistaking the Kennedy voice."

Later, at dinner, she sat next to Teddy and Jack.

"I must say I was tremendously impressed by Jack's poise and wit and charm. He talked to all the women at the table, and when he listened, it was as if every nerve and muscle in his whole body was poised at attention. As I was to learn, Jack Kennedy was the world's greatest listener."

The following day they had lunch together on the patio of Sinatra's suite. The main topic of conversation was religion.

"It was the last thing I wanted to pursue with Jack Kennedy on that beautiful day."

Exner, a lapsed Catholic, discovered that JFK was very proud of being Irish and Catholic – in that order.

After that first encounter, Exner was smitten. "I woke up feeling like Scarlett O'Hara the morning after Rhett Butler carried her up the stairs."

It wasn't until they met again at the Plaza Hotel in New York on 7 March that they made love.

The affair had begun, and had now become dangerous, as Exner herself acknowledged.

"I was concerned about where the affair was leading me. He was married and perhaps someday he would be the President of the United States.

"How does the President of the United States carry on an affair without arousing suspicion?"

But it wasn't just the affair, which was to continue until 1962.

What made the whole thing dangerous for Kennedy was the man Judith Exner was introduced to some weeks later. He was middle-aged, of medium build and ruddy complexion, but with penetrating dark eyes.

This was Sam Giancana.

And, again, it was Sinatra who made the introduction.

It was months before Exner got to know his real name; when she first met him Sinatra called him "Sam Flood", one of several aliases.

It was some months later still, if Exner is to be believed, before she found out who he really was.

Now she wasn't just about to become the President's moll; she was about to become a gangster's moll as well.

In November 1960 Kennedy beat Nixon for the Presidency, winning by the narrowest margin in American electoral history – one-tenth of one per cent of the entire popular vote.

Ever since, it has been alleged that, with the help of the Syndicate, crucial votes were "stolen" in Illinois (of which Chicago is the major city) which put Kennedy into The White House.

Exner has this to say: "Jack squeaked by on a prayer and a few thousand stolen votes in Cook County, without which Nixon would have awakened that morning as the next President of the United States. Mayor Daley has quietly taken credit for Jack's victory, but Sam often told me, 'Listen, honey, if it wasn't for me your boyfriend wouldn't even be in The White House'."

Then she made a statement which – crucially – she was to contradict years later.

"I didn't really want to know the details of anything. I liked being kept completely away from the seedier side of whatever his life may have been."

Throughout 1961 and the spring of 1962 Exner continued to see the man who was now the President – sometimes, according to her version, even visiting him in The White House and in Palm Beach, where the Kennedys had a summer house.

Then abruptly the affair stopped, the whole thing came to a halt.

Why?

Exner's version in her 1977 book, which is now a rare volume, is that she realised she no longer "loved" JFK.

"It happened so gradually that I wasn't really aware that it was over until long after it had ended. It just dwindled away, and at one point the telephone finally stopped ringing."

The last call came, she claims, at least three months after a luncheon in The White House on 22 March 1962.

Exner wasn't at that luncheon, but the FBI boss, J. Edgar Hoover, was – the man who "supposedly told the President of my relationship with Sam".

Years later, in 1975, a Senate Committee report stated that White House logs showed that Kennedy called Exner a few hours after that luncheon.

To say what? Exner supplies the answer.

"The inference is that Jack immediately contacted me and said don't ever darken my door again."

The calls from The White House stopped, she insisted, not because "of any outside force, but because of natural attrition".

The other curious thing, in view of a new version of the triangular relationship between Kennedy, Exner and Giancana, which Exner would tell years later, is that her 1977 account contains not a single claim that there was ever any contact, direct or indirect, between the President and the Mafia boss.

That came later, in 1991.

She claimed then that she had not only acted as a courier between the two men, but that, on the evening of 28 April 1961, she was present in the Ambassador East Hotel in Chicago when Kennedy met the mobster.

And that's not all.

Back in 1988, in an interview with Kitty Kelley (who has written biographies of Sinatra, Jackie Kennedy Onassis and Nancy Reagan), Exner said Kennedy and Giancana had prolonged contacts with each other, using her as a go-between. However, she claimed she had no knowledge as to the contents of the packages she carried between the two men.

By 1991, however, she was able to inform all and sundry that Kennedy had told her the packages contained intelligence material concerning the elimination of Cuba's Fidel Castro.

It is now known that by August 1960, around the time JFK was being nominated as the Democratic Presidential candidate, the CIA initiated an infamous arrangement to have Castro killed by the Mafia.

The code name for this project, involving two powerful covert organisations, was "Operation Mongoose".

And one of the key players recruited by the CIA for this was Sam Giancana.

Indeed, Giancana's own violent death is believed to be linked to his involvement in Operation Mongoose and a related plot to kill Kennedy.

He was shot seven times at his home in June 1975, shortly before he was due to give evidence to the Senate Intelligence Committee about CIA plans to hit Castro.

So what do we make of Exner's account?

Was she being economical with the truth in 1977 and 1988 – and prodigal with it in 1991?

There can be little doubt that Exner had an affair with Kennedy, and that it lasted from 1960 to 1962.

White House logs show that she made a series of telephone calls. She may also have visited the Presidential residence.

A total of 70 phone calls from Exner to The White House were recorded in the logs from 1960 to 1962. Some of the calls came from Giancana's home.

But other than Exner's own word, there is no evidence whatsoever to back up claims made by her that there was a Kennedy-Giancana connection.

Hoover, not surprisingly, since he kept files on every VIP, knew something was going on. In a memo dated 22 May 1961, he revealed that he knew Giancana was being used by the CIA against Castro.

On 27 February 1962, Bobby Kennedy received a memo from the FBI Director in which he detailed the President's relationship with Exner.

Hoover also informed him that he had information in his possession which showed that Exner was also the mistress of Giancana.

Hoover told the Attorney General that the FBI was concerned over the possibility that Giancana might use the Exner connection and his CIA relationship as a double blackmail against future prosecution.

Bobby wasted no time. It was his intervention that ended what had become for his brother the most dangerous of liaisons.

It has never been established how much the President or Bobby knew of Operation Mongoose.

The CIA Director of Covert Operations, Richard Bissell, was responsible for the secret war against Castro's Cuba.

This included plans for the assassination of Castro, plans which were formulated with the preparations for the Bay of Pigs invasion, preparations which started while Eisenhower was still President.

One of several bizarre plans involved recruiting the help of Mafia bosses. The latter were only too keen to help because they had controlled the lucrative casinos and brothels of Havana during the Batista regime.

But White House approval for the covert operations against Castro has never been established.

Kennedy's aide, Theodore Sorensen, doubted that the President had any detailed knowledge of Operation Mongoose when I discussed it with him.

"He would have disapproved of any plot to kill Castro."

We know that in May 1962 CIA General Counsel Lawrence Houston finally told Kennedy the whole ugly truth – that the Agency had entered into a contract with Giancana to murder Castro.

Kennedy fixed him with a cold look and said: "I trust that if you ever try to do business with organised crime again – with gangsters – you will let the Attorney General know."

Kennedy is also on record as publicly denouncing assassination of foreign leaders as an instrument of national policy.

But the risk Kennedy took in persisting with his affair with Exner betrays recklessness.

"That Kennedy continued seeing Judith Exner knowing that she was also seeing Sam Giancana, and possibly knowing that Giancana had been hired to kill Castro, was, of course, reckless in the extreme, especially since his brother had targeted Giancana as a top-priority candidate for investigation in his war against organised crime," stated John H. Davis in *The Kennedys: Dynasty and Disaster.*

This is echoed in *Of Kennedys and Kings* by Harris Wofford: "If the President confessed to even one-tenth the relationship with Judith Exner that she claimed, he had been bold and reckless in his private life."

If Kennedy was not a political adventurer, and I don't think that can now be sustained, he was a sexual adventurer.

There is little point in attempting to deny or downplay this.

But it cannot be convincingly argued that this undermined his moral fitness for high office.

If Kennedy is to be disqualified on this basis, then where does that leave other presidents?

13

MM and the Kennedys

Her face stares out from millions of television screens, bookshop windows and advertising posters.

The halo of bleached hair and the full lips are instantly recognisable.

The hour-glass figure has become a universal symbol of sexuality.

The woman herself died 31 years ago, but today the legend is glowing brighter than ever.

The end, when it came, was sordid and sensational.

On 5 August 1962, the body of a naked blonde woman was found in a modest house in Brentwood, a quiet suburb of Los Angeles.

Her name was Marilyn Monroe, and ever since, the circumstances of her death have been the subject of endless speculation.

Long before her death – she was 36 when she died – she was already a movie legend.

In the three decades since that fateful day, she has become not just Hollywood's greatest icon, but also a woman at the centre of what many now regard as a great cover-up.

The circumstances of Marilyn Monroe's tragic death continue to be scrutinised and re-scrutinised.

Dozens of books have been written about her death (and hundreds about her life, her career and her movies). Many of the people who have written books about her have been inspired by rumours of a Mafia or American Government cover-up.

The only other twentieth century American name as famous as Monroe is Kennedy. And in a story that could not have been more juicy if a Hollywood scriptwriter had dreamed it up, the two names came together.

Marilyn was allegedly involved with both Jack and Bobby Kennedy, and there is still speculation about their involvement in her death.

Some authors have bluntly asserted that Marilyn was killed on the direct orders of President Kennedy.

Nobody, however, has ever been able to back this up.

Questions about how and why she died are still being asked in the 1990s.

Today, unlike the 1960s, and as in the case of JFK's own death, many people now believe that the original verdict in Marilyn's case was erroneous. That much at least has been achieved – and those writers who persisted with their investigations deserve credit for that.

So if it wasn't suicide, what was it?

Was it murder? And if so, why was Marilyn murdered – and by whom?

The answer may well lie in the character of Marilyn herself, a complex, uncertain and frightened woman – something of a lost soul.

Hollywood over the years has produced its share of stars and starlets and heroines, but when one talks about a film goddess, for millions it can only mean one thing: Marilyn Monroe.

More than any other actress she personified the glamour and lure and seduction of the silver screen.

"Every man's love affair with America," is how writer Norman Mailer described her.

"The Stradivarius of sex," he added.

She certainly occupied more column inches, more unauthorised biographies and more wall space that any actress, before or since.

But behind the glamour there was a history of neglect, abuse, pain and humiliation.

As for her death, the theories abound.

Here is one of the most recycled of them. Marilyn Monroe did not commit suicide in August 1962, 31 years ago – she was killed by the Mafia.

Her stage-managed death was an attempt to embarrass, and possibly frame Bobby Kennedy, America's Attorney General, who was having an affair with her.

The actress had previously had an affair with President Kennedy, Robert's brother.

Bobby Kennedy was set to clean up America. He was the first Attorney General to openly declare war on the bosses of organised crime.

He wanted to rid it of the Mafia.

The hapless Marilyn was a pawn.

The Mafia arranged to have the sex lives of the Kennedys, especially their involvement with Monroe, taped.

Marilyn, the orphan child of several foster homes, told friends over her tapped telephone that she was falling in love with the Attorney General.

But the relationship with Bobby was foundering. And Marilyn caused fury when she tried to contact Bobby at his home, an embarrassment for a man who had just been voted "family man of the year".

However, the Mafia's attempt to implicate Bobby in the film star's death failed.

It is undisputed that documents were taken from her house. Her diary, for instance, was never found.

Suggestions that Bobby Kennedy arranged to have all connections with him removed from the house are, at best, speculative.

The manner of her death remains shrouded in mystery.

Initially, the official verdict was suicide. We were told that she died of an overdose of pills she took deliberately.

Later, however, it was alleged that she was given a lethal suppository of the barbiturate Nembutal.

In other words, she was murdered, but the murder was made to look like suicide.

The method chosen – as ingenious as it was macabre – meant the drug was absorbed rapidly and directly into the blood stream. This meant that even if she had been discovered in a coma, there was nothing in her stomach to pump out and, since no needle was used, there was no suspicious mark on her body.

"There was a mystery about her when she was alive and there remains an unsolved mystery," says journalist W.J. Weatherby, who knew her well.

"We are still unsure about the extent of her relationship with President Kennedy and his brother, Robert. We still do not know how she died – whether it was an accidental drug overdose, or whether it was suicide or even murder.

"Suicide seems out of character for the woman I knew, and much of the circumstantial evidence suggesting she was killed may simply be due to the cover-ups and conspiracies of silence that always occur when major political figures or Mafia figures or corrupt union bosses are involved in a potentially scandalous situation, and all three played a role in Marilyn's last days.

"President Kennedy had apparently shared a Mafia leader's mistress and Jimmy Hoffa of the Teamsters' Union wanted to get something on Robert Kennedy; Marilyn was a mere pawn in this ruthless power play.

"President Kennedy was killed just over a year after her death and exactly how that came about also remains a mystery, as Oliver Stone recently reminded us with his film *JFK* – perhaps he should now make another one entitled *MM*.

"When so many people who knew the truth are no longer alive 31 years later, it is unlikely we shall ever solve the mystery of Marilyn's death or Kennedy's."

Far less mystery surrounds Marilyn's death, though her place as a major sexual icon of the twentieth century remains fixed.

"It is when you add her uniquely vulnerable quality, so vividly revealed on screen and off, the quality that made possible the mystery of her death, that her hold on so many people's affections for so long seems quite understandable."

According to Barry Norman: "She was a confused and bewildered creature who used the remarkable physical gifts with which nature had endowed her to keep at bay a world that, on the whole, simply frightened her."

In 1975, 13 years after the death of the actress, *Oui* magazine published an article by Anthony Scaduto, an investigative reporter. He theorised about the identity of the killers. "She may have been killed by those protecting Bobby, JFK and the future Kennedy presidential dynasty from scandal."

This remains speculation.

Oui was also the first to say that Monroe's house in Brentwood had been bugged, and that the surveillance produced sensational tapes of Robert Kennedy and Monroe fighting on the last afternoon of her life.

No such tapes have ever entered the public domain.

During Robert Kennedy's Presidential campaign in 1968, it was reported that a right-wing group offered a $75,000 reward to anybody who could produce tapes of his affair with Monroe.

If such tapes existed, nobody produced them. Some said they vanished; others claim they remain locked up in an FBI vault.

It is difficult – nay, impossible – to believe that if such tapes were ever made, and if they survived, that they wouldn't be made public today.

The evidence of actress Susan Strasberg, in whose house Marilyn stayed, must carry considerable weight.

When she visited Ireland in 1992 to publicise her book *Marilyn and Me*, she told Pat Kenny on RTE Radio 1 of Marilyn's dependence on drugs and the effect these had on her.

"She overdosed at least ten times in the years that I knew her. Sometimes she said she wanted to kill herself. But most of the overdoses were accidental."

Ms Strasberg believes that on the fateful night in August 1962 Marilyn may have been like the little girl who cried "wolf" once too often.

"This time nobody came and she died . . . "

What about JFK? What about Marilyn's dreams of becoming First Lady?

"Marilyn, without the pills and alcohol, would not in her worst nightmare have had any desire to be with Jack Kennedy on any permanent basis.

"Okay, for a little girl from Southern California – one who had a crazy mother – to sleep with a charismatic President . . . well, that's enough fantasy to seduce women with many more advantages.

"And she loved the secrecy of it. When you're an addict like her you manipulate and use people, fantasize. Lies become the truth. But Kennedy was not a man she wanted for life."

One of the early books about her which I bought (I paid 35 cents for it in a second-hand bookshop in Peoria) carries the title: *Who Killed Marilyn – And Did The Kennedys Know?*

The author, Tony Sciacca, is in no doubt.

"She was murdered, there can be no doubt about it. And in some way, impossible to understand with precision, the Kennedy family was involved in that murder.

"We didn't realise it back then, but both John and Robert Kennedy had been her lovers.

"John first – there were innuendoes about that affair when Marilyn sang on 19 May 1962 at JFK's forty-fifth birthday party in Madison

Square Gardens, wearing a form-fitting sheer dress studded with thousands of sequins.

"She sang Happy Birthday, Mr President. Later that night she shared his bed, as she often had in past months.

"And, apparently after the President permitted caution and political realities to overtake his almost insatiable need for women like her, Robert took John's place and Marilyn focused her energies on the younger brother."

Sciacca, like many other authors, concludes that the facts of her murder were suppressed to protect the Kennedy dynasty.

This is typical of much that has been written about Marilyn, the Kennedys and her death.

But it is based on the flimsiest of evidence, much imagination and a lot of chutzpah.

An author of much greater talent and stature than Sciacca, Norman Mailer, is in no doubt about Marilyn's infatuation with America's First Family, but less certain about a Kennedy connection with her death.

A sometime conspiracy theorist, Mailer doesn't rule out the possibility of a political dimension to Marilyn's death.

"Ironically, after Watergate, the idea that she was murdered seems a little less extraordinary now, doesn't it? Echoes, echoes – we know more about the CIA, the right wing of the FBI, blackmail and counter-blackmail in high places today, don't we?"

We also know that President Kennedy was extremely worried about factions within not just the CIA and the FBI, but also within the military.

One of the books Kennedy liked most was the 1962 political thriller by Fletcher Knebel and Charles W. Bailey II called *Seven Days in May*.

This novel, later turned into a tense and exciting film starring Burt Lancaster and Kirk Douglas, is about a plot by the military to overthrow the United States government.

Kennedy not only liked the novel, he also told some of his people in The White House that the possibility of a coup was not to be dismissed.

And it isn't generally known that in an attempt to make people aware of this, he used his not inconsiderable influence to have the film made.

He even telephoned the director, John Frankheimer, and told him that when it got to the stage where scenes in The White House needed to be filmed, he would conveniently move to Hyannis Port so that this could be done.

Right-wing plots against Kennedy were a reality – this was one of the compelling reasons why some of his advisers pleaded with him not to make the trip to Dallas in November, 1963.

"You're going into nut country," one of them told him.

Dallas – like much of Texas – was a hotbed of right-wing extremism at the time, and the thousands of "Wanted for Treason" posters which were circulated the day before JFK's visit testified in a frightening way to the awful atmosphere which existed.

Today, with all that we now know about the circumstances of Kennedy's death, we can more readily appreciate that his fears about sections of the CIA, the FBI and the military – to say nothing of the Mafia – were not unfounded.

This is perhaps the context in which we should also look at Marilyn's death.

If she was murdered – and I now believe she was – it is much more probable that she was killed as part of some kind of plot to smear, embarrass or undermine the Kennedys.

Just as in the case of JFK's death, we may never know the full truth about Marilyn's death.

A friend of hers, the actress Susan Strasberg, believes Marilyn took some of her mysteries to the grave with her.

One of those mysteries was undoubtedly the lingering mystery of her tragic death.

This is partly why she still looms so large today in our culture, our history, our collective sense of the twentieth century.

There is more of course. There is the remark – by way of explanation – made by the French actress, Catherine Deneuve: "She was the most beautiful image I ever saw on the screen.

"Indeed, dying as she did at 36, close to her prime, she will forever be that mischievous, vulnerable blonde who haunts the American Dream."

Jack and Bobby Kennedy were also part of that Dream. It is fitting that her name will forever be linked with theirs.

It now seems probable that Jack Kennedy and Marilyn Monroe had met before his election to the Presidency.

To be cautious about making sexual assumptions about the Kennedy brothers is not only prudent, it is also fair and charitable.

Dean Martin's former wife, Jeanne Martin, made what is perhaps the most apposite comment: "Unless you're in the bedroom, it's unfair to presume."

One of America's leading feminists, Gloria Steinem, wrote a book on Marilyn in 1987, describing her as the icon that never died.

"Marilyn began to hint that she might marry again, this time to a very important man in government. Friends who assumed she meant Bobby Kennedy were stunned by both her lack of discretion and her lack of realism," says Steinem.

Whatever was going on between Marilyn and Bobby, marriage was never an option.

Apart from all other considerations, it would have been political suicide for RFK.

"There was something at once magical and desperate about her," observed Arthur Schlesinger, who was present in Madison Square Gardens on the famous occasion when she serenaded the President.

"Both the President and the Attorney General had ignored J. Edgar Hoover's warnings about their vulnerability to sexual scandal in the past, but they were now forced to look at their peril. Marilyn was one part of this. She was a threat by her own indiscreet and out-of-control presence. She was also a threat because of her intimacy with Sinatra . . ."

This was because of the latter's alleged links with some Mafia figures.

Some people maintain that Marilyn was threatening to hold a press conference at which she would reveal details of her relationships with the Kennedys.

Others say she was going to show a notebook, in which she had jotted down conversations with Bobby, to Ethel Kennedy.

It has been established beyond dispute that during her last days she tried to make contact with Bobby, who was staying in San Francisco with Ethel and some of their children.

"As for the Kennedys, a dead Marilyn was probably more dangerous to them than a live one. They behaved in such a cavalier fashion with Marilyn that it's difficult to believe they feared her. It's even more difficult to believe that she would have carried through a threat, especially against people whose love and approval she craved," concludes Steinem.

Norman Mailer, whose fascination with Marilyn is well-known (apart from a book, he has also written a play about her) now believed she was murdered.

"I have come around again to the thesis that Marilyn was murdered. After reading Robert Slatzer's *The Life and Curious Death of Marilyn Monroe*, the greater burden of proof is now, I think, on the side of those who would call it suicide. Slatzer's book presents a new confusion – which is whether Marilyn was murdered at home or brought back to her house after she died. But the case for an injection becomes more powerful either way since there is no trace of vomit anywhere in bedroom or bathroom, nor in her throat or nose – a rare, almost impossible phenomenon if one takes an overdose of pills.

"A wiretapper named Bernard Spindel, who died of a heart attack in prison was, according to Slatzer, hired by Jimmy Hoffa's people to make tapes of Bobby Kennedy's conversations with Marilyn at a time when Hoffa may have been trying to get material on Bobby to put in the balance against the case Kennedy was building against him.

"Again, according to Slatzer, the chief of police of Los Angeles, Bill Parker, picked up all the telephone records of Marilyn's long-distance calls the last week of her life and would not make them public. It was also Parker's desire, as more than a few people in L.A. seemed to know, to be the next head of the FBI.

"Finally, a most uncomfortable item – from the chief medical examiner of New York's Suffolk County, Dr Sidney Weinberg: 'It is extremely rare for a woman to commit suicide in the nude . . . During the past 20 years in my own experience I have seen only one such case, and that was by gunshot, not with drugs'."

Mailer then makes a telling point.

"On the other hand, one has to be an implacable opponent of the Kennedys to assume they planned a murder. Other options were open to them, including the most basic one of suffering bad publicity for a short period if Marilyn decided to attack them openly.

"The temper of the press in 1962 was to suppress personal stories about prominent figures even if they were your political enemies.

"The sex life of the President and by extension the sex life of his brother were still part of the American chalice. But criminal activities were not.

"Suppose that enemies of the Kennedys thought the best damage to be done to them was to murder Marilyn in such a way that it would look superficially like suicide – for the first day – and would then be later exposed as a murder.

"Who in America would not then believe the Kennedys were implicated?

"If not for Chief Parker's overweening desire to be the next head of the FBI, and his rush therefore to put a blanket over the case, America might have been living in the late summer of 1962 with a murder larger in its seeming implications than Watergate.

"But indeed there is one paradoxical line of reasoning which underlines the innocence of the Kennedys. If they had done it, they would have done it better. Marilyn would have looked like a real suicide and the discovery of her body would have been better arranged . . . "

The maze of sometimes conflicting and contradictory evidence, accounts, stories, claims and allegations provide an ample basis for the three conclusions cited in all the books.

The first is that Marilyn died accidentally.

The second is that she committed suicide.

And the third is that she was murdered.

If one opts for number three, then the most plausible explanation is that it was "arranged" by Hoffa and/or his pals in the Mafia to embarrass the Kennedys. Mailer, while believing she was murdered, acknowledges the difficulties of proving anything: "You could spend ten years on Marilyn and might never find out what the facts were. Because every time you begin to come upon an item in Marilyn's life, everybody's arguing about it. You talk to two of her closest friends and they'll each have different views.

"Marilyn was a phenomenon. Nothing in her life demands that a fact be there on any given day. For one thing, since she grew up in an orphanage, she learned early in life that a lie was usually more effective than the truth. Certainly a lie which people wanted to hear was vastly more useful than any truth, as far as she was concerned. And she grew up among liars. People in showbiz are naturally liars. They lean to legend."

He re-echoes Susan Strasberg's verdict.

"You finally begin to decide that Marilyn was nothing but contradictions."

Her third husband, Arthur Miller, who cared for her deeply but who, in the end, had to give up in despair, never seems to have given much weight to the theory that Marilyn's death was part of some sort of plan or plot.

"As I was coming to the end of the writing of *After The Fall*, the horrifying news came that Marilyn had died, apparently of an overdose of sleeping pills," he tells us in his autobiography.

Long before that, he had once told her: "You're the saddest girl I've ever known."

He hated Mailer's book on her, though he admits, "He was describing a woman on the knife edge of self-destruction all her adult life".

"To have survived," Miller tells us, "she would have had to be either more cynical or even further from reality than she was."

It is understandable that he should have been saddened and angered by the manner in which the press chorused its laments for her after her death – "the same press that had sneered at her for so long, whose condescension, if not contempt for her as an actress, she had taken too seriously".

Could she have survived in a Hollywood where fantasies of fame and sex and power reached gargantuan proportions?

Miller doubts it.

"Coming out of the '40s and '50s, she was proof that sexuality and seriousness could not coexist in America's psyche, were hostile, mutually rejecting opposites, in fact."

Her tragedy was to be trapped in the middle.

In August 1992 Miller gave an interview to the French newspaper *Le Figaro* in which he said she was "highly destructive" and died of a drug overdose.

"Marilyn was sick. The public knew nothing. She was totally dependent on pills and they destroyed her bit by bit.

"She was highly self-destructive. I think she was looking for stability. She was practically an orphan. She belonged to the world and not enough to herself. Since she didn't have any confidence in herself, she constantly needed to be reassured by success in the cinema.

"She was the reflection of a divine image. She incarnated at the same time power and vulnerability, the hope of America and its self-destruction."

And what of her involvement with the Kennedys?

In his 1993 book *Marilyn Monroe: A Biography*, Donald Spoto claims he has overturned the falsehoods about her life.

Spoto was granted exclusive access to the estate of Milton Greene – Marilyn's producer, lover, confidant and business partner – including 35,000 pages of confidential documents never before available to any writer.

On her relationship with John Kennedy, Spoto says she met him only a handful of times and slept with him only once – a brief interlude at Bing Crosby's house on the last weekend of March 1962.

"A passionate love affair between Marilyn Monroe and John F. Kennedy has been assumed for so long that it has achieved as solid a place in public awareness as almost any other event in the man's brief Presidency," says Spoto.

But no serious biographer, he argues, can identify Monroe and Kennedy as partners in a love affair.

On Bobby Kennedy, Spoto says she met him five times. Each time they were chaperoned by a friend and she did not have an affair with him.

All claims to the contrary have so far proved baseless.

As for her death, Spoto says neither the Mafia nor the Kennedys were involved.

Marilyn Monroe died, he says, at the hands of the two people she trusted most – her psychiatrist, Ralph Greenson, and her nurse/housekeeper, Eunice Murray.

Spoto claims Greenson and Murray could no longer dominate her through psychology so they conquered her by drugs, and when things went wrong there was a cover-up.

He claims she was not depressed or on a downward spiral at her death. She was due to remarry Joe DiMaggio on 8 August 1962 – it turned out to be her burial day.

And we know that her contract had just been renewed for *Something's Got To Give* – for treble the salary.

Where the Kennedys are concerned, the bottom line is that the evidence of involvement in affairs with Marilyn Monroe is flimsy indeed, and so tenuous in regard to her death as to be practically invisible.

Meanwhile, as Gloria Steinem reminded us, it is the lost possibilities of Marilyn Monroe which capture our imaginations.

14

Dallas

November 1963. One of Hollywood's great beauties is filming *Night of the Iguana* under John Huston's direction in a small coastal village in Mexico.

Her name is Ava Gardner.

"One evening we were all crowded into one motorboat coming home, full of equal portions of song and tequila, when we noticed Ray Stark's ocean-going yacht, which he occasionally took back and forth to Los Angeles, closing in on us. He had picked up a terrible news flash on his radio: President John F. Kennedy had been assassinated. The boat's air of drunken cheerfulness turned immediately to sobriety, silence, and tears."

Ava was remembering years later, and still grieving.

Just like the old man in McGann's pub in Doolin, County Clare, in Ireland's mid-west on a May evening in 1992, when he was introduced to Paul Hill of the Guildford Four. Hill introduced his blonde girlfriend Courtney Kennedy, daughter of the brother of the murdered President.

The old man remembered with great clarity that dreadful day in November 1963, and brushed away the tears.

There would be many tears that day and afterwards. And almost as many questions.

Millions in America, stunned by the news, and millions more across the globe asked: Why?

Writer J.G. Ballard, speaking on *Desert Island Discs* on BBC 4 in August 1992, told us why: "The image of John F. Kennedy shot to death before his young, beautiful wife is one of the most enduring and horrific of the twentieth century.

"The image both fascinates and haunts. It also cries out for explication.

"And none – even now 30 years on – is forthcoming."

According to another writer, Norman Mailer, the assassination of JFK "remains as the largest single event in the history of nearly all Americans who were alive that day – no afternoon in the recollection of our lives is equal to November 22, 1963". Americans, Mailer contends, lost their innocence that day.

Ben Bradlee, the future editor of *The Washington Post* and a friend of the Kennedys, who worked with *Newsweek* at the time, agrees.

The sledgehammer news that President Kennedy had been shot came to him while he was browsing through Brentano's bookstore on his lunch hour.

"Virtually everyone I know under 60 can remember exactly where he or she was when the news of the assassination struck them."

When he came to Dublin in June 1992 to deliver the first Independent Newspapers Annual Lecture at Trinity College, I asked him about that day.

"It just seemed like America, the world, life, would never be the same again."

Playwright Arthur Miller, whose wife, Marilyn Monroe, had been linked with JFK, writes with great poignancy of the latter's death.

"His death pushed a finger through the delicate web of the future. Certainly in all my work was an implicit reliance on some redemptive time to come, a feeling that the cosmos cared about man, if only to mock him. With Kennedy's assassination the cosmos had simply hung up the phone . . . "

The image of broadcaster Walter Cronkite of CBS shedding a tear in the midst of telling the nation the awful news from Dallas lives on in millions of minds.

Yet it is one of the ironies of that terrible day that, despite all the scores of journalists following Kennedy's limousine – "covering the body" in journalistic lingo – it was amateur photographers like Abraham Zapruder who got the important pictures.

When the first newsflash came over the UPI teletype – "Three shots were fired at President Kennedy's motorcade in downtown Dallas" – Dick Stolley, the Los Angeles bureau chief of *Life* magazine, headed for Texas.

He found out that a local garment manufacturer named Zapruder had taken an 8 mm colour film of the assassination.

Stolley tracked him down and in a tiny room, with just some Secret Service agents present, he was shown the most historic frames of home-movie film ever taken.

"I'll never forget that as long as I live," Stolley said later.

"The only sound in the room was the creaking of this old 8 mm Bell & Howell projector. You see the motorcade coming around the corner, the President's hands going up to his throat, you see Mrs Kennedy turning to him, smiling, then suddenly realising something terrible is happening.

"You get to Frame 313, that awful frame where the top of the President's head simply disappears."

Zapruder ran the film over and over.

Stolley knew *Life* magazine would take the film at any price.

Eventually the two men agreed on $50,000 – for print rights.

"It was not the money that won the day – it was *Life's* reputation," said Stolley.

Life sewed up all rights the next day with an additional payment of $100,000.

The film, which stands as the greatest single challenge to the lone assassin theory, was made available by the magazine to the Warren Commission.

After its official use, the magazine returned the original film in 1975 to Zapruder's heirs, who donated it to the National Archives, but who retain television rights.

For most people in America and throughout the world, the first opportunity to see all 18 seconds of the Zapruder film came with the release of Oliver Stone's movie *JFK*.

That 18 seconds of home movie is the foundation on which a multiplicity of conspiracy theories have been built.

During the famous footage you quite clearly see Kennedy's head lurch violently backward at the precise instant that a geyser of blood and brain tissue erupts from the right side of his head.

Yet the Warren Commission insisted that Kennedy had been struck only from behind.

"The Kennedy assassination happened three decades ago, which is not a very long time when you think about the breadth of history," says Jonathan Vankin in *Conspiracies, Cover-Ups and Crimes*.

"But I can't think of any other single event that has been the subject of such voluminous writing, research, and contemplation in the first 30 years after it occurred.

"There are probably hundreds of books about the Kennedy assassination. New ones are published every year. Combine these books with shorter articles, television programmes, and radio talk shows, and I would guess that there are thousands of pieces of work from scholarly to speculative and fictional devoted to the JFK assassination.

"Most are dedicated to the proposition that there was a conspiracy involved . . . . Suffice to say that suspicion has been stirring since the moment that Kennedy's head snapped backward from the impact of a bullet that hit him from in front."

If you believe that, then there must have been two shooters in Dallas.

And two makes a conspiracy.

Dealey Plaza in the heart of Dallas has a haunted feeling to it.

The place gives off eerie vibes.

In a silence that has its own eloquence, tourists stand and stare on Main Street, Houston Street and Elm Street.

The latter is where the object of their fascination stands – the Texas School Book Depository, which today houses a museum where once an assassin stood.

Thirty years ago someone fired a shot, or shots, from a sixth-floor window of this red-brick building which helped kill an American president.

And just as Ford's Theatre in Washington – where President Abraham Lincoln was assassinated in April 1865 – has become a kind of shrine to the macabre, so too with the Book Depository.

In the autumn of 1988, just before the 25th anniversary of Kennedy's death, the museum, called simply 'The Sixth Floor' was opened.

It was said at the time that this was an example of Dallas coming to terms with the blackest day in its history.

For years many argued that the the 86-year-old building was a symbol of the shame and pain the city felt. They wanted it razed to the ground.

Dallas County finally purchased it from a developer in 1977, renamed it the Dallas County Administrative Building, and converted most of it into courts and offices.

But the sixth storey remained shuttered and bare, except for a wire fence surrounding the south-east corner where vandals had chipped away at the bricks around the window from which Oswald fired.

Then the Dallas County Historic Foundation decided to open a permanent exhibition about the assassination.

Up to 1988, a plaque in front of the building and a concrete and granite memorial a few blocks away were all that Dallas had done to commemorate the killing of a president.

The museum is not a traditional one with items and artifacts on display. Oswald's rifle, the Italian-made Mannlicher Carcano, for example, remains at the National Archives in Washington.

Instead, the exhibition area features multi-media presentations about the period, the assassination and its aftermath.

Visitors are taken back in time. The south-east corner window area has been recreated as it appeared when Oswald fired at the Presidential motorcade.

Radio and telex announcements of the assassination carry visitors back to the initial moment when the President was shot.

According to the Chamber of Commerce, it used to be that Southfork Ranch, where the hugely popular TV series *Dallas* was made, was the most popular tourist attraction in Dallas.

Today it has been surpassed by The Sixth Floor.

But history isn't altered by an exhibition.

The real Dallas and what happened there in 1963 stands as a dark knot at the heart of the American psyche, a haunted bridge marking the transition from an age of innocence to turbulent and evil times.

Political scientist Bradley Klein has given a concise description of the American metamorphosis.

"It was a different world," he says of the days before Dallas. "It was a world in which people still had savings, and you got by with a family of four on one income. There was a sense of America's place in the world. Now things have become vicious and ugly and nasty."

As Norman Mailer once said, "We really cannot calculate the price of living with this unsolved crime".

"No American," writes Anthony Summers, "whether he loved or loathed President John F. Kennedy, has been immune to the impact of his assassination."

Summers goes on: "The very date – November 22, 1963 – is now perceived as a turning point, a lurch towards decline in the fortunes of the world's most powerful people."

Carl Oglesby, one of the founders of the Washington-based Assassination Information Bureau, is in no doubt about the magnitude of the event.

"If only in terms of sheer span of national attention and the persistence of controversy, the assassination of John F. Kennedy easily appears to be the political crime of the century."

Oglesby doesn't overstate one bit when he asserts: "All students of contemporary US politics must visit its mystery, whether they come to solve it, to expose it as a chimera, or merely to reflect on its haunting persistence."

And he has sketched out the question that remains central.

"So was Kennedy killed by a lone nut or by a conspiracy? The debate is long-standing and ongoing. It is intense and often nasty. The lone-nut side calls the conspiracy side naive, paranoid and alarmist. The Warren revisionists call the lone-nut side cynical, paralysed and complicit. There is not much room for indifference . . ."

In fact, with the passage of time the room for indifference shrinks and shrinks.

As the response to Oliver Stone's movie *JFK* demonstrated, people who were not even born at the time are today fixated by the Dealey Plaza shooting.

15

The Aftermath

Even as Air Force One flew him from Dallas to Washington, President Lyndon Baines Johnson knew that suspicions and fears of a *coup d'état* were already widespread.

He also knew this was due in no small measure to the fact that the bloody deed that toppled a president had been committed in Texas, his own home State.

The raucous ambience of Texas politics made anything possible, or seem possible, including a *coup d'état.*

Politics in the Lone Star State was fuelled by oil, money and blood, and a paranoid tendency to equate Liberalism with pro-Communism.

The Kennedy Administration was perceived to be Liberal and therefore soft on Communism, and ever since 1960, the antagonism towards the Kennedy philosophy was deep and abiding.

Nowhere in all of Texas was this more true than of Dallas.

That was one reason why JFK had been a reluctant visitor.

There had been no shortage of voices urging him not to go. The most clear-cut warning came from Senator William Fulbright, a Liberal from a State which borders Texas. He had good reason to distrust the city; he knew at first hand its history of political violence.

"Dallas is a very dangerous place," he told the President. "I wouldn't go. Don't you go."

The Mayor of the city was apprehensive. It was important, he said, that Dallas should shed its reputation as the "south-west hate capital of Dixie".

When plans for the Dallas visit were made public, Billy Graham, the evangelist, tried to communicate his foreboding to The White House.

The mood was ugly – and no secret.

The distinguished *Sunday Times* correspondent, Henry Brandon, got a call urging him to make the Texas trip on the grounds that there could be trouble. He acted on the tip and was the only foreign correspondent there on 22 November.

William Manchester, in his book *The Death of a President*, summed up the mood: "The origins of Dallas' implacable hostility to the New Frontier lay in a profound longing for the values, real and imagined, of the old frontier."

But Kennedy had to take the risk.

And he was very conscious of it. But also fatalistic.

"Last night would have been a hell of a time to assassinate a president . . . . If anyone wants to shoot a president, it's not a very difficult job. All one has to do is get on a high building with a telescopic rifle, and there is nothing anybody can do to stop it."

As for the mood, any doubts would have been swept away by the full page advertisement which appeared in the *Dallas Morning News* on 22 November 1963.

The ad, with its funereal black border and sarcastic heading, amounted to a "Wanted For Treason" broadside, in line with the thousands of leaflets with that very heading that had been distributed in the city streets prior to the visit.

When he saw the advertisement JFK remarked to his wife that they were heading into "nut country".

The *Dallas Morning News* dates back to 1842 when Texas was a republic, and it had made radical extremism reputable in the early 1960s.

The publisher and chairman of the board of *Dallas Morning News* at the time was E.M. "Ted" Dealey, and the statue of his father George B. Dealey (1859-1946) dominates Dealey Plaza.

Thanks in no small way to this newspaper, the city, which was to become the scene of the crime of the century, harboured great hatred for Kennedy. His decision to go was influenced by expediency – the need to heal a damaging rift in the State's Democratic Party organisation.

Kennedy and his advisers knew that he would have to carry Texas to secure re-election in 1964.

He also knew that he couldn't do a swing through the cities of the Lone Star State without including Dallas.

He was heading into a hotbed of hate and extremism.

"Dallas was known already to the nation and the world as a centre of intense right-wing activity," said Harrison E. Salisbury of *The New York Times.*

"Many Dallas citizens had made no secret of their violent antagonism to individuals whose opinions they regarded as left-wing or liberal."

The place was simply very dangerous.

"All of the theories about Mr Kennedy's assassination fall roughly into three categories: right-wing conspiracy, left-wing conspiracy, lone individual attack," wrote Mr Salisbury about a year later.

Since then, however, the options have been narrowed to two: the lone assassin theory, or a right-wing conspiracy.

"We let the Right inject this poison into the American bloodstream – and this is the result," said John Kenneth Galbraith.

In fact, the suspicion of a right-wing conspiracy was born almost at the moment of the attack. Because the President was shot in Dallas many people leaped to the conclusion that he was the victim of a right-wing plot.

The controversy over President Kennedy's death began with the shots that took his life. It was born at about 12.30 p.m. on that Friday in November when the lethal bullet exploded in the President's skull.

It has grown steadily since then. As an editor of *The New York Times* remarked when he read the bulletin announcing the President's death at 1.35 p.m. that day: "The year 2000 will see men still arguing and writing about the President's death."

Nothing that has happened since invalidates that prediction. On the contrary, the controversy has grown and grown.

And instead of stifling it, the Warren Commission's Report has itself become part of it.

Lyndon Johnson lost no time in establishing the seven-member Commission. In the immediate aftermath of the tragedy in Dallas, he, like others, was seized with terror, thinking that the assassination was the precursor to a Soviet nuclear attack.

The sense of panic was widespread. Was it an organised attack from abroad – or a conspiracy from within?

These, significantly, were the first thoughts of many of the key figures in the motorcade.

Not thoughts of a single assassin, a deranged loner.

The first horrible words of the Governor of Texas, John Connolly, who was very seriously wounded in the Presidential limousine, have ever since been a rallying cry for conspiracy-theorists: "My God, they're going to kill us all!"

Uncertainty reigned. Fears of a Soviet attack or a *coup d'état* were uppermost in the minds of the principals.

In fact, in the hours after Dallas, the American Government was exceedingly vulnerable. This was the main reason why Johnson was so anxious to get sworn in and get back to Washington. And his alarm grew when he learned that six members of the Cabinet, including Secretary of State Dean Rusk, were in an aircraft over the Pacific en route to Japan when their President was shot.

In his enthralling account, *The Death of a President*, William Manchester tells us of the most scary scenario: "If the assassination of

Kennedy was the first blow in a Soviet or Sino-Cuban machination, the airborne Presidential aircraft would be a prime target for a second blow."

Not only was Air Force One and the Cabinet plane flying over the Pacific unarmed – they were without fighter escorts.

Even on the day of Kennedy's funeral, Monday 25 November, the notion of a conspiracy had taken hold. To the head of The White House Secret Service detail, James Rowley, Oswald's murder strongly suggested an elaborate plot and, accordingly, he did not want President Johnson to follow the gun carriage on foot.

Johnson lost no time in setting up an investigation. By Executive Order No. 11130, dated 29 November 1963, he created the Commission to investigate the assassination of the 35th President of the United States.

He appointed Earl Warren, the Chief Justice, as its chairman, and directed the Commission to evaluate all the facts and circumstances surrounding the assassination and the subsequent killing of the alleged assassin and to report its findings and conclusions to him.

The Commission spent the better part of a year carrying out its task, submitting its report to Johnson on 24 September 1964.

It was released three days later, and here is how Anthony Lewis opened his report on it for *The New York Times*: "Washington, Sept, 27 – The assassination of President Kennedy was the work of one man, Lee Harvey Oswald. There was no conspiracy, foreign or domestic.

"That was the central finding in the Warren Commission Report. Chief Justice Earl Warren and the six other members of the President's Commission on the assassination were unanimous on this and all questions.

"The Commission found that Jack Ruby was on his own in killing Oswald. It rejected all theories that the two men were in some way connected. It said that neither Rightists nor Communists bore responsibility for the murder of the President in Dallas last November 22.

"Why did Oswald do it? To this most important and most mysterious question the Commission had no certain answer. It suggested that Oswald had no rational purpose, no motive adequate if 'judged by the standards of reasonable men'.

"Rather, the Commission saw Oswald's terrible act as the product of his entire life – a life 'characterised by isolation, frustration and failure'.

"'Oswald was profoundly alienated from the world in which he lived,' the Report said. . .

"The Commission found that Oswald had shot at former Major General Edwin A. Walker in Dallas on April 10, 1963, narrowly missing. It cited this as evidence of his capacity for violence . . ."

In attempting to answer the central mystery of who killed the President, the Report left in its wake a whole catalogue of mysteries.

Instead of closing the case, as Johnson hoped, and leaving the assessment of President Kennedy's place in history to the scholars, the Report sparked off a spate of conspiratorial speculations.

The Warren Commission opened a Pandora's Box. And today the truth behind the most shocking crime of the century is as elusive as ever.

Nearly three decades after his initial story about the Warren Commission Report, I met Anthony Lewis at a seminar on "Democracy, Censorship and Secrecy" at Trinity College Dublin.

I remembered a comment he made when the Report was published: "Few who loved John Kennedy, or this country, will be able to read it without emotion."

I had one question – who, in his opinion, was responsible for killing Kennedy?

Even as he paused to consider his answer, I could sense traces of that emotion welling up again within him.

He smiled grimly and shrugged.

"We are never going to know what happened on that awful day in Dallas. It is an American enigma."

This much we do know: the Report of the Warren Commission is now a discredited document.

According to Norman Mailer (1992): "The FBI was the first to endorse the idea of the lone assassin, and this but two weeks after the death of JFK. In 1964 the Warren Commission came down foursquare behind that finding. Over the years, however, the Warren Commission lost its credibility. The polls give the figure: a majority of Americans now believe there was more than one killer."

Yet still the Establishment clings to the lone assassin theory.

Mailer again: "It does not matter that in 1978 the House Select Committee on Assassinations decided, on the basis of acoustic evidence, that there had been a fourth shot. Since it was agreed that no rifleman, no matter how skilled, could get off four aimed rounds from a Mannlicher-Carcano bolt-action rifle in 5.6 seconds, that meant there had to be a second assassin."

The Select Committee on Assassinations, which was established by the US Congress on 17 September 1977, actually concluded that a conspiracy was "highly probable" in the case of Kennedy.

It had nothing to say about the nature of the conspiracy, but Mailer, accepting that at least two gunmen fired in Dealey Plaza, pointed in a numerical direction.

"Two assassins not only have to be able to function in concert, but, by their effectiveness itself, suggests a support system, which is to say a larger conspiracy."

Back in 1966, Presidential adviser Jack Valenti, just back from Europe, reported to President Johnson in a top secret memo that there was widespread disbelief in the Warren Commission findings and suspicion of either blundering or a cover-up. He told Johnson that the consensus in Europe was that Oswald had not acted alone.

Johnson was so upset that he even thought of reconvening the Warren Commission or appointing another commission.

He did neither. But 11 years later, the US Congress, responding to polls which showed that 87 per cent of Americans did not believe the Warren Report, set up its own investigation.

Even while it was reaching its verdict of a "probable" conspiracy, the Committee's 30-month mandate expired. Its work has never been extended.

Instead, it handed over its files to the Department of Justice. And the House Committee's own back-up records and unpublished transcripts have been sealed as "congressional material".

They won't be made public until the year 2029.

Nothing that has happened during the interim has allayed public disquiet and suspicion, not even a 1992 statement from Senator Edward Kennedy in which he supported the release of classified material concerning the assassination of his brother.

In making this call, he also said he believed the Warren Commission Report would bear up as the "most responsible" account of the 1963 killing.

The Kennedy family has never publicly opposed any investigation into the murder of President Kennedy, and although it has opposed disclosure of graphic autopsy photographs and x-rays, it has not denied their use to responsible investigators.

But Senator Kennedy, in a television interview in January 1992, appeared for the first time to express support for making other classified material available.

Asked if he believed that "there should be more items declassified", Kennedy replied: "We are all for that – any items that are out of our control, clearly – and other items, obviously, ought to be made available.

"I think you'll find out over any period of time that the Warren Commission Report is clearly the most responsible result, but I respect other people's conclusions," Teddy Kennedy said.

"I have always been satisfied with the Warren Commission Report," he told the Massachusetts television station WGMC.

"Robert – my brother Bob – spent a lot of time with Chief Justice Warren and there was no reason whatsoever as far as we were concerned to doubt the conclusion."

Earlier in Washington, a key House leader, incensed by a film suggesting a cover-up in the 1963 Kennedy assassination, said he was now willing to consider opening secret House files on the killing not scheduled to be publicly released until 2029.

The lawmaker, Representative Louis Stokes, who was chairman of the House Select Committee on Assassinations, had previously opposed unsealing the remaining House records on the grounds that everything substantive had already been made public.

The film in question, of course, was Oliver Stone's *JFK*. It is founded, as we shall see in the next chapter, on the notion of a conspiracy of frightening proportions.

But three decades later can that be substantiated?

Was JFK killed as a result of a conspiracy?

It was not a possibility that was exactly foreign to him, certainly not the possibility of a *coup d'état*.

Having read a popular novel at the time, *Seven Days In May* (an account of a high-brass attempt to take over the US Government), the President was asked if such a coup were possible.

Did the Pentagon have generals and flag-officers who could do that?

Here is Kennedy's reply: "It's possible. We could have a military take-over in this country. But the conditions would have to be just right. If, for example, we had a young President, and he had a Bay of Pigs, there would be a certain uneasiness. Maybe the Pentagon would do a little criticizing behind his back, but this would be written off as the usual military dissatisfaction with civilian control. Then if there were another Bay of Pigs, the reaction of the country would be, 'Is he too young and inexperienced?' The military would almost feel that it was their patriotic obligation to stand ready to preserve the integrity of the nation, though God knows what segment of democracy they would be defending if they overthrew the elected establishment. If there was a third Bay of Pigs, it could happen".

Did it?

For two years, ten months and two days Kennedy was President.

Was his fall the work of a lone assassin? Or the work of conspirators, perhaps linked to what Eisenhower called the military-industrial complex?

Will we ever know the truth?

Will there ever be convincing evidence, one way or the other?

Norman Mailer doesn't think so.

"To the degree that the murder of JFK was a conspiracy, so could one assume that the most salient evidence and the most inconvenient witnesses had been removed long ago."

But the question persists, because, as Mailer himself has stressed, if we are left in intellectual limbo and learn no more about what happened in Dallas, then the President's death will remain obsessive in our history.

It became an obsession for one man – Oliver Stone.

He believes there was a conspiracy. And with a very great, compelling movie, he has convinced lots of others.

Which leaves the key question – what kind of conspiracy and how big?

16
The Second Shooting of JFK

The Abbey Theatre in Dublin has been the venue for dramas in the past, ranging from the bewitching to the bizarre. Plots that would boggle the mind and test the limits of credibility have unfolded on its famous stage.

But on a February evening in 1992 a plot was outlined there with such fervour and conviction that it held the audience spellbound, at least for the duration of the performance.

The central player was the three-time Academy Award-winning writer and director, Oliver Stone.

The occasion was the Dublin Film Festival. And I, along with hundreds of film buffs, Kennedyites, conspiracy theorists and polemicists, went to the theatre to see him in person.

His controversial three-hour evaluation of what exactly happened on 22 November 1963 was on view in John Fitzgerald Kennedy's ancestral homeland for the first time. And we all wanted to know what the man behind it had to say for himself.

Even since the film went on general release, he has stood accused of distorting history.

One critic in *The Los Angeles Times* even went so far as to say that the real conspiracy was not to assassinate Kennedy, but to assassinate the Warren Commission.

Stone to this day dismisses the charge that he has audaciously set out to rewrite American history.

Born in New York City in 1946, Stone served in Vietnam from 1967 to '68 and also worked as a teacher and merchant seaman in South East Asia from 1965 to '66. He graduated from New York

University Film School in 1971. His films include *Platoon, Born on the Fourth of July, Salvador, Wall Street* and *The Doors*.

But in choosing to explore America's most controversial event of this century Stone opened a can of worms.

By starting out with the thesis that there was a conspiracy behind the assassination of President Kennedy, he walked straight into a firefight.

Oliver Stone first discovered Garrison's book (*On the Trail of the Assassins*) in 1988, while still working on *Born on the Fourth of July*. Intrigued by Garrison's story, he optioned the book and began the arduous research process which led to the script for *JFK*.

The film is not simply Garrison's story; Garrison is used, rather, as a protagonist to enable Stone to present the mountain of information which he and his research staff discovered surrounding the Kennedy assassination.

Jim Garrison (who died of natural causes in his New Orleans home on 21 October 1992 at the age of 71) sought, as a prosecutor, to know how, by whom and why John Kennedy was murdered. That is, after all, the job of a prosecutor.

To Academy Award-winner Stone, the question was not who, but why?

And in pondering that he became convinced that the malaise, the unease, the disillusionment, the cynicism and ultimately the turning from authority of two generations of Americans, all stemmed from those awful events of November 1963.

"And we are no better off for having formed a growing consensus that the Warren Commission was wrong," he says.

"But what has this done to us? Can some Americans, wherever they are and however powerful, really change our history, change the kind of people we are – and are seen to be – in the world?"

JFK became for him not just the story of a political assassination; it became the chronicle of a time in which Americans lost their way.

"On November 22, 1963, the United States of America was to be for ever changed as a nation.

"On that sunny afternoon in Dallas, Texas, the country's innocence was shattered, the course of its society altered, its destiny profoundly changed.

"The assassination of President John F. Kennedy placed this country on a path towards other events which would, in turn, shake the very foundation of American society and forever alter the way we look at our government and at each other.

"Even now, questions still haunt those old enough to remember the event and challenge those to whom it is only raw history.

"The Warren Commission, appointed to settle America's doubts, did little to answer those questions, and quite possibly raised more.

"Now that a recent Gallup Poll shows 73 per cent of Americans are convinced the Warren Commission was wrong, and believe that there was a conspiracy, the most important of these unanswered questions is – why?"

Even before shooting of the film began, Stone was being vilified.

A leaked copy of an early draft of the script (co-written by Zachary Sklar) led to a hostile anti-Stone campaign in the mainstream media.

"I don't think I'm paranoid. But I ought to be. They tried twice to kill my film – once before I started shooting, and again when the film came out."

Undeterred, Stone has stuck to his basic thesis: solve the riddle of the most vexing mysteries of modern times, and you will discover why America plunged so irrevocably into Vietnam.

What Stone leaves us is Kennedy as a victim of a military-industrial complex plot, triggered by his plan to withdraw from Vietnam.

He presents us with a *coup d'état* – with Lyndon Johnson waiting in the wings.

"What the film says is that there was a limited conspiracy to kill the President, and a second, wider conspiracy to cover it up. The cover-up was largely out of embarrassment because of the likely international effect. And I believe Lyndon Johnson and J. Edgar Hoover were part of it.

"The thing is that I've invaded a lot of the turf that's only supposed to be inhabited by the politicians and so-called 'experts'. They screwed up the case and they know they did and we uncovered at least three dozen discrepancies that they didn't investigate.

"How, for instance, did Oswald get a job at the Book Depository only a few weeks before, at a spot overlooking the place where Kennedy's car was to slow to 11 mph? Even the House felt the Warren Commission had done a lousy job there."

Stone feels strongly that Kennedy would have manoeuvred his way out of Vietnam. He says the book, *JFK In Vietnam*, by John Newman, supports that view.

He did send 16,000 "advisers" in response to the pressures he was under, but he had decided by 1963 that, if he won a second term, he would pull out altogether by 1965.

"He knew he couldn't do it before that," says Stone. He told that to a number of people, including Senator Mike Mansfield, who confirmed it to me on the phone, and also to Wayne Morris and Tip O'Neill.

"He was making public statements that were hawkish about the domino principle, but that was because he could not publicise what he wanted to do in the face of the threat from Goldwater and the Right. He did what a lot of politicians do. He feinted one way while intending to go the other way.

"He said clearly that if the American public would not support an invasion of Cuba 90 miles away, they would certainly not support an invasion of Vietnam 9,000 miles away.

"Also, he was a man who had the ability to change. After the Bay of Pigs and Cuba, he didn't have to prove himself as macho, like Johnson had to over in Vietnam.

"I think that if he'd lived, the Cold War would have ended in the seventies and the era of Reagan and Gorbachev would have been brought forward by over 20 years. Trillions of dollars would thus have been saved, and quite a few lives.

"But he was rocking the boat, and he paid for it with his life . . . "

And when it comes to President Kennedy's murder, the Establishment does not want to re-open the doors.

Stone admits that in making *JFK* he was trying to create an alternative myth to the Warren Commission.

"I set out to explore the true meaning of the shooting in Dealey Plaza. What the murder of JFK meant to the country. Why he was killed."

Norman Mailer, backing Stone, believes he dared something very dangerous: "He has entered the echoing halls of the largest paranoid myth of our time – the undeclared national belief that John Fitzgerald Kennedy was killed by the concentrated forces of malign power in the land."

Yes – but were those forces concentrated in a single individual or a group?

Mailer himself doesn't hide his doubts about the kind of major conspiracy – stretching all the way to The White House – posited by Stone.

"*JFK* is false probably to the likelihoods of whatever conspiracy did take place, since it is all but inconceivable that a major plot involving the Pentagon, the CIA, the FBI, and The White House could ever hold together through the decades."

James McKinley, in *Playboy's* 'History of Assassination in America', makes the same telling point.

"In many instances, the theories in rings of persons and places rippling out from the central incident to encompass so much that one wonders if any conspiracy so huge could remain a secret. Three or four men, perhaps . . . "

A journalist who was in Dallas on the fateful day, Tom Wicker of *The New York Times*, finds another kind of "gaping hole" in the Stone movie.

"If a conspiracy as vast and consequential as the one claimed could have been carried out and covered up for three decades, why did the conspirators or their heirs allow Stone to make this movie?

"Why not murder him, as they supposedly murdered others? Why, for that matter, didn't they knock off Garrison himself when – as Stone tells it with so much assurance – the New Orleans district attorney began so fearlessly to follow their trail?"

Richard M. Mosk, who served on the staff of the Warren Commission, in accusing the entertainment industry of distorting history for profit, said Stone's movie "constructed a conspiracy of the gay underground, the FBI, the CIA, the military, President Johnson, state officials and local police". Also included are the Warren Commission members and staff and even those in later Administrations – all of whom were allegedly engaged in the continuing cover-up.

"That all these individuals and organisations could effectively carry out such a monumental task and keep quiet for decades defies logic and common sense."

Much the same point was made in a straightforward common-sense way by John Kenneth Galbraith, who was one of Kennedy's close advisers and who does not subscribe to any of the conspiracy theories.

"I think it was the work of one crazed man, the man who shot Kennedy. If it had been a conspiracy somebody would have confessed it before now.

"There would have been several million dollars profit in doing so. There would have been a very high reward."

I have no doubt that a lot of people will find that very compelling, human nature being what it is.

It certainly rules out, to my mind, the notion of a large, multi-layered conspiracy.

But it still leaves untouched the possibility of a conspiracy organised by a small, tightly-knit group.

That's something that could be controlled, kept under wraps, by one means or another.

Such as other killings.

The alternative is an assassin acting alone, and for reasons that have more to do with madness than politics.

Dr Richard H. Popkin of the University of California questions the place of the "lone-nut" theory in American political culture.

"In the case of Kennedy, the lone-nut theory is still adhered to as the official explanation, with its corollary that political assassinations by conspiracy just do not occur in the United States.

"In one of the first critical works – Thomas G. Buchanan's *Who Killed Kennedy?* written in 1964 – the author surveyed the history of American political assassinations and showed that they have continuously been explained as the work of lone mad assassins.

"The lone-nut theory seems to have a strange status in American political thinking. It is offered by important figures almost as an unchallengeable axiom.

"Why does this explanatory theory have such a strong hold, independent of the evidence?

"Politicians in America, we are told and taught, can only be killed by solitary psychopaths, while anybody else can be killed by conspirators.

"Our ideology allows for any bizarre form of subversive political conspiracy short of murder, and any sort of murder short of political content."

Professor Popkin believes the Watergate scandal during the Nixon Presidency has changed a lot of things, because it was revealed as a "fantastic conspiracy" run from The White House itself.

"Up to then, it was perfectly all right for America to be manipulated and controlled by a criminal conspiracy to re-elect a president. But it was still unthinkable that the same kind of plot might have ever existed in American history to assassinate a president."

He has pointed out that in both cases the same motives could exist (to determine policy), the same kind of dramatis personae, the same kinds of techniques, and the same results.

"But the Watergate conspiracy could be explained as normal American politics, and a similar conspiracy involving assassination is still claimed to be incredible, and not the sort of event that is possible in the United States."

But since Watergate more and more people have been willing to think the unthinkable – to consider the possibility that Kennedy might have died as a result of a conspiracy.

"We are supposed to recoil from the possibility that political assassinations in the USA are the result of conspiracies," says Professor Popkin. "Some fundamental facet of our mythology is at stake, something that differentiates our national destiny from everybody else's."

In his view, the Warren Commission was designed to save this mythology.

But instead of answering the theories, the rumours and the suspicions, and laying them to rest, it created more and more.

The real triumph of Stone's *JFK* is not that it gives us "false history", as its critics claim, but that it has forced many people to look again, in the light of all that has happened, at the official version.

Stone's version, stripped of its speculative hyperbole, is simply that the Warren Commission covered up rather than investigated.

"We don't say this is exactly what happened and this is who did it," Stone emphasised that day in Dublin's Abbey Theatre. "I wouldn't be that presumptuous, nor do I know.

"I have taken, I think as a good detective would, all the clues that have presented themselves, put them into one mosaic, followed the clues and come to some conclusions of my own.

"But I present them as speculation, not as a definite conclusion.

"As the movie unfolds as a mystery, you unravel layer after layer, and you come out in the end with a very strong speculation as to what might have happened.

"But there is no doubt in my mind that it was a military-style ambush. . ."

The effect the movie has had has been excellently summarised by Robert Scheer, the former editor of *Ramparts* magazine.

"Before I saw *JFK*, I believed, just as Kevin Costner did in *Bull Durham* when he tells Susan Sarandon, in a litany of his character traits, 'I believe in the Warren Commission report that Lee Harvey Oswald acted alone'. And like Costner in real life, I was forced to re-examine the evidence Stone accumulated – and had to conclude that the official version is bunk.

"If the movie has the same effect on other people and we all start questioning what we have been told, that ought to be worth a couple of Academy Awards."

Above all, the Stone movie dramatically illustrates the truth of Anthony Summers' observation: "Long after John Kennedy's death, Americans still argue about the manner of his passing."

Summers might have added – and non-Americans as well.

The JFK assassination has been called the greatest "whodunit" of the twentieth century.

So what does *JFK* the movie tell us about this "whodunit"?

The *Guardian's* distinguished film critic, Derek Malcolm, provides an answer that will strike a chord with many: "At the conclusion of the film, you have to face the fact that a conspiracy of some sort, orchestrated by powerful special interests, was involved.

"But who exactly was it?"

Stone himself insists the killing in Dallas involved a military-style ambush.

Who could have organised that?

Once, as a guide for approaching political questions that do not have a quick answer, Lenin laid down the axiom: "Whom? Whom does this benefit?"

It is the very question posed by the mysterious "Mr X" (played by Donald Sutherland) in the movie.

Oliver Stone at least attempted to answer the question.

But was his answer the correct one?

17

Cork instead of Dallas?

Shortly after 10.00 p.m. on the night of Thursday, 27 June 1963 a telephone extension rang in the newsroom of *The Cork Examiner* in the centre of Cork City.

A sub-editor named Mick Kelly who was working the night shift picked up the instrument.

Extension 324 was his. He thought the call was personal.

The voice at the other end was that of a male, and the accent was local.

No name was given. Just a terse message.

"I just want to tell you that I overheard a conversation a little while ago in the bar of the Metropole Hotel . . . "

Kelly, like the rest of *The Examiner* staff, knew the hotel quite well. It was in MacCurtain Street, on the other side of the River Lee, about a half-mile away.

"Go on," said Kelly, who was beginning to think that the call had been put through to the wrong extension by the switchboard operator.

This call should go to one of the reporters, he told himself, as he listened.

"A group of individuals who I was told were from Cuba were talking about assassinating President Kennedy. It was all very hush-hush. I don't think they realised I could hear, because there was a small screen between them and me . . ."

Kelly wasn't sure what to say.

"They were talking about doing it here. In Cork, I mean. They said it could be arranged in front of the Imperial Hotel. They seemed to know what they were talking about . . ."

Kelly also knew the Imperial very well. It was just blocks away from *The Examiner*, over on the South Mall, one of the city's main thoroughfares and very much a banking, financial and insurance centre.

The mysterious caller was still talking.

"There may be nothing in any of this. But this is what these fellas were talking about. I said I'd call anyway . . ."

Then he hung up.

Kelly, an experienced journalist, thought for a few moments about what had just happened.

He knew full well the call could just be a hoax, somebody just play-acting, trying to pull a fast one.

But his instincts told him otherwise. There was something about the quality of the voice he had heard over the phone, something about the way the message was conveyed.

No giggling, no undertone of sarcasm, no sense of suppressed laughter. Kelly was sure the caller wasn't acting tongue-in-cheek.

Yet he also knew this was no time to be alarmist.

The country was in a celebratory mood.

The reason was clear. It was spelled out in a bold headline right across the top of that morning's *Examiner.*

JFK "HAPPY TO BE HERE", it read.

Kelly fingered it as he pondered the situation.

The sub-heading on the lead story said: TUMULTUOUS RECEPTION FOR PRESIDENT.

The first two paragraphs told the story: "After a day of heavy rain the sun shone at Dublin Airport last evening and as a rainbow appeared in the eastern sky, President Kennedy's blue and white Boeing swung rapidly around Dublin and made a perfect landing five minutes ahead of schedule.

"Out stepped a smiling President to be greeted by 80-year-old President de Valera who braved a slight chill to be present for the occasion. Mr de Valera, welcoming the first US President to pay a visit to Ireland, hailed President Kennedy as "the scion of our race who has won first place among his countrymen".

Kelly unfolded the full broadsheet page on the desk and glanced over it.

There were two photographs on page one. The main one, under the headline at the top of the page, showed Kennedy standing in front of microphones, replying to President de Valera's address of welcome.

Standing behind him were his sisters Mrs Eunice Shriver and Mrs Jean Smith. Next to them were the Taoiseach, Mr Sean Lemass, the Tanaiste, Mr Sean McEntee, the Minister for External Affairs, Mr Frank Aiken, and the American Ambassador, Mr Matthew McCloskey.

The second, much smaller photograph, down the page, showed Mr Andrew Minihane, the chairman of New Ross Urban District Council, who had the distinction later that day of welcoming JFK to the County Wexford town from which his ancestors hailed.

The other front page stories told of the death of 38 Belgian skytroops after their plane crashed near a NATO base in West Germany, and of the Pope's plans to pay for a dinner for all prisoners in Italian jails to celebrate his coronation the following Sunday.

Another story was headed: PROFUMO LEAVES PRIVY COUNCIL AT OWN REQUEST.

But it was a box in the centre of the page that held Kelly's attention.

It contained details of the President's programme for that day.

And just before he received the disturbing message from the mysterious man, Kelly had been working on the box that would appear on the front page of the following edition.

It read:

President Kennedy's programme for today is:

9.00 a.m. – Leaves Dublin by helicopter for Cork.

10.15 a.m. – Arrives Collins Barracks Cork, motors through city.

10.35 a.m. – President Kennedy receives Freedom of the City at City Hall; address by Lord Mayor; presentation of scroll and casket; President's reply.

11.30 a.m. – Leaves Cork (Victoria Road) by helicopter.

12.45 p.m. – Arrives in Dublin.

1.00 p.m. – Gives lunch for President de Valera and the Taoiseach at US Embassy.

3.00 p.m. – Leaves Embassy.

3.10 p.m. – Lays wreath at Arbour Hill.

3.25 p.m. – Leaves Arbour Hill.

4.00 p.m. – Address joint session of both Houses of Oireachtas.

5.00 p.m. – Receives Honorary Degrees of NUI, UCD, and Freedom of City of Dublin at Dublin Castle.

8.00 p.m. – Attends dinner given by Mr de Valera at Aras an Uachtaráin.

As Kelly read the last line of the schedule, he had, for one fleeting moment, a sickening thought: would JFK ever make it to that dinner in the Phoenix Park?

It was an absurd thought, of course, and he brushed it aside.

The idea that the President of the United States might be assassinated in Cork was crazy.

Kelly, an ardent film fan, told himself this sort of thing only happened in Hollywood.

It was 1963, for God's sake. The caller must be out of his mind.

How many American presidents had been assassinated, Kelly asked himself. Four? Five?

He knew the last was William McKinley, the 25th president, and that was on 6 September 1901.

It happened during a visit to the Pan-American Exposition at Buffalo, New York. Thousands had turned out to catch a glimpse of the President and possibly a chance to experience his famous handshake. Among them was a man named Leon Czolgosz. His mission was to kill the President, not because he had anything against McKinley, but because he hated all the Government and by inference hated the man at the top.

As they carried him off to a makeshift hospital with two bullets in his body, the President wondered aloud about who had done this to him.

"Must be some misguided fellow," he said.

Mick Kelly came to the same conclusion about the mysterious caller.

The Editor would laugh at him if he took it across as a possible news story.

This was not the time to spoil a glorious, festive occasion, an historic occasion which had the whole country agog.

Kelly wouldn't try to have it carried as a news story. But he decided, just as a precaution, to pass the message on to the police. So he rang the regional headquarters of the Gardai at Union Quay, and told the desk sergeant about the message he had received.

The following day Kennedy came to Cork as planned.

Kelly doesn't remember much about the day, except that he had no special feelings of apprehension.

He knew the route of the Presidential motorcade would bring the cars down Summer Hill from Collins Barracks, along MacCurtain Street, past the Metropole Hotel, over the north channel of the Lee and into Patrick Street, then left into the Grand Parade, left again into the South Mall, past the Imperial Hotel, and then right at the bottom over the south channel and to the City Hall.

The South Mall is a long wide street, with the Imperial Hotel situated on the left-hand side about halfway down.

It was at this hotel that General Michael Collins – one of the founders of the modern Irish State – stayed on the night of 21 August 1922.

The following morning Collins set out on the fateful journey to his native West Cork which ended that afternoon with his assassination at Beal na mBlath.

No such thoughts occupied Kelly as he watched the motorcade pass by.

The South Mall, like the rest of the streets along the route, was crowded as President Kennedy passed, standing up in the back of his big, open-topped limousine, waving to the crowd.

A perfect assassin's target, Kelly thought later.

Better even than in Dallas, where he was seated.

Kennedy came, saw and conquered the hearts of all of Cork.

He left behind, as a special gift to the Lord Mayor, an autographed portrait beautifully framed in leather.

He returned to Dublin, and went to the dinner at Aras an Uachtaráin.

The Irish visit ended the following day, with an emotional farewell at Shannon Airport.

Months passed.

Mick Kelly sub-edited many pages on *The Examiner*, all thoughts of Kennedy, of Cubans and of a possible assassination long forgotten.

Nothing more was heard from the mysterious caller.

Then came 22 November 1963 – and the terrible news from Dallas.

Mick Kelly was on duty that night. He still vividly remembers the feelings of numbness, shock, disbelief and sadness which permeated the newsroom.

"It hung like a giant pall over the place," he recalls.

The extension 324 rings again.

Kelly's extension.

He picks it up.

That voice again.

He recognises it instantly.

No introduction. No name. Just another terse message. And this time, just as before, the caller doesn't ask for anybody in particular.

Just somebody in the editorial department, he tells the switchboard.

Kelly is the one who picks up the phone.

The enormity of the coincidence doesn't strike him until much later.

"I'm the one who phoned the warning back in June," says the caller.

"They didn't get him in Cork – but they got him in Dallas, just like they said they would. I told you, didn't I?"

Then the phone goes dead. The connection is broken.

18

Who Killed Kennedy . . . ?

The two strangers at the bar knew that the woman who had just come in a few minutes ago was uneasy. Her steady blond hair was dishevelled, and the strain was visible in her over-made up face.

She was good looking – that's the main reason why they remembered her.

The other reason was her companions. Two of them. Both male. Both dark-skinned and swarthy.

Not blacks, but not whites either.

Latins? Mexicans? Cubans?

The onlookers in the Silver Slipper Lounge couldn't be sure, but yeah, they might have been Cubans.

Bulky. And hostile. No argument about that. Edgy and hostile. Angry with the blonde.

She was drinking tequila, and talking back to the two men. Her voice was raised, and she was gesturing like someone half out of control.

But the strangers couldn't hear what was being said. The din in the crowded bar drowned out the voices.

Flashes of anger – no doubt about that.

The pair with the blonde were drinking whiskey and coke, or maybe it was rum and coke.

One of them looked scared.

Then more flashes of anger, voices going up by decibels.

Suddenly one of the men grabbed the blonde by the arms, pulled her away from the counter and started to frogmarch her towards the door.

The other dumped his drink and quickly followed.

The strangers' eyes met. One gave a faint shrug of his shoulders. The other smiled thinly and turned back to his drink. A lover's tiff, he thought.

He sipped his Jack Daniels and pushed the trio who had just left out of his mind, picking up a copy of the local paper at the same time.

The date on the paper was 20 November 1963.

It would be all of two years before he would see the blonde again. And by then she would be dead.

In another newspaper in 1965 he would read that on 4 September a woman named Rose Cheramie was found dead by a highway near Big Sandy, Texas – a small town about midway between Dallas and the Louisiana border.

The authorities were told that Cheramie was lying in the roadway, apparently having been thrown from a car, when another car drove over her head.

The driver of the second car was questioned by the police, but they could establish no connection between him and the dead woman, so the file on Rose Cheramie – aka Melba Christine Marcades – was closed.

The man in the Louisiana bar who had originally seen her in the company of two dark-skinned companions knew nothing of this.

All he recognised was her photograph in the paper the morning after she was killed.

Nor – like millions of others – did he know that Rose Cheramie had predicted Kennedy's death.

She also claimed she worked for Jack Ruby.

It would be sometime later before the police discovered that the Texas address given to them by the man who killed Rose was non-existent.

Her story is one of the strangest of all connected to the JFK killing.

On 20 November 1963 – two days before the assassination in Dallas – a Louisiana State police lieutenant named Francis Fruge travelled to Eunice, Louisiana, to pick up a woman who had received minor abrasions when she was thrown from a car.

This in fact is one of the opening scenes of Stone's *JFK*, with Sally Kirkland playing Rose Cheramie.

Rose was taken by Fruge to the State Hospital in Jackson, Louisiana.

On the way she told Fruge she had been travelling from Florida to Dallas with two men, two Latins.

While in the State Hospital, Rose Cheramie told doctors that Kennedy was to be killed in Dallas.

She appeared quite lucid.

And hospital records showed that she had been diagnosed as "without psychosis".

This woman, a prostitute, claiming to have foreknowledge of the JFK assassination, is one of the strangest and most intriguing of all the witnesses.

On the day Kennedy died, Lieutenant Fruge remembered Rose Cheramie and her prediction.

He went back to question her. She said the two men were on their way from Florida to Dallas to kill Kennedy. She said she heard the two men discussing a plot to assassinate the President.

However, a row had broken out on route; the men had slapped her around, and thrown her from the car onto the roadside.

Fruge confirmed this story with the owner of the Silver Slipper Lounge.

Thinking that he had valuable information, he then went to Captain Will Fritz, the Chief of Homicide of the Dallas Police Department, who was in charge of the assassination investigation. Fritz told him he wasn't interested, and Fruge dropped his own investigation.

Interest in the strange case of Rose Cheramie was not revived until New Orleans District Attorney reopened the investigation of Kennedy's murder in 1967 and the House Select Committee on Assassinations began its hearings in 1976.

Meanwhile, the most convincing account of a CIA/Cuban link to the Dallas killing has come from a top CIA source.

"I had little sympathy for the President. The Bay of Pigs fiasco, which he tried to hang on the CIA and which led to the resignation of CIA Director Allen Dulles, was his own doing. I think the decision to withdraw air support of the invasion coloured Kennedy's entire career and impacted on everything that followed."

That's the view of James Angleton, director of covert operations for the CIA.

It establishes a clear motive.

In January 1993 I spoke to veteran *New York Times* journalist, Anthony Lewis, who visited Dublin to give a lecture at a conference on "Censorship, Secrecy and Democracy" at Trinity College.

Although he talked at length about the "culture of secrecy" that pervades government circles in Washington, and talked about such cover-ups or attempted cover-ups as Watergate and the Pentagon Papers, he was resolute in refusing to place the Report of the Warren Commission into this category.

When I asked him if it should not be seen in a similar light, he shook his head. "No," he said, very firmly. "I am not a conspiracy theorist."

I then asked him if he had seen the Oliver Stone movie, *JFK*. "Yes," he replied, "and I hated it."

Why?

"Where did he get all that stuff from. We had this mysterious character in Washington (played by Donald Sutherland) who lays out all the links, all of the pieces of the conspiracy for Garrison (played by Kevin Costner). But in reality there is no such character."

Rose Kennedy

The happy clan

A somewhat older Kennedy clan

Jack and 'Kick'

'The Boys'

'The Girls'

'Just another day at the office'

Press Conference March 23, 1961

Cabinet Meeting around the time of the Cuban Missile Crisis October 18, 1962

Arrival at Dallas, November 22, 1963

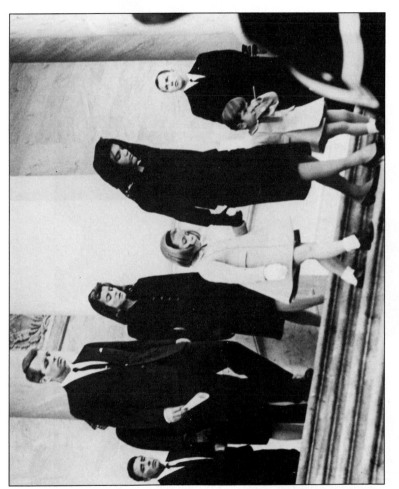

A tragic end – November 24, 1963

'Happier Days'
Caroline and Edwin Schlossberg – July 19, 1986

'Newlyweds'
Kerry Kennedy and Anthony Cuomo – June 9, 1990

Hong Kong – August 7, 1993

John F. Kennedy Jr. and actress Daryl Hannah

Stone insists there is.

"They said that Mr X doesn't even exist. Well, he does exist. He's based on Colonel Fletcher Prouty, who served in the Pentagon from 1962 as chief of special operations for the Office of the Joint Chiefs of Staff, liaising with the CIA."

Prouty, along with John Newman and Jim Marrs (whose books *JFK and Vietnam* and *Crossfire: The Plot That Killed Kennedy* along with Jim Garrison's *On The Trail of the Assassins* served as the basis for the screenplay of *JFK*), is listed as a technical adviser on the film.

Lewis, who was a classmate of Bobby Kennedy's and is still very friendly with Ethel Kennedy, made it clear that he finds all the conspiracy stuff "very painful".

Clearly, the killings of JFK and RFK are not matters he finds it easy to talk about.

"We'll never really know what happened in Dallas. It's one of those unfathomable episodes of our history. We'll never know what happened that awful day . . ."

Many other journalists, writers and film-makers do not share his uncertainty.

At this stage the list of those who were allegedly involved in the assassination is legion.

Some, like ex-President George Bush and Senator Edward Kennedy, stick to the Oswald as the lone-killer story.

So does Donald Paul Bellisario, the only Hollywood producer, so far as is known, who has ever met Lee Harvey Oswald and has based a TV episode on JFK's official assassin.

Bellisario is executive producer of TV's *Quantum Leap* series, a time travel show in which one principal "jumps" inside the skin of fictional characters every week to change the course of history.

NBC TV on 22 September 1992 featured actor Scott Bakula leaping into Oswald's body in a highly fictionalised episode.

"Although not as highly fictionalized as Oliver Stone's *JFK*," Bellisario said, "this is the first time in five years I've used a genuine historical figure."

His hour-long episode is totally at odds with Stone's controversial second-gun, CIA-Lyndon Johnson conspiracy in the JFK film.

Bellisario, who produced *Magnum PI*, *Battlestar Galactica* and *Airwolf*, encountered Oswald when they were in the Marine Corps.

He came away convinced Oswald was a Communist fanatic.

The time was December 1958 in Tustin, California. Bellisario visited his old outfit to look up some buddies in Marine Air Control Squadron 9, a unit of 120 Marines to which Oswald had been attached after Bellisario was reassigned.

Bellisario said: "I encountered him once, and I never forgot him for a good reason. I stopped to ask him where I could find a duty roster to check out my buddies.

"Oswald was sitting cross-legged on the floor reading *The Worker*. I sat down, surprised. You just didn't see marine privates reading Communist newspapers 30 years ago – at least a 22-year-old sergeant at the time didn't.

"He looked up and made some inflammatory comment, the exact words of which escape me now. It was like listening to Russian propaganda on the radio. So we got into a heated polemic on Communism versus Democracy, which still stands out in my mind.

"To this day I remember his arrogance and his sneer. I remember our verbal battle, which went on for 10 or 15 minutes.

"As I walked away I passed another Private and asked, 'Who is that little fucker?' He told me he was a harmless little jerk who argued and fought with everybody.

"Kennedy was shot in 1963, about five years later, and when Oswald's picture appeared on my TV screen, I came out of my chair. I said to my wife, 'I know that guy'. But I couldn't remember where or when. The name meant nothing to me."

That came later.

And Bellisario has never had any doubts that Oswald killed Kennedy.

"Lee Harvey Oswald was a fanatic."

Twenty-nine years ago, the Warren Commission came to the same conclusion.

It sparked off a debate that even after three decades has not been settled.

Unlike the media scrutiny associated with Watergate and Irangate and subsequent intensive investigative journalism, the established press at the time did little to refute the Commissions' findings.

However, there was critical reaction to the Report, and it has gathered force over the ensuing decades.

Mark Lane's *Rush To Judgment*, published in August 1966, was the really serious challenge to the Commission's findings.

The most controversial and most challenged of these findings throughout the years is the "magic bullet" theory, the contention that one bullet hit both President Kennedy and Texas Governor John Connolly.

According to this "magic bullet" theory, Governor Connolly, riding in the front seat of the President's car, was hit by the same bullet that pierced the President's neck – after it changed direction.

The path of the bullet makes it highly unlikely that it could have done all the damage it did to both men.

The Warren Commission also concluded that the two men were hit less than 2.3 seconds apart. But Oswald's rifle, a single-shot, bolt-action Italian model, was found by the Commission to be incapable of firing faster than one shot every 2.3 seconds. Thus, unless the same bullet went through both the President and the Governor, they had to be shot by two different gunmen.

More than any other issue, the "magic bullet" theory split the seven-member Commission.

Senator Richard Russell did not believe in the lone gunman theory, and requested a footnote to the section on the magic bullet theory noting his dissent. Chief Justice Earl Warren, however, insisted on unanimity in the Report.

And Senator John Sherman Cooper, a Kentucky Republican, always remained "unconvinced" of the conclusions of the Commission.

Growing doubts over these conclusions, combined with burgeoning conspiracy theories and the assassinations of Dr Martin Luther King and Senator Robert F. Kennedy, finally resulted in a Congressional examination into the deaths of President Kennedy and King in 1976.

Specifically, in September of that year, the US Congress passed special legislation, termed House Resolution 1540, creating "The House Select Committee on Assassinations".

Resolution 1540 directed the Congress by means of a special committee to conduct a full and complete investigation into the circumstances surrounding the deaths of JFK and Dr King.

In December 1987, after two years of work and the expenditure of $5.8 million, committee members were poised to concur with the Warren Commission's key finding that Lee Harvey Oswald, acting alone, had assassinated President Kennedy, wounded Governor Connolly, and that there was no conspiracy.

However, less than three weeks later, a major reversal occurred. The 600-plus page report was rejected, and on 29 December 1978 a majority of the committee approved a seven-page "Summary of Findings and Recommendations".

While still implicating Oswald, the summary stated that President Kennedy "was probably assassinated as a result of a conspiracy".

As with the Warren Commission, there was a lot of focus on the "lone gunman" scenario.

The committee, in rejecting this, based its newly-formed conclusions on the testimony of acoustical experts, Mark Weiss and Ernest Aschkenasy. The two had analysed the dictabelt recording of sounds picked up by a microphone on a Dallas police motorcycle.

That recording was compared with others made of shooting tests. The two experts concluded that there was a high probability (95 per cent) that there was gunfire from two spots along the route of the Kennedy motorcade – one from the Texas School Book Depository, and the other from what has become known as "the grassy knoll" in Dealey Plaza, to the front right of the passing Presidential limousine.

The committee's investigation and subsequent findings did little, however, to explore conspiracy theories or conclude what other individual or individuals acted with Oswald.

The report stated that "based on the evidence available to it, the Soviet Union, Cuba, organised crime or anti-Castro groups were not responsible for the Kennedy assassination".

But the panel did conclude it was possible that individual members of organised crime or anti-Castro groups might have been involved.

Also, while not implicated in the assassination, the FBI, the CIA and the Justice Department were highly criticised in the summary for their failings following the assassination.

So who were the real assassins?

And was Oswald, as he maintained, just "a patsy"?

And who pulled the strings?

The answers range from the Garrison/Stone military-industrial complex to the Mafia, or the Mafia/CIA, or disaffected anti-Castro Cubans.

"There are motives galore," wrote Jonathan Vankin in *Conspiracies, Cover-Ups and Crimes*, his 1992 book.

"CIA cold warriors and anti-Castro Cubans had a grudge against Kennedy for back-stabbing them on the Bay of Pigs invasion.

"The CIA had an extra beef: Kennedy had become appalled at its outrageous conduct. He vowed to smash the CIA's power and started by firing Allen Dulles.

"The Mafia had its own vendetta against Kennedy for letting his brother carry out the vigorous, almost fanatical prosecutions that J. Edgar Hoover had shunned.

"In fact, Hoover had prominent friends with underworld ties, though he publicly denied that the Mafia was real. Chicago boss Giancana had reason to feel sharply betrayed. His vote-rigging probably meant Kennedy's margin of victory in the razor-close 1960 election.

"Oilmen such as Clint Murchison and H.L. Hunt had a grievance of their own with Kennedy. They were ultra-right ideologues who despised the President, but they had an even more compelling motive. The oil depletion allowance let them multiply their wealth to unthinkable dimensions. Kennedy promised to strip that allowance . . ."

So who were the real assassins?

We are never likely to have proof that will stand up in a court of law.

But my own assessment of all of the evidence, including important new evidence from Kennedy's 1963 visit to Ireland leads me to two conclusions –

(a) Oswald did not act alone and may not have been involved in the shooting of Kennedy at all, and (b) the most likely conspirators were anti-Castro Cubans.

Jim Marrs, whose book served as an essential part of the basis for the screenplay for Stone's *JFK*, is not alone in thinking that in all of this Lee Harvey Oswald was just a patsy.

"The preponderance of evidence suggests that the Oswald in Dallas – whether lone-nut, American agent, Soviet operative, real, or substitute – did not kill President Kennedy."

In the words of the Kevin Costner/Jim Garrison character in *JFK*: "Maybe Oswald didn't pull the trigger."

As for the anti-Castro Cubans, the story told by Rose Cheramie points to a definite link.

And of all of the conspiracy theories, this is the only one for which a claim was made – in advance of the shooting.

In 1978, a physician who treated Rose Cheramie at the State Hospital in Jackson told the House Select Committee on Assassinations that shortly after being admitted to the hospital – the woman said Kennedy was to be assassinated in Dallas on 22 November.

Dr Victor Weiss confirmed that she had been lucid at the time.

It is the fact that she made her comments before Kennedy was killed – and that she knew the date and the venue – which sets Rose Cheramie's story apart.

If her story had been followed up, the real story of what happened in Texas in November 1963 might be known now.

19

JFK – A New Assessment

The first time I heard the 1993 Suzanne Vega single "When Heroes Go Down" was while I was immersed in a file of quotations and remembrances of John Fitzgerald Kennedy.

The title of that single seemed apt then, and still does.

Every age needs its heroes, and JFK was without question one of the heroes of that incandescent decade – the sixties.

His name and his reputation have, of course, been vilified and shredded during the interim.

Certain books have sought to paint a picture of a sordid White House and a besmirched Camelot.

For some authors Kennedy the womaniser, the satyr, is all that exists. The politician, the statesman, the visionary, the husband and the father have been all but obscured.

But all the attempts to rubbish his reputation have left the essence of the Kennedy Presidency untouched.

If I were a dealer in Presidential shares, I would buy Kennedys as eagerly as I would sell Nixons, Reagans and Bushes.

When the definitive history of the American Presidency comes to be written, JFK will rank next to Franklin D. Roosevelt.

"His brief time in power seems to me now to have been filled more with hope and promise than performance," wrote Ben Bradlee. "But the hope and the promise that he held for America were real, and they have not been approached since his death."

Some say the Kennedy reputation has been damaged irreparably. Ordinary people both within the United States and outside of it do not agree.

The mud-slinging has been fierce, and sustained. But if the pendulum of popularity has ever swung away from Kennedy, it is certainly swinging back now.

His friend and close aide, Theodore Sorensen, says the pendulum never swung away.

"I don't think his reputation ever really declined," he told me in his spacious law office in New York in November 1992.

"It declined among a certain sector, a certain number of self-appointed intellectuals, a certain number on the far Left who blame him for Vietnam, a certain number of people on the far Right who wanted to tarnish his reputation, and a certain number of gossip-mongers.

"But my guess is that if a poll had been taken every year for the past 30 years asking people which President in the 20th century did they have the most affection for, did they most admire, he would have won every year. Every year."

Ben Bradlee of *The Washington Post* concurs.

"Kennedy's reputation stands amazingly high today given all the unpleasant revelations about his private life. It's really quite amazing. I am perhaps typical in this. I feel that some of his behaviour – especially the sharing of a mistress with a gangster – is really unforgivable and unforgivably reckless. Yet I somehow have forgiven that because I know of no permanent damage that liaison did to the country. And all of Kennedy's virtues and promises override his frailties in my mind."

Sorensen spells out the abiding interest in JFK: "He had been there in The White House about the same time as Gerald Ford and less time than Jimmy Carter. How many books, how many television shows, how many articles do you see about the Ford and Carter Presidencies? I can't tell you how high the interest in Kennedy remains."

Lest you think Sorensen exaggerates, it is well to remember that a Gallup Poll conducted for *Newsweek* in 1983 confirmed that Kennedy was easily America's most popular President.

Two-thirds of the respondents believed that the United States would have been "much different" had he lived.

According to one commentator, the 1983 poll revealed an almost Messianic image of Kennedy – one committed to the downtrodden, to racial justice, to facing down the Soviets, and to infusing the nation with a new spirit.

In this part of the world, we witnessed this ourselves when JFK's photographs appeared in many homes alongside that of Pope John XXIII, another inspirational figure.

And not even a massive media concentration in recent years on Kennedy's shortcomings has blurred that image.

Like Pope John XXIII, he represented hope and the promise of a better, saner and more humane world.

The idea of a Catholic running for president is acceptable now – thanks to JFK.

We shouldn't forget that the issue was strong enough to contribute to Al Smith's defeat in 1928 and to make John Kennedy face a panel of sceptical Protestant ministers in 1960.

Kennedy's visit to Houston in mid-September that year for his appearance before Baptist ministers would create a new chapter in American Presidential history.

That appearance was a triumph, defining the role of a modern Catholic leader in a democracy, separating the candidate's beliefs from certain edicts of the Catholic Church on secular matters, reaffirming the absolute separation of Church and State in America, doing much to expunge religious bigotry generally, and even applying the lesson of the monument to the sacredness of the Alamo.

"Side by side with Bowie and Crockett died Fuentes and McCafferty and Bailey and Badillo and Carey. No one knows whether they were Catholic or not," said Kennedy, "for there was no religious test here."

Albert J. Menendez takes up the theme in his book *John F. Kennedy – Catholic and Humanist.*

"Most interpreters of the Kennedy era have ignored what I believe to be his most enduring achievement. His election ratified and made credible America's image of itself as a nation predicated on religious tolerance and liberty. That image had been tarnished by restrictive political movements based on religious prejudice. The Kennedy election and the manner in which he sought to resolve long-standing interfaith and Church-State disputes earn him a place in history.

"His Presidency substantially aided the development of pluralism. By breaking the unwritten law against non-Protestants, he severed the Protestant stranglehold on The White House and made it symbolically the genuine home of all Americans.

"He made it at least conceivable that members of other minority religious groups could aspire to the nation's highest elective office.

"He illuminated the discussion of Church-State issues and brought them to the fore of public exposure. He proved that a Catholic president could be just as devoted to religious liberty as a non-Catholic, and his ecumenical posture furthered the cause of religious tolerance and understanding in America."

One question has been asked often in theological as well as political circles. It is this: did Kennedy's Presidency cause or merely coincide with parallel movements within US Catholicism?

Was it a fluke of history or was it almost providential that JFK and Pope John were contemporaries?

As Menendez and others agree, historical judgements of this nature are difficult to make, but it is undeniable that JFK enhanced and gave impetus to the movements of inter-religious and inter-Church harmony and Catholic liberalism.

The late Cardinal Cushing subscribed to this view: "John F. Kennedy and Pope John XXIII were the great pioneers of what we now call the ecumenical spirit which is intended to wipe away all forms of bigotry by knowing, respecting and esteeming the religious beliefs of all peoples . . . . I always felt that JFK was a forerunner in this field . . . because he never allowed his faith to interfere in any way with his relations with others. He was the greatest representative of brotherhood."

Kennedy's record also had an indisputable impact on Catholic political attitudes. His adherence to relatively liberal goals and values gave them a new respectability within the Catholic community.

In view of all of this, it is fatuous to assert, as Alastair Cooke did in his "Letter From America" on BBC Radio 4 on 13 December 1992, that JFK was "a false blip on time's radar screen".

This is both extremely arrogant and dismissive and also extremely inaccurate.

It is typical of the attitude of much of the British Establishment towards the Kennedys, and to JFK in particular on becoming President.

Fr Andrew Greeley, the Chicago-based priest-sociologist and novelist, is right when he says it is now time for a new "revision" of John Fitzgerald Kennedy, after the attempts by certain revisionists to destroy the image and record.

"The pundits, the experts, the Op-Ed page political geniuses have written him off as an unimportant President. Now another generation of more serious thinkers and writers are re-analyzing the Kennedy contribution to American life."

Their conclusion, according to Greeley, is that the Kennedy legacy to American life is immensely important.

"The American people – who still consider John Kennedy one of their greatest leaders – certainly agree."

Kennedy deserves to be remembered for the idealism, vigour and intellectual acumen he brought to his Presidency.

"His emphasis on excellence," Menendez tells us, "his ability to grow and change when new challenges required it, and his belief that each person can make a difference were attributes deserving of praise and appreciation."

His willingness to jettison the uncreative anti-Communism of US foreign policy, and his recognition that civil rights was a moral crisis that demanded resolution, should also assure him a place in history.

Despite the attempts made by certain historians to tear his reputation to pieces, the fact remains many black homes in America contain a pictorial memorial to the slain President.

They knew, even if certain historians did not, that they had a friend in The White House.

The assessment by Tom Wicker of *The New York Times* will stand: "John Fitzgerald Kennedy was the last president the American people looked up to, in the old, unquestioning way. He was our young emperor, before the throne became bloodied and the cause tarnished by its own excesses. He was the last leader in a time when Americans were eager to follow."

Professor James N. Giglio of Southwest Missouri State University is surely right when he reminds us that it is erroneous to attribute President Kennedy's elevation solely to the circumstances of his death.

"After all, he exhibited considerable popularity during his Presidency, with an approval rating that never fell below 59 per cent in the Gallup Polls.

"He will always be remembered for his style. His youthful and handsome appearance stood out among a generation of ageing leaders such as Truman, Eisenhower, Adenauer, de Gaulle, Macmillan, Nehru and Khrushchev. Yet more than this, he projected an almost indescribable aura that affected practically everyone who came in contact with him either personally or through television.

"Much of that appeal can be attributed to his good manners, vitality, wit, self-deprecating humour, a disarming casualness, which journalist Mary McGrory insisted made him 'the most attractive man of his generation'.

"Kennedy gave the impression of liking and caring about people, and they in turn felt that way about him. The Byrds, a musical group of the late '60s and '70s, expressed a common sentiment when they sang, 'Though I never met him, I knew him just the same. He was a friend of mine'."

But as Sorensen has argued persuasively, there was far more to Kennedy than just style.

Giglio agrees: "Kennedy also succeeded in articulating a sense of hope and purpose that made a profound impression, particularly on the young and disadvantaged, causing them to connect with government in a way that they have not done again since then.

"He conveyed a lofty standard of excellence that became the perfect antidote to the mass conformity and mediocrity that seemed to characterise the society of the fifties."

In a 1986 ABC TV Special, Theodore White author of *The Making of the President* (1960) talked about JFK in the following terms:

"I felt that he was a key figure of the twentieth century. He was the first Catholic to be elected president, an Irish Catholic. It meant that all the other subdued ethnics who hadn't yet seized the opportunities of American politics would follow him . . .

"He opened the gates for all the new surges in American life, surges in American culture.

"He came down hard on the environmental thing very early. He got the Test Ban Treaty through. He did remarkable things in three short years. And he left his work unfinished. He was cut off just as things were about to come to harvest . . .

"If he had gone on till 1968 it might have been one of the three most memorable administrations in American history . . . "

Averall Harriman, a former Ambassador to Moscow, drew the obvious parallel with Roosevelt:

"Franklin Roosevelt had talked over the heads of Government to the hearts of people, and the same was true of John Kennedy," he said six months after Dallas.

"He also had been an expression of the ideals that the world hoped us to live up to. His inaugural and his subsequent speeches were read everywhere, and the world felt that a new FDR had come to power."

No two Presidents had had world opinion and affection centred on them as had Roosevelt and Kennedy. In both cases, people abroad felt they had lost a personal friend when they died.

Kennedy's death, and the manner of it, sent shock waves across the globe.

Harriman said of the impact of Dallas: "Then came the stunning fact, and the reaction in one's self, one's country, and in the world was in some ways more vocal and more intense than the reaction to Roosevelt's death.

"This was particularly true among the youth. Someone had cared about them, genuinely cared, and was doing something about it. Youth knew and was responding. Suddenly, he was gone, gone, gone . . . "

Robert McNamara, who served as JFK's Secretary for Defense, also captured the sense of loss: "Nothing will be quite the same with him gone. Among other things, he reached the hearts of people around the world with a quality and a style and a sophistication which epitomized the age and the times . . . "

In the nineties, for a man like Oliver Stone, who served in Vietnam, the appeal of Kennedy remains undimmed.

"Kennedy, to me, was like the Godfather of my generation. He was a very important figure, a leader, and a prince, in a sense.

"And his murder marked the end of a dream, the end of a concept, of an idealism that I associate with my youth, and that's the reason I particularly was plunged into betrayal and war – race war, Vietnam, Watergate – the whole laundry list of problems that have bedevilled America since his death . . .

"Not that I'm saying he would have solved everything, like the King Arthur legend. But there's no question in my mind; John Kennedy would never have committed combat troops to Vietnam. He refused to in 1961 and again in 1963, and he told several people he would withdraw them in '65 if he won the election.

"So, you know, my whole life was shaped by his death, as was everybody's who's alive today of that age.

"I think the 1990s are very much determined by what happened in the 1960s.

"And I think we should all go back now and try to understand what went wrong in 1963 – and if we can begin to understand the consequences of that day in November, it will shape the rest of our lives."

A Kennedy critic, Garry Wills, who felt the Presidency was more style than substance, nevertheless acknowledges that the best had yet to come.

"There is no way of knowing what President Kennedy might have done had he lived. Could he have withdrawn from Vietnam without losing face?"

The answer to that in 1993, for Stone and many others, is a resounding yes.

More than anything else, this was because, like Churchill, he believed that courage was the one quality which guaranteed all the rest.

And he showed again and again that he possessed not just courage alone.

"May none but honest and wise men ever rule under this roof."

The words were penned by John Adams, the first President (1797-1801) to live in The White House.

A hundred and forty-five years later Franklin Roosevelt had the words carved in the mantlepiece of the State Dining Room.

Was Kennedy honest and wise?

A bit of both, certainly; perhaps a lot.

No politician, not even Abraham Lincoln, can be totally honest.

As for wisdom, that's measured by different yardsticks.

This much can be asserted: Kennedy was better fitted than most men for the high office which he assumed that cold January day in 1961.

John Kenneth Galbraith, who served as Ambassador during the Kennedy Administration, was once asked if he longed for a return to "Camelot". Here is his reply: "During that period, the Government of the United States was tinged with a certain excitement. The Government was a force for good and without wanting to use the term Camelot, I hope that excitement might not be dead."

Norman Mailer's verdict has stood the test of time: "There can be no doubt that Kennedy's magic was not alone that of wealth and youth and good looks, or even of all these things joined to intelligence and will.

"It was, more than this, the hope that he could redeem American politics by releasing American life from its various bondages to orthodoxy."

That appeared possible because, above all, John F. Kennedy loved the noble art of politics, which is government of the people, by the people, for the people.

More than any other politician of this century, he breathed new life, imparted new meaning, to that definition of democracy first uttered by Lincoln at Gettysburg on another November day exactly a century before the tragedy at Dallas.

20
Bobby

"He would have made a great President. Yes – a great President."

I was sitting across from Kathleen Kennedy Townsend in her office in Baltimore, and we were discussing her late father.

No one can say for sure, but there are plenty of people who believe that Robert F. Kennedy would indeed have made a great President.

More than that, they believe that his death robbed America of an opportunity to take a direction which would have obviated much of the pain and social turmoil of the Vietnam and post-Vietnam years.

The last time RFK spoke on the floor of the US Senate was on 7 March 1968. He had already decided to run for President on an anti-war platform. During the course of his speech, he posed the following question:

"Moreover, there is a question of our moral responsibility. Are we like the God of the Old Testament that we can decide in Washington DC what cities, what towns, what hamlets in Vietnam are going to be destroyed?"

Moral responsibility meant much to RFK, for he was in reality a moral crusader.

"In one sense," Simon Tisdall of *The Guardian* wrote on the 25th anniversary of his death, "and as shown most recently by Bill Clinton's campaign last year, the political history of America in the past 25 years has been one long search for a new Bobby.

"His death has also become both a symbol of and justification for the subsequent alienation and disillusionment with the political process, among both blacks and whites. Their angry disenchantment was confirmed by Nixon's Watergate and has grown ever since."

RFK's friend, the columnist Anthony Lewis, made much the same point writing in *The New York Times* at the same time: "We know what happened. The country turned from the politics of responsibility to the politics of selfishness. The conservative movement, coming to power with President Reagan, gave an apostolic blessing to greed."

It may be, as Tisdall says, that RFK's memory has been sanctified through a generation's expectations – hopes which he raised, inspired, and shared but never had the chance to fulfil.

"By dying young, his reputation was not sullied by exposure to the unromantic, grubby realities of actually being a president."

I have no doubt the man described as the last white politician who was trusted by black people would have coped superbly with those "grubby realities".

The line spoken by the mysterious "Mr X" in the Oliver Stone movie *JFK* is one Bobby would probably have made his own: "Fundamentally, people are suckers for the truth."

I also think Theodore Sorensen is correct when he says Bobby would have been a more controversial president than JFK.

Of JFK it used be said that he was detached, even about his religion.

No such thing could be said of Bobby; he combined fire, passion and anger in face of injustice, deprivation and oppression.

In the summer of 1967, after race riots in Newark, Harlem and Detroit, he spoke out on behalf of the blacks, the poor and the marginalised:

"If we can spend $24 billion for the freedom and liberty of the people of Vietnam, certainly we can spend a small percentage of that for the liberty and freedom and the future of our people in this United States . . . "

Professor Arthur Schlesinger offered this assessment: "By November 1967, when Robert Kennedy had his 42nd birthday, he was the most original, enigmatic and provocative figure in mid-century American politics."

"Bobby had a psychic violence about himself," says actress Shirley MacLaine. She characterised his approach as follows: "Let's be violent with our minds and get this thing changed. Let's not be violent with our triggers."

He agreed with Martin Luther King that "segregation is a cancer in the body politic", and with singer Joan Baez that "we shall overcome".

One of his critics, a novelist and polemicist, Gore Vidal, once conceded: "I think he has a real affinity for the hurt people of the world: the blacks, the poor, the misunderstood young."

More than his brother, Bobby believed in the "social gospel", in the radical, transforming powers of the Sermon on the Mount.

His own Church, he once told Pope Paul VI, ought to be "the foremost champion for changing this kind of difficult, poverty-stricken life".

Robert Scheer, editor of the New Left magazine *Ramparts* at the time, said that Kennedy "gave a shit about the Indians", and "gave a shit about what was happening to black people".

Breaking with President Johnson, and some of his own brother's closest advisers (who had stayed on in The White House after Dallas) on the Vietnam War was a turning-point for him.

In January 1966, Senator George McGovern (who would contest the Presidency in 1972) wrote to him: "Bob, I do hope you will continue to raise questions about Vietnam. Your voice is one of the very few that is powerful enough to help steer us away from catastrophe."

The following month, at a meeting of the Senate Foreign Relations Committee, Kennedy proposed a negotiated settlement in Vietnam.

The anger within the Johnson Administration and the military establishment was reflected in the *Chicago Tribune*, which entitled its editorial "Ho Chi Kennedy".

Yet negotiations for a settlement would begin during the Nixon Administration after Bobby Kennedy's death, and would eventually lead to an American withdrawal in 1975.

When President Johnson, devastated by the manner in which Vietnam had divided America, announced that he would not seek re-election in 1968, it was a triumph for Bobby.

Later, in retirement, Lyndon B. Johnson said as much to his biographer, Doris Kearns.

"I felt that I was being chased on all sides by a giant stampede. . . I was being forced over the edge by rioting blacks, demonstrating students, marching welfare mothers, squawking professors, and hysterical reporters.

"And then the final straw. The thing I feared from the first day of my Presidency was actually coming true. Robert Kennedy had openly announced his intention to reclaim the throne in the memory of his brother. And the American people, swayed by the magic of the name, were dancing in the streets."

But the magic was short-lived.

Death was never far from Bobby's mind. He spoke about it regularly, often quoting a line from Sophocles' *Oedipus of Colonus*: "Not to be born is past all prizing best".

In September 1966 Dean Markham, a very close friend from his time at Harvard, and Ethel's brother George Skakel, (Bobby married Ethel Skakel in June 1950) died in a plane crash in Idaho.

Bob Kennedy said to Sorensen: "You had better pretend you don't know me. Everyone connected with me seems jinxed."

A few days after he had announced his decision to run for Democratic nomination for President, and at a time when his followers were elated, Jackie Kennedy met Arthur Schlesinger at a New York dinner party. She took the historian aside.

"Do you know what I think will happen to Bobby?"

Schlesinger shook his head.

"The same thing that happened to Jack. There is so much hatred in this country, and more people hate Bobby than hated Jack. I've told Bobby this, but he isn't fatalistic, like me."

In fact, he was fatalistic, and that made him believe that he – no more than any other human being – could not escape his destiny.

Somebody once asked RFK whether he believed in God.

"Yes," he said hesitantly. "I think. But one question which really shakes me, really shakes me – if God exists why do poor people exist? Why does a Hitler arise? I can't give an answer for that."

In April 1968, Bobby went to Memphis to see Coretta King the day after the assassination of her husband Martin Luther King.

Afterwards, a despondent RFK said: "You know that fellow Lee Harvey Oswald set something loose in this country . . ."

Today it still seems strange to many that Robert Kennedy never publicly questioned the Warren Commission's findings about the death of JFK in Dallas.

"He refused to involve himself in the problem of who had murdered his brother," Schlesinger tells us.

Theodore Sorensen adds: "His brother was gone and no investigation or revelation could bring him back. But if he had known any grounds for legitimate suspicion suggesting that others were involved in his brother's murder, it is hard to believe that he would let such a matter rest."

Some say that shortly before his own death in June 1968 in Los Angeles, RFK seemed preoccupied with the "secrets" of his brother's death.

Schlesinger recalls being in PJ Clarke's bar in New York with Bobby much earlier when RFK was wondering how long he could continue to avoid comment on the Warren Report.

According to the historian, RFK believed the Report was a poor job and he was not prepared to endorse it. At the same time, he was unwilling to criticise it and thereby re-open the whole tragic business.

Bobby's friend, Anthony Lewis, the distinguished *New York Times* columnist, says we'll never have the answer to Dallas. "It will remain a mystery," he told me in Dublin in 1993.

Later, I recalled that in 1975 – after Dallas and Los Angeles, Lewis had written: "The search for conspiracy only increases the elements of morbidity and paranoia and fantasy in this country . . . . It obscures our necessary understanding, all of us, that in this life there is often tragedy without reason."

Robert Kennedy's assassination in the kitchen of the Ambassador Hotel appears to have been such a tragedy.

Questions of course have been raised, even though it looked like an open-and-shut case.

On the night of 5 June 1968, Robert Kennedy, the Democrat Senator from New York, who had just won the California Primary, was shot in the presence of 76 people while passing through the pantry of the Ambassador Hotel in Los Angeles.

Sirhan Sirhan, a young Palestinian immigrant embittered by the US support for the Israelis, pleaded guilty.

He is still serving a life sentence.

Over the years, American reporters have pointed out discrepancies in the District Attorney's case which, because of the guilty plea, was not tested in court.

Then in 1992 two British television producers, Chris Plumley and Tim Tate, decided to undertake a fresh investigation.

The programme which they put together – *The Robert Kennedy Assassination* – was screened by Channel 4 on 17 August 1992.

Their film for Channel 4's Secret History slot was made after they re-interviewed witnesses and examined police documents.

It challenged the official version of the assassination, giving additional weight to yet another conspiracy theory.

Yet a lot of people were left unconvinced by the evidence presented on television.

"The necessary momentum and simplification of documentary narrative are different from the pettifogging process of scientific inquiry," wrote Laurence Marks in *The Observer.*

The Los Angeles Police Department concluded that Sirhan fired eight .22 bullets from his eight-shot Iver-Johnson revolver.

One lodged in Kennedy's spine, another in his heart, a third entered through his back and exited through his chest.

Five other bullets wounded bystanders.

Seven bullets were recovered; the eighth was lost in the pantry's ceiling space.

The Channel 4 film focused on three inconsistencies.

First, the autopsy report states that the Senator was hit by bullets fired from behind at point-blank range.

Plumley and Tate say that the witnesses all agreed that Sirhan fired from at least six feet in front of the Senator, but that this contradiction was not disclosed in court.

Secondly, the FBI found four bullet-holes in a wooden room-divider. That would add up to more than eight shots.

In an attempt to explain this away, the Los Angeles Police Department (LAPD) said they were nail holes.

Thirdly, the LAPD's trajectory analysis was contradicted by evidence from the wounded bystanders.

If the bullets that hit Kennedy did.not come from in front of him, and if there were more than eight, then there must have been at least one other gunman who got away.

That is not impossible in a mêlée of more than 70 shocked and distracted people crowded into a narrow kitchen space.

Sandra Serrano, aged 18 at the time, was at the foot of a staircase immediately after the shooting when a woman in a white polka-dot dress followed by a man ran downstairs.

Serrano claimed the woman was shouting: "We've shot him! We've shot him!"

Sergeant Paul Scharaga put out a radio call for police to look out for the couple, but was quickly ordered to cancel it.

The film includes an LAPD tape-recording of Hank Hernandez, a detective leading the investigation, trying to persuade Serrano to retract.

It is at this point that Plumley and Tate propound their conspiracy theory.

The question they pose is: "Did the CIA kill Bobby Kennedy?"

They answer: "Yes."

Why?

The CIA opposed Kennedy's intentions to withdraw from Vietnam.

Hernandez and another senior detective had suppositious links with the CIA.

After the trial they ordered most of the evidence to be destroyed.

Sirhan Sirhan claims he is unable to recall the events of that night.

Amnesia can follow hypno-programming. The CIA has experimented with the possibility of hypnotising political assassins.

That is the kernel of the case put forward by Plumley and Tate.

Is it convincing?

Garry Wills may be right when he says: "Robert Kennedy's assassination gave lesser scope to conspiracy theorists – no one knew, beforehand, his route through the kitchen."

Yet Sirhan Sirhan got to him.

Still, according to officials then and now, the case was cut and dried. Sirhan Sirhan, a Palestinian now serving a life sentence in a California jail, violently opposed Robert Kennedy's views on Israel, and so killed him.

Yet the notion of a conspiracy refuses to go away.

In June 1993, the possibility of CIA involvement in the death of RFK was again dealt with when 150 American radio stations broadcast *The RFK Tapes*, a documentary suggesting that Sirhan Sirhan was not acting alone and may have been brainwashed.

The programme argues that Sirhan was simply a stooge who had been brainwashed, possibly with CIA involvement.

In the documentary, journalist-narrator William Klaber claims Sirhan was programmed to carry out the assassination by the late William Bryan, a Californian sex therapist who conducted experiments in hypnosis for the CIA.

Some radio critics felt the programme was more plausible than many conspiracy theory exercises, and raised significant doubts about the way the case was handled at the time by the LAPD.

Several prominent scholars and writers, including Norman Mailer and the historian Arthur Schlesinger Jr, have petitioned a Los Angeles grand jury to review the police investigation.

The coroner, for example, said in court that Bobby had been killed by a bullet fired inches from the back of his head. Many witnesses, however, agree that Sirhan was in front of the Senator when he discharged all eight bullets in his .22 revolver.

Also, who was "the girl in the polka-dot dress" seen talking to Sirhan and another man before the killing?

She has never been identified and, Klaber suggests, may have been Sirhan's "mind-controller".

The most elaborate conclusions in the programme are expressed by Paul Schraga, a retired sergeant who was the first police officer on the scene.

He claims right-wing extremists in the Los Angeles police intelligence unit were deeply involved in the assassination.

"Conspiracy? You bet your bottom dollar there was a conspiracy," he told *Time* magazine.

That RFK was a target for assassination goes without saying. He showed promise of being more radical than his brother and, as Jackie Kennedy emphasised, he had more enemies and was more of a hate figure.

The Right hated him, so did the Mob, and his anti-Vietnam War stance made him an alien figure in the eyes of the CIA and the Pentagon.

His loss, in terms of his potential, may have been even greater than JFK's.

Comparisons are invidious.

"Both Kennedy brothers had great capacity to inspire people," Professor Schlesinger told me. "RFK was the more emotional of the two, and, had he lived, he would have become President in more emotional times."

Let us leave the final words on Bobby to his brother, Edward.

"That year, 1968, was not only one of tragedy for the Kennedy family; it was also a watershed year in contemporary American history.

"I often think of the 'might have beens' of 1968. If Robert Kennedy had lived, he might well have been elected President of the United States, and the nation's subsequent history would have been different and better. We might have been spared much of the confrontation that has plagued America since.

"I remember 1968 as a time of great energy and hope, when a majority of the American people first realised that the Vietnam War was wrong and that it ought to end. And Robert Kennedy believed that individuals could make the difference.

"As he told the students at the University of Capetown in South Africa in 1966: 'Each time a man stands up for an ideal, or acts to improve the lot of others, or strikes out against injustice, he sends forth a tiny ripple of hope and, crossing each other from a million different centres of energy and daring, those ripples build a current that can sweep down the mightiest walls of oppression and resistance.'

"In the years since he was taken from us, much has changed in politics and the country. If my brother were here today, he would be gratified that there is no longer a searing issue like Vietnam. But he would be distressed with politicians who trust polls and consultants over their own instincts.

"He would be proudest of the civil rights revolution, but he would be appalled at the lack of progress in the wars against hunger and poverty, disease and illiteracy – wars that he knew America could win.

"He would have disagreed with the passive 'government keep out' philosophy . . .

"Bobby sought the office himself because he knew how much he could accomplish as an active President."

The last campaign of Robert Francis Kennedy, which looked certain to take him to The White House, ran for 85 days.

Then an assassin's bullets cut short RFK's glittering career, signalling the death of the other American dream.

It was the film director John Frankenheimer who drove him to the Hotel Ambassador that fateful day.

As they sped furiously along the Santa Monica Freeway, Kennedy turned to the film director. "Take it easy, John," he said. "Life is too short."

Little did he know.

When he died he was only 42 years old. And his favourite song was "The Impossible Dream".

21
Chappaquiddick – A Bridge Too Far

"What Chappaquiddick did was to shatter the dynastic claims of Edward Kennedy . . . "

The conservative commentator, William F. Buckley, drew this conclusion in October 1969 – just months after the tragedy which cost Mary Jo Kopechne her life.

She died of drowning when a car driven by Senator Edward Kennedy plunged off a bridge on Chappaquiddick Island on the night of July 18. With her died Teddy Kennedy's hopes of ever becoming President.

He didn't think that at the time. In fact, Buckley's conclusion showed prescience.

A decade later – on 19 November 1979 – *Newsweek* carried the following report: "Years of political flirtation and speculation ended last week on a grisly gray morning in Boston. With his three children and his wife beside him, Edward Moore Kennedy told why he had chosen to challenge a sitting President of his own party.

"The grin, the accent and the stabbing gestures were hauntingly familiar of his brothers, John and Robert – and so was the call to activism."

Yet, as *Newsweek* noted, with the special advantages born of the Kennedy legacy came special problems. Central to these problems was a spate of adverse comment in the press which focused on Chappaquiddick and on Kennedy's failure to articulate his substantial differences with President Jimmy Carter.

"We are willing, even anxious, to be on the march again," said Kennedy.

The question was how far would Kennedy's march take him.

Far – but not nearly far enough.

He entered all 34 primaries, and lost 24 of them.

The shadow of Chappaquiddick could not be erased.

Still Kennedy did not quit.

On 6 January 1986 *Newsweek* carried another story.

"The opportunity was there this time, but so was the reality. After weeks of private deliberation, Massachusetts Senator Edward Kennedy concluded a fortnight ago that while he might well win the Democratic nomination in 1988, winning the Presidency would be far more difficult."

He declined another bid for The White House, and instead said he would run again for the Senate in 1988.

"I know that this decision means that I may never be President," Kennedy said. "But the pursuit of the Presidency is not my life."

Up to that point it had been.

Many observers believed his 1986 decision not to run for President signalled the end of an era – both for the older generation of the Kennedy political dynasty and the old guard of liberal Democrats he had come to represent.

Although polls put him ahead of the Democratic pack, they also reflected a high negative rating.

Newsweek told why: "Residual rumours about Kennedy's personal problems – his divorce, and reminders of Chappaquiddick – continued to dog his tracks."

He was divorced from his wife, Joan, in 1983 – but it was Chappaquiddick which sank his hopes of ever making it to The White House.

Shortly after he was elected the US Senator for Massachusetts in 1952, at the age of 35, the future President Kennedy was asked at a press conference if he was stepping into the shoes of his elder brother who had died in the war.

"Just as I went into politics because Joe died, if anything happens to me tomorrow, my brother Bobby would run for my seat in the Senate. And if Bobby died, Teddy would take over from him," he said, in an answer which defined a political dynasty.

All three brothers were conscious of this. Bobby tried for the Presidency; Teddy wanted to. It was not to be.

His life and his career have been haunted by the spectre of the biggest, blackest blotch on his life – the night in July 1969 when his Oldsmobile went off the Dike Bridge on the island of Chappaquiddick, drowning campaign worker Mary Jo Kopechne.

The party at Lawrence Cottage was beginning to break up. Ted Kennedy, tired, slightly flushed, but flashing that famous smile, emerged into the hallway, pulling on a coat.

At the door of the cottage Mary Jo was waiting to go. Teddy had offered to drive her. He took the keys to the black Oldsmobile from his 63-year-old chauffeur, Jack Crimmons, and said it was time to get moving.

Mary Jo needed a lift to catch a ferry going from Chappaquiddick Island to Martha's Vineyard, a larger island off the heel of Cape Cod in Massachusetts.

It was just 11.57 p.m. Teddy was talking to Esther Newberg, one of the six girls in the cottage, all of whom had been his brother Bobby's campaign workers in 1968 before the assassination in Los Angeles.

He waved to Mary Jo, who had stepped outside, to indicate he was on his way, and kissed one of the other girls – Maryellen Lyons – on the cheek, causing her to blush.

At the door he shouted goodbye to Paul Markham, an old family friend, picked up his briefcase, took Mary Jo by the arm, and walked into the darkness towards the car.

She was 28, a very lovely, very lively woman, according to friends. She'd worked as a legislative secretary for Bobby for three years before his death. "She was very much attached to the Kennedy family," said her mother.

To get to the ferry, they would have to cross the Dike Bridge over Poncha Pond.

According to Kennedy's statement at the time, he was unfamiliar with the road and took a wrong turn.

"After about half a mile, I went down a hill and came upon a narrow bridge. The car went off the side."

The vehicle turned over and sank, landing with its roof resting on the bottom.

"Death by drowning" was the official verdict, even though no autopsy was carried out.

And Kennedy's own account was that he was rushing to get his female passenger to the last ferry at midnight from Chappaquiddick when his car went out of control and off the narrow bridge.

Later, conflicting accounts emerged. And the implication of these was unmistakable: Teddy had been taking Mary to the beach, not the ferry.

The other implication was that sex was the motive. When Mary Jo's body was found, she was fully dressed but was not wearing underwear.

According to a scuba diver who helped to recover the body, there was a good chance the girl could have been saved if help had been called soon after the accident.

It wasn't: in fact, the alarm wasn't raised until hours later.

The rest, as they say, is history.

When the story broke it was the page one lead in newspapers everywhere.

Here is how the opening paragraphs of *The Boston Globe* account on 20 July 1969 read: "Edgarton – Sen. Edward M. Kennedy, the only surviving brother in a family pursued by tragedy, narrowly escaped death yesterday when his car plunged into a pond on a sparsely inhabited island off the coast of Martha's Vineyard.

"A passenger, Mary Jo Kopechne, 28, of Washington, a former campaign worker for the late Sen. Robert F. Kennedy, was drowned.

"The car went off a wooden bridge, turned over, and sank to the bottom of Poncha Pond.

"Police say the accident occurred between midnight and 1.00 a.m. yesterday on Chappaquiddick Island, where Kennedy was visiting with friends at a small cottage . . . "

According to Kennedy, he dived repeatedly to the sunken car to try to free its passenger.

It was eight hours later before he called the police.

Two questions have ever since been central: (a) why did he take so long to report the accident, and (b) why didn't his friends phone the police themselves after he had come back to the cottage?

That delay, when it became public, did Teddy Kennedy's reputation much damage.

Some claim that the account given by Kennedy and his advisers was a blanket of lies and contradictions. This claim was reinforced by a book entitled *The Last Brother*, written by journalist Joe McGinniss and published in mid-1993.

It challenges the Kennedy account head-on, and contends that the Senator deliberately hid the truth about what happened on the fateful night of Friday, 18 July 1969.

The truth, it is contended, and the scandal it would have led to, would have ruined Teddy Kennedy's career.

He was a member of the most famous family in America, a senator, handsome and ambitious, known to have his eye on his nation's greatest political prize.

She was a young secretary, intelligent and attractive, part of a special breed that politicians cannot do without – bright, efficient, dedicated, hard-working and discreet.

The party was the second annual reunion for Mary Jo and five other single girls, known as "the boiler-room girls". All had worked on Bobby Kennedy's campaign.

Within an hour of leaving Lawrence Cottage Mary Jo was dead, and Teddy Kennedy's political career – which up to then promised so much – was in ruins.

From that day forth the aura of greatness and moral rectitude was greatly diminished.

He had been 31 years old and was presiding over a debate in the US Senate when the terrible news of JFK's assassination came through from Dallas.

The torch was passed to Bobby. But within five years, he too was dead, also cut down by an assassin's bullets.

Now, in the midst of tragedy, he was the family standard-bearer. His very name evoked the Camelot legend, and the old mystique which surrounded JFK.

And then came Chappaquiddick . . .

It would perhaps have finished lesser mortals, other politicians without the sustaining power of the Kennedy dynasty and the Kennedy millions.

Edward Kennedy was heir to a myth, but he also had to deal with personal and political realities.

One of those realities – which he finally faced 17 years later – meant he could never occupy The White House, never be President.

But if he couldn't get the Presidency, he could still amass great power and influence within his party, on Capitol Hill, within official Washington. And he did, slowly and skilfully.

He showed that, unlike many sections of the media, he was not prepared to believe that history stopped at Chappaquiddick.

And his success can be gauged from the fact that in a 1990 analysis of the American legislature, entitled WHO RUNS CONGRESS?, political scientist Mark Green called Kennedy "the most influential Senator of the decade".

In the years after the Mary Jo Kopechne tragedy, Teddy learned some very hard lessons.

After he was soundly beaten for the 1980 Democratic nomination by Jimmy Carter, he was asked what he had learned after a long and difficult campaign.

"Well, I learned to lose," he replied. "And for a Kennedy that's hard."

In 1988, he was back on the campaign trail – but this time for Michael Dukakis, his Governor in Massachusetts. He found many supporters in the crowds, and in Iowa, according to *The New York Times*, "the signs said 'Dukakis' but the nostalgia for the name Kennedy will not die".

But for every devotee, there's still someone ready to remind Kennedy of that fateful night, a quarter of a century ago, when his car – and his career – took a turn towards disaster.

Chappaquiddick, as William F. Buckley saw, had broken the natural line of succession.

James MacGregor Burns, one of JFK's earliest biographers, agrees:

"Two things Edward Kennedy did know. In behaving differently from the way his brothers would have done, he had betrayed the Camelot legacy of honour. And for him and for the country, the tragedy of Chappaquiddick would never end."

Could things have been different?

22

Teddy Now

Could Edward Kennedy have been elected President of the United States if Chappaquiddick had never happened?

One of the great "ifs" of modern American politics.

I put the question to Ben Bradlee, former editor of *The Washington Post.*

"I think Ted Kennedy could have made it to The White House – but without Chappaquiddick."

In New York, Theodore Sorensen concurred. "Yes, I think he could have done it."

These days Kennedy himself is philosophical. What is past is past. And no man can rewrite his own history.

1986 was his last chance. After that, his hunger for The White House waned noticeably.

He came to Washington as the baby brother of the President and the Attorney General and saw them both into their graves. Now at the age of 61, he has entered the silver decade.

With a leonine head of grey-streaked hair, he is the Dean of US Senate liberals, and he has to his credit an impressive list of legislative achievements on major issues such as health care, education, civil rights and foreign policy.

He rebuilt his political career, winning the respect of the Senate for his decision to take up the radical causes of his brother Bobby and become the liberal conscience of the Democratic Party.

It is his political, not his personal life, which commands the respect of his peers in the Senate.

Over the years he mustered the largest and best staff of aides and advisers in the Senate, many of whom joined up with White House stars in their eyes. But they stayed on because Kennedy was good: he got laws passed, stopped bad bills, and made a difference. Kennedy fought constantly for the principle of a national health care system – and finally, as we are seeing now under Clinton, converted the Party to it.

He supported arms control with the Soviets and gun control in American cities.

On the latter, even he ran up against a stone wall.

Despite the rising tide of violence in American cities, the gun lobby remains enormously powerful.

The John Wayne syndrome is deeply embedded in American culture.

And it will remain so for as long as the American courts continue to interpret the Second Amendment (in constitutional terms it is known as the right to keep and bear arms) in a manner more appropriate to the conditions of the eighteenth century than the late twentieth century.

Gun control – not surprisingly, given what they have been through – is a matter of principle with the Kennedys.

For Senator Ted Kennedy, fighting for it is something he feels he owes to his two slain brothers.

"Our gun laws are crazy," he says. He is ashamed of the fact that the United States remains the only modern nation in the world without firm regulation of the sale and use of firearms.

One statistic remains burned into his brain. The year after his brother, the President, was gunned down, over 600,000 firearms were purchased in the USA.

He has also – like another Catholic, Governor Mario Cuomo in New York – taken a stand on an issue which has brought him into conflict with some conservative Catholics and members of the US hierarchy.

This is the highly emotive issue of abortion. He has stood up for it, and sees no conflict between his stance here and his stance against capital punishment.

Kennedy, like Cuomo (whose son is married to Bobby's daughter, Kerry), fully understands the concept of a pluralist society.

Like his brother, John, he believes in the separation of Church and State, and can see distinctions between his private beliefs as a Catholic and the need as a legislator to bring in laws to serve the entire society.

"He has been a major force in the Senate," political scientist Thomas Mann of the Brookings Institute says. "He is hard-working and effective. Odds are that will continue."

"I recognise my own shortcomings – the faults in the conduct of my private life," Kennedy said in a *mea culpa* speech to political supporters in 1991.

"I recognise that I alone am responsible for them and I am the one who must confront them." Opponents as well as friends admit that he has done this.

"Unlike my brothers, I have been given length of years and time. As I approach my 63rd birthday, I am determined to give all that I have to advance the causes for which I have stood for almost a third of a century."

He had to shake off the effects of the sex trial of his nephew, William Kennedy Smith, who was acquitted in December 1991 of charges that he raped a woman he picked up at a Palm Beach bar while out drinking with his Uncle Ted.

The publicity surrounding the case, the run-up to the trial and the trial itself, forced Kennedy to take a low profile.

But his appearance at the trial to give evidence got huge media attention – and his performance on the stand was universally regarded as quite impressive.

Smith's attorney made the Senator a key figure in the trial, asking prospective jurors what they thought of him and the rest of America's most famous political family.

Congressman Joe Moakley, a fellow Massachusetts Democrat, said Kennedy's strong performance at the rape trial not only impacted powerfully on the jury – it ensured that the trial will not be an issue when Teddy stands again for re-election to the Senate in 1994.

"He hit the ball out of the park," Moakley said, describing the testimony in baseball terms.

"He's still very popular."

In March 1992 Ted Kennedy announced his engagement to Victoria Reggie, a 38-year-old, Washington DC lawyer and divorced mother of two, with the simple, romantic declaration: "I love Victoria and her children very much, and she has brought enormous happiness into my life."

Kennedy had been quietly a-courtin' Victoria since June 1991 with flowers, twice-daily phone calls, dates to the theatre and Washington Redskins' games, as well as sailing vacations in the waters off Hyannis Port.

The first public viewing of the relationship came at the Senator's 60th birthday party at his home in McLean, Virginia. A bit of the famous Kennedy rakishness was on display as well; he was dressed as Rhett Butler, she was Scarlett O'Hara.

He and Victoria, an elegant, brown-eyed brunette of Lebanese descent, were married in 1992.

She comes from a monied background in Crowley, Louisiana, a region best known for oil and rice.

Her father, Edmund Reggie, a former banker and a retired city judge, headed the short-lived Louisiana campaign for Kennedy in 1980 – and even after the Senator bowed out in favour of Jimmy Carter, Victoria's mother, Doris, 62, insisted on casting her vote for Ted when she went to the Democratic National Convention as a delegate.

"That's how much we think of him," says her husband. "We know him, and we love him. He's one of my dearest friends."

The Reggies have been Kennedy supporters since 1956, when the Judge met John F. Kennedy, then a vice-presidential hopeful, at the Democratic Convention in Chicago.

He managed JFK's 1960 campaign in Louisiana (the future President even stayed at the Reggie's home) as well as Robert Kennedy's campaign there in 1968.

The Reggies have been present at assorted Kennedy weddings, and Victoria's brother Dennis, a photographer, shot the Maria Shriver-Arnold Schwarzenegger nuptials in 1986 and the Kerry Kennedy-Andrew Cuomo wedding in 1990. (Maria Shriver is the daughter of President Kennedy's sister, Eunice, and Kerry Cuomo is Robert Kennedy's daughter.)

Like the Kennedys, the Reggies are staunchly Catholic. Victoria's parents have even made a pilgrimage to Medjugorge, Yugoslavia, where the Blessed Virgin is said to have been appearing at regular intervals over the past decade.

Victoria attended parochial schools in Crowley, and studied law at Tulane University, New Orleans, graduating *summa cum laude* in 1979.

That was followed by a prestigious assignment clerking in the US Seventh Circuit Court of Appeals in Chicago.

It was in Chicago she met Grier Raclin, a fellow attorney. They married in 1980 and divorced 10 years later after they had moved to Washington DC. Victoria has two children by Raclin; Caroline, 7, and Curran, 10.

Ted Kennedy and the lawyer started dating in the spring of 1991 after he attended a 40th wedding anniversary party she threw for her parents in Washington, and several months after he and previous girlfriend, Dragana Lickle, a 36-year-old from Palm Beach, broke up.

"It's been very obvious that he's really smitten with her," says Kennedy-watcher Andrew Migs, Washington bureau chief of the *Boston Herald American*, "and apparently he's devoted to her children."

Kennedy has always kept close ties with his own children by his first wife, Joan, now 56.

She took the news of the second marriage very well, and sent best wishes to the pair.

Joan Bennett and Edward Kennedy were married in Bronxville, New York in November 1958, with Cardinal Francis Spellman performing the ceremony. She was 22, he was four years older. Joan had been introduced to him by his sister, Jean Kennedy Smith, now the US Ambassador to Ireland.

The marriage was happy in the early years, though Joan once told a friend: "The only reason he wanted to marry me was because he couldn't get me any other way."

At the time of Chappaquiddick in July 1969, Joan was pregnant.

She attended the funeral of Mary Jo Kopechne, but said afterwards: "It was a terrible experience, one of the worst in my life. And it was the beginning of the end for Ted and me."

Close friends said she suffered as the "second victim" of the plunge off the bridge at Chappaquiddick.

The end, however, was still a decade away.

In August 1974 Richard Nixon resigned as President, and afterwards pressure built up on Ted to enter the 1976 race for The White House.

Whatever positives there were in favour of his candidacy in Joan's eyes, they were far outweighed by the negatives, first and foremost, the fear of another assassination.

When she was asked by a reporter if perhaps she exaggerated that fear, she replied: "Exaggerate? Exaggerate? How can you say that? Let's get in my car and I'll drive you down the road just over a mile to Hickory Hill where Ethel lives. Let's go there and you can look at a house filled with eleven children without a father, and then tell me if I exaggerate the dangers of being a Senator Kennedy."

By this stage their marriage was clearly disintegrating, and Joan had an alcohol problem.

For their three children – Kara, Edward Jr and Patrick – it was a most difficult time; they, too, were terrified that their father would be shot like their uncles.

On 7 November 1979 Ted announced his candidacy for President at Faneuil Hall in Boston.

In the *Boston Herald American* a columnist called Ted's announcement the latest episode in the "elongated soap opera tale of the Kennedys . . ."

Earlier that month, CBS screened an hour-long special entitled "Teddy", during which presenter Roger Mudd recalled a remark Teddy had made just after the accident at Chappaquiddick when he said he felt "an awful curse hanging over the Kennedy family".

It is a remark he bitterly regrets ever since.

At this stage the marriage was in deep trouble, and matters were not helped by an article published in the December 1979 issue of the *Washington Monthly* and titled "Kennedy's Woman Problem: Women's Kennedy problem".

The author, Suzannah Lessard wrote:

"The type of womanising that Kennedy is associated with is a series of short involvements – if they can be called that – after which he drops the lady . . . it suggests an old-fashioned, male-chauvinist view of women as primarily objects of pleasure . . ."

Joan, like a dutiful wife, was prepared to suffer on, not wanting to do anything to jeopardise her husband's chances of The White House.

And, despite all her fears, she harboured a secret ambition to follow in Jackie Kennedy's footsteps.

At the August 1980 Democratic Convention at Madison Square Gardens in New York, the Kennedy bubble burst.

Kennedy's Presidential aspirations were squashed when he failed to topple President Jimmy Carter in the race for the nomination.

After the roll call, Carter had 2,129 delegate votes to Kennedy's 1,146.

The latter withdrew, and made a gracious and electrifying 32-minute speech.

Observers said he had staked a claim to be the "conscience of the Democratic Party".

The defeat by Carter meant the end not just of Joan's fantasies of becoming First Lady, but also her dreams of a reconciliation with Ted.

The announcement of their plans to divorce was made in January 1981 – on the day after Ronald Reagan's inauguration as President.

Articles speculated that Joan's settlement was in the region of $5 million with an annual alimony of $175,000, plus a house.

In the years since, Ted and Joan have remained good friends, though for her, having to cope with the reputation of being the only defector from America's Royal Family hasn't been easy.

Today, Ted Kennedy knows he can never be King, but in Washington he is regarded as a king-maker.

And his sense of his family's destiny has not lessened.

He still believes passionately in the words he spoke at the opening of the JFK Memorial Library in 1979: "The spark still glows, the journey never ends, the dream shall never die."

He knows that he has disappointed the millions who loved John Kennedy and harboured the hope that Edward Moore Kennedy could resume the journey and fulfil the dream.

But he knows, too, that he has made a very significant contribution to the political, economic, social and cultural life of his nation.

His stature had never been higher, and with his new wife he continues to be a commanding and influential figure on the American political stage.

That influence works today to Ireland's advantage.

Kennedy is a key member of the executive committee of the Friends of Ireland, a lobby group whose support for the Anglo-Irish Agreement has proved crucial.

This group has access to the President, to heads of government departments and to leaders of the business community.

And they have played a most important role in determining how a sizeable proportion of the 42 million Irish-Americans view Ireland and particularly the "troubles" in the North. If there is far less support and sympathy now in the USA for the old nationalistic slogans and simplistic solutions to the Northern Ireland problem, that's largely due to Kennedy, to former New York Governor Hugh Carey, former Speaker of the House, Tip O'Neill, current Speaker, Tom Foley, Senator Patrick Moynihan and Congressman Brian Donnelly.

None of that happened overnight, of course, as SDLP leader John Hume (who is very close to Ted Kennedy and the others) reminded me during a discussion we had in New York.

In Kennedy's own case there was also a painful process of political education and adjustment involved *vis-à-vis* the complexities of the Irish situation.

Indeed, his early views on Northern Ireland alarmed the then Taoiseach, Jack Lynch.

Kennedy tended to see the North in those early days as an Irish Vietnam – the bad guys were the British; the good guys were the IRA.

But just as he came to see the violence in Vietnam as immoral, so too did he, due to the influence of people like Hume, come to see the violence in the North in similar fashion.

It was only over a period of time that the full implications of having one million Unionists on the island dawned. With that came the realisation that the overwhelming majority of the Irish people abhorred the IRA's "armed struggle".

Apart from Hume, other Irish political figures like Lynch, Dr Garret FitzGerald, Dr Conor Cruise O'Brien, and top officials in the Department of Foreign Affairs and the Irish Embassy in Washington helped to provide Kennedy with a new perspective on the "Irish Question".

Kennedy's influence, as John Hume readily acknowledges, on Anglo-Irish affairs continues to be important.

And now that there is a Democrat in The White House and a Kennedy in the American Ambassador's residence in Dublin, Hume and others believe that influence will increase.

Today Teddy Kennedy is a respected elder statesman. Those close to him say he has finally come to terms with that fateful night nearly a quarter of a century ago when his car and his career took a turn towards disaster.

His performance in Washington, and the respect in which he is held by all sides, give the lie to the claim made by ex-Nixon speechwriter, William Safire, that after Bobby's death in 1968 the torch had been passed to "a clammy hand".

23

Back to the Future

It is 20 January 2001. A cold wind whips through Washington DC, sending shivers through the large crowd assembled in the Capitol Plaza.

On the steps in front of the huge domed edifice, the home of the US legislature, a slim dark-haired woman places her left hand on top of the Bible held by the Chief Justice, and raises her right hand.

A hush has fallen over the crowd. In the seats behind, her family and friends are gathered, as well as political colleagues and foes.

Former President Bill Clinton and his wife Hillary are there, along with Jack Kemp the defeated Republican contender.

So too are Hollywood stars Michelle Pfeiffer and Kevin Costner. They, along with several other big names from Tinseltown, did not spare themselves during the gruelling campaign.

The dark-haired woman, solemn of mien, intones the Oath after the Chief Justice.

"I, Kathleen Kennedy Townsend, do solemnly swear that I will faithfully execute the office of President of the United States, and will to the best of my ability, preserve, protect and defend the Constitution of the United States."

The Chief Justice extends his hand. The new President smiles and takes it. Out in the Plaza the applause rises to a crescendo.

The 44th President has just been sworn in.

Every inauguration creates its own history, but this one is special.

Even if she achieves nothing of note in the four years that lie ahead, President Kennedy Townsend has already created a special niche for herself in the history books.

David, her husband steps forward to embrace her, followed by their three daughters, Meaghan, Maeve and Rose Catherine.

Her uncle, Teddy Kennedy, is next. And he is followed by her sister, Kerry, and the children of another and even more famous uncle.

Caroline and John F. Kennedy Jr are the centre of media attention.

Back in 1960 their father had stood where Kathleen Kennedy Townsend is now standing. Four places away, to the left, two elderly women are standing together, faces beaming. Ethel Kennedy and Jacqueline Kennedy Onassis are proud and it shows.

Ben Bradlee, executive editor of The Washington Post, is also there with his wife, Sally Quinn. Seated close by are actresses Blair Brown and Susan Sarandon, and the feminist writer Gloria Steinem. Another writer called Peggy Noonan is with them.

As they watch, they reflect on different things, different memories.

In the TV movie "Majority Rule", which was aired in the USA in November 1992, actress Blair Brown portrays presidential candidate Katherine Taylor.

Taylor is a General who, in a recent Desert Storm-like war, leads a ragtag group of men and women in a victorious charge against the enemy.

Her bravery and bravado make her a national hero and, though a political nobody, she decides to run for the highest office in the land.

One striking scene in the movie shows her posing in front of a poster flanked by the American flag and the Presidential flag.

In bold letters, the poster proclaims:

AMERICA'S FIRST WOMAN PRESIDENT.

Susan Sarandon reminds her of it.

Ms Brown – who once played Jackie Kennedy in a biopic – tells her that the outsider scenario makes her uncomfortable.

"You don't just pop out of nowhere and become President. I want a professional brain surgeon if someone's working on my head. I'd like a professional politician in The White House," says Blair, who, like Ms Sarandon, actively supported Clinton in 1992 and 1996, and Townsend in 2000.

But she admits she took the challenge of creating a believable, appealing female Presidential candidate very seriously.

"You have such freedom putting a character like this together," she says.

"It's the kind of challenge any actress – or any screenwriter or film director – would love."

"Where would you look for the 'character components', the jigsaw pieces to create a female President?" asks Susan.

"Initially I used Geraldine Ferraro as a model," admits Blair. "I also listened to some of the great speeches of Churchill, Kennedy, Martin Luther King . . . "

Blair Brown, or any screenwriter or director, might also have been well advised to take a hard look at Kathleen Kennedy Townsend, suggests the star of "Thelma and Louise".

Ben Bradlee is thinking the very same thing. He had been primed in advance.

"She could do it. She could make history by becoming the first woman President," Charles Daly, curator of the JFK Library, tells him years before when they meet at a seminar.

So who is Kathleen Kennedy Townsend?

Sally Quinn is thinking of the profile she has just written. The new President is Bobby Kennedy's oldest child.

And even her birthday is special – 4 July (Independence Day) 1951.

Kathleen, who is named after her father's sister (who had died only a few years earlier), attended the Sacred Heart Country Day School in Bethesda, Maryland; the Putney School and Radcliffe College.

She holds a law degree from the University of New Mexico School of Law. And, most interesting, she wrote her final law school thesis on Emma Goldman, the controversial feminist and social activist.

And it is from Goldman that she takes her favourite quote: "Woman's development, her freedom, her independence, must come from and through herself".

That she has acted on this herself is something Ms Quinn is convinced of, having recently interviewed her.

She doesn't think the idea of a woman as President is far-fetched at all.

Neither does actress Susan Sarandon of "Thelma and Louise" fame.

An enthusiastic Democrat and socially committed, she tells Clinton, when she first campaigns for him back in the early nineties, that she hopes they are both around to see a woman in The White House one day.

"Why not? A woman could do the job just as well as a man any day," is how Clinton replies.

And now that day is here.

They are both chuffed.

Sarandon believes women can be agents of real change in America and the world, and she admires the Kennedys.

"As a family they have shown great commitment," she tells Blair Brown. "They have gone out there and stuck with it when others would have given up long ago."

Peggy Noonan, who worked as a speechwriter in the Reagan White House, is another Kennedy admirer.

She is close by and talking to a senior editor from CBS News. "We were in love with the Kennedys. They were Irish Catholics just like us, and they were smart and glamorous with their tuxedos and silk dresses, and they always said the right thing and had a wonderful sense of humour – and with a little time and money and education we could be just like them. They opened the doors of American glamour to the working class."

Noonan, who also wrote speeches for George Bush, once saw Kathleen Kennedy Townsend posing for a photograph with Bush in The White House when he was President.

Even then the thought that Kathleen or some other member of the Kennedy family would make it back there as president crosses her mind.

It is Noonan who will write the line "a kinder, gentler nation" for one of Bush's speeches.

He didn't achieve that; perhaps nobody could in the context of the eighties.

As a line, it might have been more appropriate for a woman president. As against coming from Bush, it would have a truer ring to it.

Gloria Steinem agrees.

For her, the empowerment of women will mark a new beginning in America and in the world. It's a dream now, perhaps, but she knows that politics is about dreams as much as it is about power.

It has to be if it is going to be humanising, liberating and enriching for people.

This is a vision long treasured by Ms Steinem.

Did she not once write an essay for "Look" magazine saying this would be the effect of having a woman in The White House as President?

Now she is watching it, watching history in the making. And for her, as for the others, it is a joy to behold. On the rostrum, an aide hands the President a slim leather leaflet case with the letters "KKT" embossed in gold on its cover.

She takes out a copy of the speech for which the nation and the world have been waiting.

On both sides of the rostrum the transparent screens of the TelePrompter are quivering in the breeze.

The President, in an emerald green two-piece suit, worn over a lime-green high-necked blouse, seems not to notice the cold.

For a moment she hesitates, waiting for the applause to die away.

Fragments of other Inaugural Addresses flash across her mind.

" . . . The only thing we have to fear is fear itself – nameless, unreasoning terror" (Franklin D. Roosevelt).

" . . . *Let us strive on to finish the work we are in, to bind up the nation's wounds" (Abraham Lincoln).*

" . . . *We stand again at the steps of this symbol of our democracy" (Ronald Reagan).*

" . . . *Moral stamina means more energy and more productivity, on the farm and in the factory" (Dwight D. Eisenhower).*

And then lines from the Address she knows best of all, the Address by which her own will be judged.

" . . . *Ask not what your country can do for you; ask what you can do for your country" (John F. Kennedy).*

The new President has no worries. She is reassured by the presence in the seats behind her of a tall, bespectacled man, whose hair is now streaked with grey.

Theodore C. Sorensen – the man who served as Special Counsel in The White House and who played a key role in fashioning President Kennedy's justly acclaimed Address back in 1960 – has contributed material again this time.

A week ago he had travelled to Crosmore Lane in Baltimore, to the home of the Townsends, to work on the final draft of the President-elect's speech.

She wanted him there, first as a link with the past, as a sign of continuity, and as a witness to the fact that the torch had been passed to another Kennedy.

And she also wanted his imprimatur on the words she would soon be delivering to the nation and the world.

Sorensen liked what he read.

And the President-elect was pleased.

Now the moment is at hand.

She begins to speak.

"My fellow citizens, we are gathered here on an auspicious occasion, an occasion which will stand out in the history of our land as marking the beginning of a new era. From this day forth the Presidency and Presidential politics will never be the same.

"*You, the American people, have seen to that. In voting for change, you have broken the mould. In deciding for the first time in our history to put a woman in The White House, you have set an example which the whole world will regard as a key symbol of new times and new beginnings . . . .* "

She speaks for eleven minutes.

It is a short but inspirational speech delivered by a President who feels confident and worthy of the challenges which lie ahead.

More applause.

The President smiles and waves.

The TV crews and photographers are delighted.

She steps back from the rostrum to more applause and embraces from her family.

Briefly, she looks at Sorensen. He nods and smiles.

Now another woman steps to the rostrum, tall and lithe and black.

Silence descends again.

Even the wind seems to be stilled as Whitney Houston begins to sing "The Star-Spangled Banner".

Backed by a military band, she ends with a flourish.

The President, standing with shoulders erect, is pleased. She knows she has made the right choice.

The memory of another occasion has stayed with her over the years.

It was the time Whitney Houston sang the National Anthem during the Super Bowl, just before the start of "Operation Desert Storm" and the Gulf War.

Some of her advisers didn't want Ms Houston.

The President had insisted.

Now she knows she did the right thing.

She waves again to the cheering crowd before turning away.

The members of her family crowd around her as she takes Whitney Houston's hand and they walk together into the Capitol.

Lunch awaits in the Senate dining-room.

Afterwards, she will walk with her husband David down Pennsylvania Avenue to The White House – just as Jimmy Carter had done with his wife back in 1977.

Somebody will remind her that back in 1809 Dolly Madison became the first wife to attend her husband's inauguration.

The President will gaze at her husband and smile.

Things have changed. America has changed. The world has changed.

"The Washington Post", hailing the election of the first woman to the Presidency:

"We were told over and over during the campaign that the time was not yet right, that America was not yet ready for a female in The White House.

"The sceptics derided the possibility, the pundits pontificated against it, the faint-hearted were fearful of it.

"But the people have spoken. They have shown they are ready for change, the most significant change in the history of the American Presidency. They have embraced change.

"And so today we welcome President Kathleen Kennedy Townsend.

"Her victory has evoked memories of another Presidency and of the New Frontier.

"Dare we say that her victory signifies the rebirth of Camelot, the restoration of the Kennedy dynasty . . .

"We have embarked on a journey back to the future . . . "

24

The Kennedy Women

Much has been made of the remarkable Kennedy men and their remarkable achievements – the stuff of which Hollywood epics are made.

Fame, wealth, power – and more than a whiff of sex and scandal – we are dealing here with the ingredients of a Tolstoy novel.

But if the Kennedy men have captured the headlines, if the men have been at the epicentre of success, drama and more than any one family's share of tragedy, the Kennedy women have been no less remarkable.

And the most remarkable of all the distaff members of this famous family has been Rose Kennedy.

Born on 22 July 1890 – when Leo XIII was still Pope, and Queen Victoria sat on the British throne – Rose Elizabeth Fitzgerald was destined to become matriarch of the Kennedy clan, America's foremost twentieth century political dynasty.

If her husband's legacy was one of ruthless ambition, Rose's was one of dedicated public service.

Joe Kennedy was destined for public heroics; Rose played a more private, but no less pivotal, role.

This remarkable woman was overshadowed for much of her life by her colourful, controversial and buccaneering husband.

Yet, strong-willed and deeply religious, she exerted considerable influence over her children, especially her sons, and imparted to them a vision of duty and a sense of noblesse oblige.

For her daughters, and for the women who married her sons, she would come in time to represent both a model and an inspiration for them.

She embodied the emotional centre of the family. It was a family which was to be marked by high achievement and tragedy – but through it all she was the rock, the unshakeable centre to which all the others turned – for solace as well as to get their bearings.

For Patricia and Jean and Eunice, and for Jack's wife, Jacqueline Bouvier, and Bobby's wife, Ethel Skakel, and Teddy's wife, Joan Bennett, Rose was the touchstone.

She was always the perfect Kennedy woman, mothering, dominating, the strict disciplinarian who hammered home the lessons of personal achievement and family solidarity.

They all in their different ways experienced the loss of Jack and Bobby.

But for courage and steadfastness, they didn't have far to look.

Rose Kennedy's personal arc of triumph – and tragedy – now seem inseparable from the American century with which her family's name has been so intimately intertwined.

"Life is too full of things waiting to be seen," she once wrote. "When I was a girl I used to pause and stare at the windows of steamships or travel agencies, with their displays of posters, and wonder what it was like to be there . . . . I never recovered from that wanderlust."

Rose Kennedy travelled the world as daughter, wife, mother and grandmother. She dined with ward bosses and kings, Hollywood stars and disabled war veterans.

Her curiosity was insatiable, her capacity to learn from – and, ultimately, to influence – history was prodigious.

According to biographer Doris Kearns Goodwin, who wrote the definitive history of the Kennedys and the Fitzgeralds, the figure of Rose Kennedy looms large in any appreciation of what the dynasty has wrought.

Often overshadowed by her husband – financier and diplomat Joseph P. Kennedy who died in 1969 – Rose took a passion for history, geography and politics and made it into a cornerstone of the Kennedy legacy.

Little was left to chance.

"Her influence was enormous," says Goodwin, "much more than she's given credit for.

"Remember, politics was in her blood from an early age, even more so than in Joe's."

Goodwin also cites Rose's intellectual discipline and lifelong devotion to learning as major components of the Kennedy mystique.

A more recent example of that is supplied by Kerry Kennedy Cuomo after a visit to her grandmother's Palm Beach home. By Rose's bed she found several books on history and religion, all heavily underlined, with detailed written summaries at the end of each chapter.

"She's never been the bubbly, cuddly, pillow-type grandmother," says Kerry. "She's extremely disciplined. Mealtimes with her were always quiz sessions – grammar, mathematics, geography. If you went to Mass with her at age ten, you'd better have listened to the sermon, because you'd be grilled on it during lunch."

Historian Arthur Schlesinger Jr agrees. "Both Rose and Joe were systematic educators, especially around the dining-room table.

"My guess is she had the stronger influence over the children when they were younger, before they came of age politically, when their father was often away from home," says the man who was a White House special assistant during John F. Kennedy's Presidency.

"She was cosmopolitan, of course – she spoke French and knew Paris well – but she also had this deep, almost inexhaustible religious faith that she imparted to her kids."

The topography of Rose's own youth has long since passed into the history books. A second-generation descendant of Irish immigrants, she was a strikingly handsome and self-possessed girl who, in due course, became the Belle of Boston.

She hoped to attend Wellesley, then, as now, one of America's most progressive women's colleges, but was sent instead to the Sacred Heart Convent in Blumenthal, the Netherlands.

Compared to liberal Wellesley, Blumenthal was as austere as a prison camp: a daily regime of study, prayer and meditation, unrelieved by social niceties.

Rather than rebel against this asceticism, however, the otherwise outgoing Rose seemed to embrace it.

Years later, it was the discipline of her Catholic faith, forged in this least pampered of settings, that would sustain her and the rest of the Kennedys in the face of unspeakable tragedy.

Her stoicism was sorely tested, of course, by the wave of tragedy that engulfed the Kennedy family.

Rosemary was institutionalised in 1941, suffering from mental illness, and Joe Jr was killed in 1944 on a high-risk bombing run against German installations.

Add to these the death of Kathleen in a 1948 plane crash, and the cross might have been almost too much to bear.

Some say that these losses hit Rose perhaps even harder than the assassinations of Jack and Bobby, which devastated an entire nation.

In each instance Rose wept but did not flinch. Where there was grief, there was also resolve. And if there was guilt, there was also a singular generosity of spirit.

"The loss of my brothers Jack and Bobby was obviously a terrible one," says Teddy Kennedy today. "But what Mother felt most was how difficult it would be to bring up their children without a father. It was almost as if she moved beyond her own personal tragedy to the larger question of how this would happen."

This is echoed by Goodwin: "She really had no moments of self-pity. Talking to me about her own emotions, she was always quite fiery.

"I believe Rose is convinced that if the kids could come back again – I mean Joe Jr and Jack and Kathleen and Bobby – knowing what would happen to them to cut their lives short, they would still want the same life.

"And I think that feeling gave her a remarkable sense of peacefulness."

Goodwin is not surprised that America continues its fascination, if not outright love affair, with the Kennedy clan, a singular family that comes about as close to royalty as American society has produced.

Some of that fascination has to do with political power, but not all of it.

"So long as the Kennedy family shows a sense of bonding together," says Goodwin, "Americans will be intrigued by them. And when I think about Rose Kennedy's long life, to me her most remarkable creation is not that she produced three sons who became US Senators, or even one who won the Presidency. It is the conscious creation of a family tradition that has survived over several generations."

Rose Kennedy survived the inordinately painful loss of two sons to assassins, and of course her grandchildren were deeply affected, too, at the loss of fathers and uncles.

"I don't think any of us would have survived if we hadn't had the drive to make a difference in the world," admits one of her grandchildren, Kerry Kennedy Cuomo.

Kerry and Kathleen and Courtney and Maria (wife of bodybuilder-turned-movie star Arnold Schwarzenegger) and the others are living proof of the manner in which her powerful influence has filtered down.

"My grandmother has really been a source of enormous strength," says Kathleen Townsend, "through all the good, fun times we had growing up, as well as through many of the sad times our family has faced."

Indeed, while activism, idealism and ambition have always been associated with the Kennedys, in this generation it is the women more than the men who are turning the words into action.

For more than half a century the term "Kennedy women" has been widely regarded as a catchphrase for the original stand-by-your-man women.

By and large, the Kennedy women were seen as devoted mothers, loyal sisters and dutiful wives.

With the exception of Joan Kennedy, Teddy's ex-wife – the only female "drop-out" from Camelot – the Kennedy women, sometimes in the face of hurt and even humiliation, have steadfastly stood by their men.

But now there is a new generation, with new names, and new, independent attitudes.

Apart from Kathleen Kennedy Townsend and Kerry Kennedy Cuomo, there's Courtney and Rory, the other daughters of Bobby; Caroline Kennedy Schlossberg, of course; Maria Shriver, Sydney Lawford McKelvey and Victoria Lawford, the offspring of Patricia Kennedy and film actor, Peter Lawford; Kara Kennedy Allen, the only daughter of Ted and Joan; and Kim and Amanda Smith, the daughters of Jean and the late Steve Smith.

This clutch of bright, committed and independently-minded females are giving a new meaning to the phrase "Kennedy women".

"I think there's a pretty serious group of us," says Kathleen, Bobby's firstborn and the oldest of her generation.

Caroline is the oldest child of Camelot, but despite her fame, she regularly wheels her own daughters through Central Park in New York wearing sweatpants and pullovers.

Often called "the private Kennedy", in 1986 she married Edwin Schlossberg, the son of a wealthy Jewish textile manufacturer.

In 1992 she co-authored *In Our Defense: The Bill of Rights in Action* with law school friend, Ellen Alderman.

The book explains and defines each of the ten amendments to the US Constitution through a specific court case.

"We really did want to show how people use these rights in action," she says. "I wanted to take my experience and the advantages I've had and try to communicate them to other people."

While she is planning to practise law one day, and consider more books on the subject, right now she prefers to be at home with her children.

At all times during the publicity campaign for the book, she refused to make any appearances without her co-author.

"I hope to keep the focus on the book," she told the media.

But it's no accident that on the book jacket Caroline calls herself Caroline Kennedy – not Caroline Kennedy Schlossberg.

Maria Shriver, the 39-year-old daughter of Eunice Kennedy and Sargent Shriver, has carved out a name for herself as a television journalist for NBC.

Married to Arnold Schwarzenegger, she has done a series of interviews with people like pop singer Sinead O'Connor, television star Kirstie Alley of *Cheers* fame, Cuban leader Fidel Castro and Corazon Aquino of the Philippines which won her critical acclaim.

As a member of the glamorous, high-achieving clan the world knows as The Kennedys, she is determined to distinguish herself as an individual.

"Kerry, Kathleen – all Bobby's kids ➤ like doing the Kennedy thing. They're into it, and that's great. But I've tried to stay away from that."

If Maria is the most visible, and Caroline the most embedded in the public imagination, Kathleen and Kerry are the most politically committed.

They are not only comfortable with the Kennedy legacy, they are expanding it and pushing it forward.

More than any of the others, perhaps, they have contributed most to the "restoration" of the Kennedy name and reputation by their very visibility and idealism, and through the causes they champion.

Kathleen was born on the July 4 – and that certainly made an impression.

One journalist said of her: "She's like that relentlessly patriotic kid who's always jumping up and down waving an American flag in your face."

Kathleen has been called the most serious thinker of them all.

When she was twelve and her uncle Jack was killed, her father wrote her a note.

"You seemed to understand that Jack died and was buried today," Bobby wrote. "As the oldest of the Kennedy grandchildren, you have a particular responsibility . . . . Be kind and work for your country."

In 1986 she ran for Congress in Maryland – and lost. But in running, she made an historic move – she became the first Kennedy woman to make the switch from campaigner to candidate.

And she'll try again. "What I was really taught when growing up was that if I fell off my horse, I got back on and kept going."

A workaholic, she has done ground-breaking work in carrying out a 1985 mandate written into the Maryland State Board of Education's bye-laws that requires every high school to introduce some form of public service into the curriculum.

She discovered in 1987 that not one school had initiated such a programme. She saw this as a great opportunity and a great challenge, and with typical Kennedy energy and dedication, she set about transforming the situation.

"High-school students can volunteer to work in soup kitchens and homes for the aged, hopefully doing some good and building their self-esteem, and receiving academic credit at the same time," she says of the programme.

She has also worked tirelessly to highlight what she regards as a serious moral crisis in the USA, and criticising schools for not teaching values.

"Far too many school-leavers," she insists, "cannot tell the difference between right and wrong."

"Kathleen," says sister Kerry, "has an intellectual curiosity unmatched by anyone in our family. She has a willingness to always be open to ideas, not to become entrenched."

Others have said much the same of Kerry. Her brother, Robert Kennedy Jr says she is the child of whom their father "would have been most proud".

She runs the RFK Memorial Centre for Human Rights from a 7th floor office in mid-Manhattan. It is joined by a circular staircase to the office below, occupied by her husband Andrew Cuomo. He is the son of New York Governor, Mario Cuomo, and he runs an organisation that builds housing for the homeless.

Like Kathleen, she would like to run for public office, but insists that one can achieve an awful lot without going into politics.

"I think there are certain moral values Robert Kennedy stood for and his life was a testament to. To the extent that I share those values, and to the extent that I can carry out those values or give a hand to those who share them, I'd like to."

All the other Kennedy women play public service roles, albeit in a more low-profile way.

Courtney, for instance, who is now married to Paul Hill of the Guildford Four, is on the board of directors of the John F. Kennedy Library and is head of fund-raising for the Robert F. Kennedy Memorial Foundation; Kara is a television producer, Amanda Smith, as well as being a talented artist, looks after the needs of special children, and Victoria Lawford has worked in the Washington office of her aunt Jean Kennedy Smith's Very Special Arts programme.

They all know, in the words of Kathleen Kennedy Townsend, that "being a Kennedy raises expectations, but it is also a source of great pride".

Of them all, Maria Shriver is the only one who has consciously worked to disavow the Kennedy label.

She once did an interview with McCall's magazine which was headed: "Maria Shriver, No Kennedy Clone."

Maybe not, but she is still a Kennedy. They all are, whether they embrace it or resist it.

25

Jackie O

It was the one rendezvous that Hillary Clinton wanted to keep secret. There was to be no publicity, she told aides in The White House. And no Secret Service team to provide protection for the First Lady.

President Clinton wasn't altogether happy about that. Reluctantly, he agreed – after listening to what his wife was planning.

Hillary Clinton had a problem – how to appear "wifely" and yet remain a powerful political figure.

She was hoping her heroine would be able to solve it.

So with her husband's approval she dispensed with Air Force One and the motorcade whose sirens now advertise her every move.

She took a commercial flight to New York, exited from Kennedy Airport through a side door, and was driven away in an unmarked car.

The reason for all the secrecy was that Hillary Clinton did not want anyone to know she was on a pilgrimage to America's most elevated First Lady, Jacqueline Kennedy Onassis.

The hush-hush meeting between the new First Lady and the most enigmatic holder of that post took place in the privacy of Jackie's opulent apartment in Manhattan.

It was hastily arranged at Hillary's request after Mrs Clinton pleaded with mutual friends in the Washington Establishment to convince Jackie O to invite her to a private lunch.

Details of the meeting eventually leaked to the press, and it was seen as yet a further indication of the extraordinary position and stature which JFK's widow still holds three decades after his death.

For many Americans the meeting in the drawing-room of Jackie's apartment at 1040 Fifth Avenue had a poignant symbolism. Clinton's victory brought the first Democratic Administration to The White

House in 12 years. And in so doing the Clintons assumed the Kennedy mantle, having linked themselves during the 1991 campaign to the mythology and even the phraseology of Kennedy's "Camelot".

Little wonder that Hillary wanted to meet and pay homage to Mrs Kennedy.

Though she may be regarded by some as inscrutable, for millions of Americans, Jackie O is revered and idolised as a "queen in exile".

"You can have no idea how much Hillary looks up to Jackie," said a White House aide.

And what she wanted was advice about the mistakes she should avoid and how to cope with the mechanics of running The White House as wife and mother.

"She would like people to admire her the way they have finally come to admire Jackie," added the aide.

Hillary Clinton knows that Jackie had to win back her place in the nation's heart after the widespread shock and disappointment of her marriage to Greek tycoon Aristotle Onassis.

That was the low point of her popularity, but in time she overcame it, winning back the respect and acclaim of her White House years.

Of all past First Ladies, Jackie understands the pressures and the problems of the job.

She knows better than most the risk – which she warned Mrs Clinton about – of a populist President's wife being perceived as too elitist – a charge that was often thrown at Jackie.

She knows, too, what it is like to be watching from the sidelines as the threat of sexual scandal hung over her husband.

It never broke her poise in public.

Hillary Clinton is well aware of this; she too lives with the allegations of marital infidelity, allegations in particular of an affair between her husband and singer-actress Gennifer Flowers.

Jackie knows all about such allegations, and of the need for the First Lady to remember at all times that private hurt must not impinge on public performance.

Now aged 64, Jackie Kennedy Onassis has lived in the full glare of publicity from that moment in September 1953 when she married the young, handsome, dashing Senator from Massachussetts.

It all started in 1951 at a Washington dinner party when the young and ambitious politician leaned across the asparagus and asked the beautiful young lady near him if she would like to go out with him.

At the time, Jacqueline Bouvier was working as an "inquiring photographer" for the *Washington Times Herald*.

Friends described her as aloof, private, independent, possessing aesthetic interests and a barbed wit.

She had been educated at the George Washington University, Vassar, and the Sorbonne in Paris.

Although initially she never felt entirely at home with the intensely political Boston-Irish family, the courtship took hold and flourished.

In June 1953, while she was in London photographing the Coronation of Queen Elizabeth II, her beau, now a junior senator, proposed by cable.

Soon she was swept into the Kennedy family life, and the Camelot years lay ahead.

One of the best-kept secrets of Camelot is that Jackie and her husband were working colleagues in much the same way as the Clintons.

Jackie was often consulted by the President, and she observed top-level meetings, including meetings of the National Security Council (NSC), which is in charge of defence and intelligence policy.

For five consecutive years she had topped the Gallup Poll as the one woman in the world most Americans admired.

Then came the wedding to Onassis.

A beloved icon who had been placed on a pedestal was suddenly being viewed in a new light.

Onassis became a close friend during the period of mourning after Dallas.

That was well-known within the Kennedy circle, but none of the family thought JFK's widow would ever marry again.

When it happened it caused shock, and an outpouring of criticism and even protest.

These days she lives quietly and alone, though she has men friends from the world of the arts, from politics and from business who regularly escort her to first nights, fashion shows and exhibitions.

One man, an industrialist, is her closest companion.

The most vivid images of Jackie will always be frozen in time from November 1963.

Jackie and John F. Kennedy – whom she married in her early twenties when he was a rising political star – had dazzled the world during his one thousand days in The White House.

Now assassins' bullets had struck the President.

Photographs flashed around the world showing Jackie cradling her dying husband in her arms in the back seat of the blood-stained limousine.

Hours later, still wearing the same blood-stained pale pink outfit, she watched on board Air Force One as Lyndon Johnson was sworn in as her husband's successor.

And then there was that nightmarish flight back to Washington and she sat numbed, her face tear-streaked, by his casket in the rear of the plane.

Later, there would be more photographs of her, as she walked behind the horse-drawn caisson to Arlington Cemetery.

Cracks began to appear later in the Camelot myth of the Kennedy Presidency with stories of his womanising, studded with names of Hollywood stars such as Gene Tierney, Marilyn Monroe, and Angie Dickinson.

Jackie and the President had been apart for long periods. It was said she disliked the public role expected of her as First Lady, though that was never really true.

In time she came to be regarded as one of the most memorable of all First Ladies.

She was widely admired as a woman who, despite her husband's carrying on, put the country before herself and supported JFK, while bending her energies to make The White House both a home for her family and a splendid place for the nation and the world.

And she gained a reputation as a big spender.

One book claimed her personal expenditure in the first year of the Presidency was $105,446 at a time when her husband's salary was only $100,000.

Kennedy's death left Jackie in a unique position in America's national life, almost as a First Widow. Remarriage to anyone would inevitably have drawn criticism from some quarters.

And it did, when she did remarry.

After the assassination in Dallas, Jackie received many strange offers, mainly of a matrimonial nature. Proposals of marriage came from the most unlikely quarters, including one from a South American military dictator.

Today, 30 years after the nightmare of Dallas, life is sweet for Jackie and her family.

At 64, the excitement and the tragedy that marked her jet-setting years are behind her.

She has pushed into the background the trauma of the assassination, and the tempestuous second marriage to Onassis.

She still has a regal presence, grace, style, elegance, decency and dignity.

Jackie Bouvier Kennedy Onassis remains one of the most elusive, mysterious women of our time.

Like Greta Garbo, she has been known to decry and resent the public's overriding interest in her private life.

"I'm happiest when I'm alone," she told her friend Bunny Mellon on her birthday.

Another friend, Jane Wrightsman, was privy to a similar lament, when Jackie said: "I'm 64 now, and I've been in the public eye for more than 30 years. I can't believe that anyone really cares about me or is still interested in what I do."

But people do care. And books, articles and television documentaries on Jackie continue to proliferate.

Through it all she remains silent and aloof, unresponsive to her interlocutors and allowing no interviews.

It has been said that America is fascinated with her because it doesn't understand her.

She distances herself from the public, and moves in a private, exclusive world of the selected rich and famous.

If anything, the quest for privacy has enhanced the myth of the President's widow and increased the curiosity.

Three decades after Dallas, the real Jackie is as remote and inscrutable as she ever was.

She has retained some of her girlish charm – the whispery voice that reminded Maria Callas of "Marilyn Monroe playing Ophelia"; the shoulder-length hair, the eternal sunglasses and the movie star smile.

Her name has been linked with numerous wealthy men, though her most frequent escort for some years now has been Maurice Tempelsman, a New York-based diamond dealer and entrepreneur.

He and her work as book editor have been the most stabilising influences in her life.

"Maurice Tempelsman affords Jackie more than mere companionship," says columnist George Plimpton. "Over the past decade he has given her excellent financial advice."

Jackie has become a wealthier woman under Tempelsman's guidance, parlaying her original Onassis inheritance into a $120 million fortune, though estimates of her wealth vary widely.

She loves her work as a book editor at Doubleday, and has used her impressive contacts to secure a number of very valuable contracts for the firm, including Michael Jackson's autobiography *Moonwalk*.

Her favourite weekend and vacation haunt, and the place where she spends most of her time when not in New York, is at the $4.5 million house she built on 425 oceanfront acres on Martha's Vineyard.

While she jealously guards her privacy, the world will not stop talking about her. She remains headline news and so do her interests.

Her life has been centred on providing support for her two children, Caroline and John, who have both grown into well-balanced and successful adults, avoiding problems encountered by some of the other Kennedy offspring.

Both are law school graduates, and Caroline has co-authored a best-selling treatise on the Bill of Rights.

Apart from her work, Jackie spends long weekends at her coastal retreat just south of Cape Cod.

The house is situated so as to guarantee privacy from even the most persistent photographer.

In New York her social life includes charity appearances in support of a variety of worthy causes, and quiet dinner parties with selected friends.

Maurice Tempelsman, who is estranged from his wife, is invariably present.

But few people seem to be expecting Jackie to marry again.

Bitter memories of the marriage to Onassis still linger.

26

For Love of a Greek

On 18 October, 1968, barely four months after the assassination in Los Angeles, Jacqueline Kennedy made an announcement that caused widespread disappointment, disbelief, shock and even anger.

On that day she announced to the world that she was planning to marry the Greek shipping tycoon, Aristotle Onassis.

An extremely rich man, Onassis was older than her by almost three decades (29 years, to be exact).

He was also divorced, and had a reputation which had some unsavoury features to it.

Worldwide, the reaction to the marriage plans was wholly negative.

People were puzzled. Many were hurt. Many more felt let down, even betrayed.

The reasons were obvious.

Here is how John H. Davis summed them up from an American perspective in his book *The Kennedys: Dynasty and Disaster.*

"The American public had conceived of Jackie as the loving wife of an American hero, as a radiant, queenly First Lady of unimpeachable virtue, and then as a grieving widow devoted to her slain husband's memory and ideals. They had thought of her as a sacred American legend, as a living saint.

"When this paragon of American womanhood virtually eloped with a disreputable old man who seemed to have no ideals whatsoever beyond piling up enormous sums of money, and collecting yachtfuls of celebrities, people were stunned."

Criticism of Jackie for her marriage to Onassis persisted long after his death.

It is not even clear today whether all members of the extended Kennedy clan forgave her.

Did she do it for love of a Greek – or because of greed?

Much of what has been said and written about her second marriage has been very unfair.

To suggest, for instance, as John. H. Davis has done that the decision to marry Onassis "so deflated the Kennedy image it has never been quite the same since" is patent nonsense.

Much the same over-inflated reaction came from Kitty Kelley: "Camelot started collapsing moments after the wedding announcement".

It is sometimes overlooked that Onassis became a close friend during her period of mourning after Dallas.

This was well-known in the Kennedy circle, but none of the family thought JFK's widow would ever remarry – or even wish to.

When she finally told Robert Kennedy about her fondness for the man he always referred to as "The Greek", he threw up his hands in despair.

On 15 October 1967 the *Boston Herald Traveller* broke the news of the wedding in a front-page story.

It predicted the marriage "in the near future" of the widow of the slain President and Aristotle Onassis.

The latter was in Greece at the time and Jackie called him to tell him the story had broken.

She urged him to bring forward their wedding plans; he agreed.

Jackie's next task was to tell her mother, Mrs Janet Auchincloss.

"Oh God, Jackie, you can't mean that!" she responded. Her shock and disbelief was shared by millions both inside and outside of the United States.

The initial newspaper story carried no official confirmation from the Kennedy family.

Jackie's sister-in-law, Jean Kennedy Smith, was the first to be told. Jackie told her the marriage had to be rushed now because the news was out.

Jean took it well, and agreed to help break the news to the Kennedy matriarch, Rose.

When Jackie called herself, Mrs Kennedy was over the initial shock. To mollify her, Jackie said she had talked with and received the support of Cardinal Richard Cushing, who was very close to the Kennedy family.

Rose gave her blessing, but declined to attend the wedding in Greece on the grounds of her husband's declining health.

On 17 October 1968, she was driven to the airport where she met her mother and Jean Kennedy Smith and flew to Greece on board an aircraft from Olympic Airlines, which was owned by the man who would soon be her husband.

In the tiny Chapel of Our Lady on the Greek isle of Skorpios, the couple were married on 20 October 1968.

"The American Queen of the world married the multi-millionaire King of international society in the most celebrated nuptials of the twentieth century," wrote Kitty Kelley.

The bride was 39, the groom 68 – and their wedding photographs were soon on the front pages of newspapers across the globe.

The wedding was a constant source of controversy and conflict throughout the seven years it lasted.

It ended in acrimony when Onassis died in Paris on Saturday, 15 March 1975.

At the time Jackie was 3,000 miles away in New York.

The marriage, apart from its initial phase, was not a happy one.

Part of the reason was that Onassis was still in love with the internationally famous diva, Maria Callas, with whom he had had a long and passionate affair.

The beautiful but fiery and temperamental soprano had left her husband for Onassis.

She had every reason to believe that the shipping tycoon would marry her.

Every reason but one – Jackie Kennedy.

When Onassis left her for Jackie, it broke her heart, though she never stopped loving him.

Later, when his marriage started to go sour, he turned to Maria Callas for solace. Too late, he realised that the gifted singer was the true love of his life.

Callas never recovered from Onassis' death. In her biography of the great opera star, Arianna Stassinopoulos writes: "His death had struck her an almost mortal blow. Existing in a world that did not contain him seemed pointless. The past had vanished and, in her deep suffering, there was no future . . ."

Callas died, at the age of 54, also in Paris, on 16 September 1977.

Some say she never forgave Jackie Bouvier Kennedy Onassis.

After all, had not Callas, back in April 1974, told Barbara Walters on the *Today* television show that Aristotle Onassis was "the big love" of her life.

And she had lost him to Jackie.

If the latter's decision to marry the Greek tycoon shattered Maria Callas, that same decision puzzled, disappointed and hurt many people who were close to Jackie.

But nearly all forgot what the wedding meant to her.

One person who knew them both said Jackie's marriage to Onassis wasn't difficult to understand. "She married him for his money, that's all. He was a charmer but that wasn't enough."

Money was undoubtedly part of it.

But there was more.

"Aristotle Onassis rescued me at a moment when my life was engulfed with shadows," she would say later by way of explanation.

She had endured very difficult, indeed traumatic, times. Onassis offered solace, comfort, security and protection.

He came into her life, crucially, when she was devastated, frightened, insecure, unsure and worried about the future.

Apart from other considerations, she had two young children to rear, and her pension as the widow of a President wasn't huge.

The marriage ended in sadness and recrimination.

By 1974 the signs that it was in trouble were evident to those familiar with the couple. They were spending more and more time apart, going their separate ways.

In Monte Carlo that year, Onassis hosted a dinner for Prince Rainier and Princess Grace aboard his luxury yacht.

He was dyspeptic and gloomy.

"It was all very sad," Prince Rainier said afterwards. "To have come so far just to end up heartbroken and ill on board this yacht with only your daughter for company seemed almost unfair."

So great became his distrust of Jackie that he arranged for private detectives to follow her. But her extramarital behaviour did not extend beyond harmless lunches, dinners and visits to shops, theatres and art shows.

Shortly after his death, *The New York Times* carried a story that he had intended to divorce Jackie. It was soon picked up by the news agencies.

She was very upset, so much so that she implored Onassis' daughter, Christina, to issue a denial.

Obediently, the latter complied.

"Miss Christina Onassis is very much distressed at the distorted stories and speculations which appeared in the international press about her father and Mrs Jacqueline Onassis. These stories are totally untrue and she repudiates them. In fact, the marriage of the late Mr Onassis and Mrs Jacqueline Onassis was a happy marriage and all rumours of intended divorce are untrue . . . "

They weren't, and later Christina disowned the statement, and a series of unseemly squabbles ensued over the Onassis fortune.

Some six months after burying Onassis, Jackie went to work as a consulting editor at Viking Press in New York. In October 1977 she resigned over Viking's decision to publish Jeffrey Archer's novel *Shall We Tell The President* which depicted Teddy Kennedy as the target of an assassination attempt.

In the spring of 1978 she joined Doubleday. A young Jesuit who was the poetry editor of *America* magazine, described to me the time she sat in on an editorial conference at which he was present.

"She was very cool, very beautiful, and very self-possessed. She didn't say much, but when she spoke there was total silence. All the rest of us were very deferential. All through she was very courteous."

Two days later we both went to PJ Clarke's Bar on Third Avenue, which she occasionally frequented with Frank Sinatra and Pete Hamill.

When we got there she had just left, but the barman showed us a copy of Vogue magazine which she had autographed for him.

"She was only in the door when a posse of photographers arrived, so she left without even finishing her drink."

It was ever thus.

Jackie Kennedy Onassis remains a superstar.

Wherever she goes she attracts attention in a way matched only by royalty. As one of her biographers, David Heymann, has pointed out, "She is still the target of more gossip and innuendo than any ten Hollywood movie legends combined".

Although she is now 64, her svelte figure and photogenic face makes her instantly recognisable.

And she doesn't look her age.

Hers is one of the truly universal faces of the twentieth century.

27

A Kennedy Returns

President Clinton has a green handkerchief in his breast pocket. When he made the official announcement, Senator Edward Kennedy, sporting a bright green tie, smiled broadly.

It is St Patrick's Day, 1993, in The White House.

And Jean Kennedy Smith – sister of Jack and Bobby and Teddy – has just been named as the new US Ambassador to Ireland.

At the photocall she stands with Teddy to her left. On her right, separating her from the President, is the Taoiseach, Albert Reynolds.

He turns now and shakes hands with the new Ambassador. Her face, with the sharply defined features, is wreathed in smiles.

It is 17 March – Ireland's National Holiday – and in keeping with tradition, the country's top politician is visiting the US President.

The visit is largely symbolic; it acknowledges the special ties between Ireland and America, and also honours the Irish diaspora, that huge army of exiles who have found new beginnings in the States.

This time there is some business to be done. As has been the case since the Nixon Presidency, Northern Ireland is on the agenda.

Will the President send a peace envoy.

In the lead up to St Patrick's Day there has been intense speculation that the President will announce the setting up of a fact-finding mission to Northern Ireland as the preamble to the later appointment of a peace envoy?

It is known that apart from John Hume, MEP, leader of the SDLP, advice has also been sought from former President Jimmy Carter.

The word is that Carter has indicated that he would be interested in becoming involved in the project – now or later.

It soon emerges that it will have to be later.

Clinton has made campaign promises to the Irish-American lobby. But the British have a powerful lobby in Washington as well.

And there is disappointment when Clinton puts the idea of a peace envoy on ice.

"I don't think the United States can make peace in Northern Ireland," says the President.

He stresses his support for dialogue between the British and Irish Governments, and continues: "I think the most significant thing I should be doing right now is to encourage the resumption of that dialogue."

Clinton emphasises that the idea of a peace envoy to Northern Ireland is an option which will be kept open and reconsidered when the time seems appropriate.

The good news is the appointment of Jean Kennedy Smith.

Her presence in Dublin will ensure that Northern Ireland will remain on The White House agenda.

Although she comes from one of the greatest political dynasties in America, she herself is not a politician.

But everyone knows that even if the position of Ambassador is not strictly a political one, her appointment underlines the substantial clout which the Kennedy family still wields in the United States.

From the moment of Clinton's election – Teddy has been lobbying for her with the transition team.

Now Clinton has agreed.

Differences between Irish-American power brokers on Capitol Hill – among whom there are intricate rivalries – have been smoothed over.

But they won't go away.

This time Teddy Kennedy is the victor. The appointment of his sister is a personal triumph for him in a tussle with another powerful figure.

Mrs Kennedy Smith is not the favourite choice of Thomas Foley, the Speaker of the House of Representatives. He wants former Congressman Brian Donnelly.

Clinton has spoken; the matter is settled.

Amid the green and the shamrocks and the tricolours, the Taoiseach seems pleased.

Reynolds knows that the Kennedy name has enduring magic in Ireland.

Aside from being a Kennedy, the new Ambassador's fame is based on her charitable work. Now 66, she runs an organisation that involves the disabled in the arts.

She suffered unwelcome media attention in 1991 when one of her four children, William Kennedy Smith, was tried and acquitted of rape charges in Palm Beach, Florida.

Her late husband, Stephen E. Smith, was generally regarded as the successor to her empire-building father, Joe Kennedy, as the family's helmsman, handling a lot of the family's financial affairs.

The couple first met in school and knew each other for several years before their friendship became serious and led to marriage.

That was in 1956, by which time Smith was a financial analyst and transportation millionaire.

Steve Smith managed Jack's successful campaign in 1960, and is also remembered for managing Teddy's bid for the Democratic nomination in 1980. He died of cancer in August 1990.

Jean Kennedy Smith has never run for public office herself but, like the rest of the family, she was active in the various campaigns, most notably Teddy's unsuccessful 1980 battle in the primaries with Jimmy Carter.

A private person with staunch family values, her name, despite her family connections, has rarely appeared in the newspapers.

All of that was to change in April 1991 when her son, William, was accused of raping a young woman in the Kennedy holiday home at Palm Springs.

The subsequent court case became an enormous media event. It was televised live and drew huge audiences.

And with Uncle Ted also implicated, it was presented as if the entire Kennedy dynasty was on trial.

This was typified by a spate of articles in newspapers and magazines postulating the end of the line for the Kennedy Dynasty.

"At least no one died at Palm Beach," wrote Elizabeth Kaye in *Esquire*, "but there had, in fact, been a death of sorts. What had died was the willingness of everyday people to retain the Kennedys as the custodians of the nation's heart."

But nothing that happened in the aftermath of the trial served to bear that out.

The family is reputed to have spent more than $500,000 on lawyers – and there was widespread relief when William was acquitted of the charges against him.

Now a doctor at the University of New Mexico in Albuquerque, he said nearly a year later: "No one lets me forget. When anyone looks at me, all they think is I'm the one from that trial."

Jean Kennedy Smith wants to forget. To her it is a closed episode.

When she visited Ireland in late 1992 to promote her disabled arts programme, she made an appearance on *Kenny Live* of RTE Television.

The show's amiable host, Pat Kenny, felt he had to raise the issue of the trial and the effect of it on her. She gently but firmly parried all his questions, refusing to get involved in any discussion on the issues.

"We are here to talk about the arts – let's not forget that," she chided him, insisting on changing the subject when Kenny attempted to discuss the case with her.

It is typical of her resolve to forget the whole unsavoury episode.

It is clear that it is an episode on which she has firmly closed the door.

It is equally clear it was a very testing and very trying time for her, coming so soon after the death of her husband. She testified that she had invited her son to leave his medical studies and join her in Florida as it was her first holiday since the death of her husband.

She also told the jury she heard no screams on the night of the alleged incident.

During the court proceedings, much of the attention was focused on the Kennedy women, led by Jean, who attended each day.

They put up a brave face, going out of their way to reinforce the sense of family unity.

As they arrived at the court-house each morning, they made no effort to shun the crowd of onlookers, smiling and waving at them.

It was Kennedy bravura at its best.

The trial also provided the American media with an opportunity to focus on the Kennedy clan – an opportunity gleefully availed of.

Some of the material written about them, and about the Smith family in particular, was lurid.

People magazine ran a profile under the heading "Dignity and Despair", and alleged that Mrs Kennedy Smith's husband was a womaniser who treated her like dirt.

In a letter to the magazine's editor, she angrily refuted the allegations, emphasising that they demeaned her, her children and her entire family.

The article is an example of what she and other members of the clan had to endure.

Born in 1928, Jean Kennedy Smith is the second youngest of the nine children born to Joseph and Rose Kennedy.

In 1974 she founded Very Special Arts, an international organisation which provides programmes in dance, creative writing, drama, literature, music and the visual arts for people with mental and physical disabilities.

Since her husband's death in 1990, she has become more and more involved in this work.

Among the many awards she received for her charitable work are the Jefferson Award for Outstanding Public Service, the Margaret Mead Humanitarian Award and the Capital Children's Museum Humanitarian Award.

That work will now be continued by others during her sojourn as Ambassador to Ireland, though she will still – in tireless Kennedy fashion – keep an eye on things.

Jean Kennedy Smith accompanied President Kennedy during his June 1963 visit to Ireland, and she doesn't attempt to hide her admiration for the place.

"I come whenever I can think of an excuse," she told Pat Kenny.

Now that she is Ambassador, she has an excuse to set up house here for at least four years.

And she is looking forward to a very exciting time.

She was thrilled when the Democrats returned to power, saying of Bill Clinton: "He's full of energy, he's full of good ideas, and he has a lot of charisma."

All of which – as Ireland is discovering – is also true of Jean Kennedy Smith.

She has already been warmly welcomed, and it is entirely appropriate that America's representative here should come from a family which has consistently cultivated an interest in this country's well-being and worked on Ireland's behalf in the USA.

28

Passing the Torch

The Fabled Four – that's how they were described to me by one of a group of students as we sat in the thin November sunshine on the campus of Fordham University in New York.

The students were part of a generation which had helped to bring Clinton to power, and I was curious to know what they thought of the Kennedys in general, and of the younger Kennedys in particular.

Earlier, one of them, a bright girl named Shoona, who was studying politics and sociology, had helped me locate Garry Wills' book *The Kennedys: A Shattered Illusion*, in the Library.

Written in 1983, and hostile to the Kennedys, it is nevertheless full of provocative insights.

Wills is an insightful though conservative commentator, noted for his acerbic style.

He doesn't spare the Kennedys, JFK being his main target.

The book makes much of the Kennedy "image", and one chapter is actually entitled "The Prisoner of Image".

He likens JFK's period in The White House not so much to an Imperial Presidency but to an Appearances Presidency.

He tells us that Camelot was the "opium of the intellectuals", and that "Kennedy was a shrewd manipulator of his own appearance and impact".

As for the intellectuals, they too, Wills maintains, were manipulated.

"They lined up to celebrate the second coming of a second-hand Lord Melbourne."

So what did these young people think – the youth of the Clinton generation?

We talked about the Wills book and his cynical assessments. They knew the even more cynical stories, of course, all painting a picture of a cold, ruthless, ambitious, amoral and manipulative family intent on attaining and maintaining power.

Yet their view, which I heard echoed elsewhere, was refreshing and untainted by the endless muckraking.

"When I see photographs of President Kennedy I think of Robert Redford," said Shoona.

"I think of Kevin Costner," said her pal, Susan, who had just recently seen the Oliver Stone movie.

Youthful romanticism, you may say. Yes. But there was more. There was the sense of idealism and commitment to a better society which Clinton had rekindled.

And, yes, more again. Another Kennedy in American politics.

But which one?

Which of the younger Kennedys would emerge as the standard-bearer, the torch-carrier?

They knew, as I did, that the election of Clinton had created new possibilities – one of which might be a new Kennedy era.

The kids knew that once – and not that long ago – the name Kennedy meant magic in American politics. Then the pendulum swung, as unsavoury stories emerged.

Soon, dogged by misfortune and scandal, the name came to represent for some a political handicap, more a ball and chain than a charm, especially for the young Kennedys living in the shadow of JFK and his brother Bobby.

Now that, too, had passed. The pendulum was swinging again.

Well, wasn't it?

Young heads nodded in the middle of Fordham.

So I pressed them again.

"Do any of the younger Kennedys have what it takes to make President?"

Heads nodded again.

"Do any of them even want to be?"

Yes, the students felt. The Kennedys had not given up on The White House.

Listening to them, I remembered a story.

Flashback to 1968:

It is the summer of a year that seems to make new hope for a nation driven by the controversies and divisions over Vietnam. RFK represents that new hope.

Then disaster strikes in an LA hotel.

The train carrying the mortal remains of Senator Robert F. Kennedy is making its way towards Washington after the shooting in LA. All along the tracks, people stand in silence paying a last tribute as a dream embodied in and by the slain Senator passes them by.

Yet another tragedy, another shooting, has turned day into night for America's most famous family.

But inside the train the dream has not quite departed the earth. In spite of the horror of LA, the dream lives on.

The dead Senator's eldest son, Joe, is walking up and down the aisles. He is wearing one of his father's dark pin-striped suits, and his mother Ethel is at his side.

Joe Kennedy is shaking hands and saying, "I'm Joe Kennedy, thank you for coming", with such composure that Ethel later exclaims excitedly, "He's got it, he's got it!"

To those listening no further words are necessary. They realise she is talking about the touch, the control, the dignity, the sense of destiny, the manifestation of the political genes that many of the grandchildren are already wondering and talking about.

Today some would say that Joseph Kennedy Junior has already fulfilled his political destiny in getting elected as a Congressman.

No one can say that with any certainty.

But in the years since that summer of 1968 one certainty has emerged – not all of the many offspring that make up the Kennedy clan either have nor particularly want the unique burden of those extraordinary genes.

The students at Fordham understood that in a family so large and diverse, it would be unusual if it were otherwise.

Not all of the younger Kennedys are drawn to politics.

They also understood that, with such a large family, it could be argued as a statistical certainty that success, failure and tragedy would continue to visit the many and dispersed Kennedy households.

So we talked for a while about the dark side of the Kennedy story.

To judge by some of the books written about the Kennedy family, you would think there was only a dark side – and nothing else.

For example, the stories and claims about the involvement of JFK and Bobby with Marilyn Monroe highlight this. Then there was Dike Bridge, Chappaquiddick, in 1969, with Teddy and Mary Jo Kopechne; two decades later there was Palm Beach (1991) and the rape case involving William Kennedy Smith which cast the latest shadow over the family.

The hatchet job done on the Kennedys is without parallel in contemporary American politics. In book after book, article after article, they have been vilified and traduced.

Gossip and innuendo have, in the case of the Kennedys, been elevated to the status of truth, firm and unshakeable.

The Palm Beach scandal was the latest episode.

Yet the extraordinary thing is that, far from being lessened, the appeal of the Kennedy name not only endures, but grows.

This came home to me very forcefully as I sat in Fordham University.

Fall-out from the Stone movie was still being discussed then, but it was the excitement over the Clinton victory and the idea of having a Democrat as President again which dominated.

The tide had turned in American politics after the Reagan and Bush years.

Thoughts went back to 1961-63 and those one thousand days, and forward to the Clinton era and what might lie beyond that.

I told the students about one photograph I had seen during the 1992 campaign – a photo of a pretty young girl in a "Vote Clinton" T-shirt holding a framed picture of JFK.

Yes, some of them had seen it as well.

To me the symbolism was full of poignancy and also full of promise.

It pointed in two directions – backwards to Camelot and forward to a New Camelot.

Another Kennedy President?

Why not?

Then I got to my main question: who if any among the grandchildren has got it?

Which one – or ones – possess the "right stuff" to go all the way to The White House?

Caroline Kennedy, John F. Kennedy Junior, Kathleen Kennedy Townsend and Kerry Kennedy Cuomo – that's how they were listed to me.

The first two are the children of the slain President – JFK.

The second two are the daughters of the slain Presidential-contender – RFK.

If there is to be another Kennedy Presidency within the next 20 years or so, many political pundits believe it will come from within this quartet.

There are other Kennedys of course – Patrick Kennedy, the freckled, red-haired youngest son of Senator Ted, and Doug Kennedy, bookish and quiet, the tenth of RFK's eleven children, are much spoken of.

But the focus of interest where political futures are concerned is very much on the Fabled Four.

29

Caroline

"She's very like her father. Very bright. She could be the best of all the extended family, though I doubt that she'll ever enter politics."

This is Theodore Sorensen speaking about Caroline Kennedy.

As he speaks, I recall a photograph by Jacques Lowe of Caroline leaning forward to kiss her father, with Jackie looking on.

She was only four when he died, and it took her a very long time to get over it.

Today she remains the most private of all the sons and daughters of the three Kennedy brothers.

As a rule, she shuns all publicity.

Two events – one in 1986, the other in 1991 – proved memorable exceptions.

Saturday, 19 July 1986 was a very special day in Caroline's life. The headline in the next day's *Boston Globe* told why – "A Kennedy Is Wed, An Era Remembered".

The opening paragraphs of the story by Teresa M. Hanafin capture the mixed emotions of the occasion:

"CENTREVILLE – With the style and grace that typified the Kennedy White House years, the only daughter of one of the nation's most popular Presidents was married yesterday.

"For millions of Americans who watched Caroline Kennedy frolic in the Oval Office as a child to the delight of her father, President John F. Kennedy, her marriage to Edwin A. Schlossberg, 41, was a joyous scene tinged with nostalgia."

The consensus of the crowd of more than 4,000 gathered outside Our Lady of Victory Church was that the 28-year-old Caroline had grown into a beautiful woman.

The crowd was also impressed by Caroline's brother, John F. Kennedy Jr, 25, who almost stole the show when he arrived with the bridegroom, for whom he acted as best man.

"I bet the President would have liked to have seen this," said several onlookers.

And the sense of nostalgia was heightened when the bride's mother, Jacqueline Kennedy Onassis came out of the church fighting back tears, and lay her head for comfort on the shoulder of her brother-in-law, Senator Edward M. Kennedy.

At that moment there were more than a few wet eyes in the crowd – testimony to the esteem in which the Kennedys are held.

The wedding provided an occasion for a rare gathering of names and faces which brought back memories of the Kennedy Administration.

On hand were John Kenneth Galbraith, the Harvard-based economist and Kennedy's Ambassador to India; Sorensen, the late President's chief speechwriter, and Dave Powers, longtime family friend and curator of the Kennedy Museum in Dorchester, Boston.

As Powers emerged from his car, he waved to the crowd and said simply: "The New Frontier", the nickname given the Kennedy Presidency – and the crowd cheered.

Although Schlossberg is Jewish, the double-ring ceremony was not ecumenical. No Mass was said, but the couple recited the traditional Roman Catholic wedding vows.

The media presence was large. Nearly all the members of America's "royal family" were on view.

Although both Caroline and Edwin prefer a quiet life-style, and try hard to stay out of the social columns of Boston, New York and Washington, they could do nothing about the fact that the wedding of JFK's daughter was going to be a major media event.

Four hundred photographers were outside the church. And coming out after the ceremony, the crush was such that the groom's mother, Mrs Mae Schlossberg, lost her footing and fell down the four steps. But she was unhurt, as she demonstrated later when she danced at the lavish reception at Hyannis Port where Carly Simon sang "Chapel of Love."

Then there were the speeches. "We've all thought of Jack today," said her uncle, the Senator. "And we've thought, too, of how much he loved Caroline and Jackie."

The most emotion-charged moment came when John F. Kennedy Jr rose to propose a toast to his sister. "It's been the three of us alone for so long – Mommy, me and Caroline – and now we've got a fourth."

At that moment, it wasn't just the bride who cried.

For Caroline, looking radiant and calm, it was an unavoidable but rare public appearance in the full glare of the media.

In the years before and since, this is something she has deliberately shunned.

She cherishes her privacy.

"Even on those very few occasions where she has spoken to media people, she absolutely refrains from any comment on her father's death," according to Charles Daly, Director of the JFK Library.

"It is one subject she will not in any circumstances talk about," he told me, as I prepared to write a letter to her.

Now 36, she is based in New York. With her husband and two daughters, she lives in an apartment on Park Avenue. Occasionally at weekends, the family can be spotted walking or cycling through Central Park.

Edwin Schlossberg is a designer, poet and artist, and the author of nine books.

He is the son of a wealthy Jewish textile manufacturer, and runs his own design firm. He holds a Ph.D. in science and literature from Columbia University, and also teaches part-time.

The marriage, by all accounts, is a very happy one. Friends say that Edwin, whom Caroline met at a dinner party in 1981, has the qualities of intelligence and humanism which she admires most in members of her own family.

And in him, one friend says, she has found "a warm, witty, down-to-earth, sensitive man – Ed's her protector".

Like many women of the 1980s, Caroline wanted to sort out her career before having a baby. So she did not become pregnant until her last year studying law at Columbia University.

Her classmates marvelled at her stamina; she didn't miss a single day, even showing up in the snow of New York winters.

In May 1988 Caroline graduated with honours. A month later, on 25 June, Rose Kennedy Schlossberg was born.

Although Caroline has a deep-rooted sense of family and legacy – her decision to name her first daughter after her own grandmother, the 100-year-old Rose Kennedy – she has not been slow in other respects to break away from some family traditions.

Instead of spending weekends at the Kennedy compound at Hyannis Port or with Jackie on Martha's Vineyard, she and her husband often go to The Hamptons, the exclusive community on Long Island's South Fork that is popular with literary and artistic people.

Her second daughter, Tatiani, was born in March 1990.

Although Caroline retains many of her father's qualities – wit and intelligence, above all – she is also very like her mother in terms of discipline and public decorum.

"Of all of the Kennedys," said one acquaintance, "Caroline is the most together and likeable."

Theodore Sorensen agrees. "She is a mature, level-headed, well-balanced and very bright person," he says.

Some observers deem this to be all the more remarkable, not just because of the tragedy of Dallas, but the difficulty of being the daughter of Jackie Kennedy Onassis.

"All girls have problems with their mothers," admitted one of Jackie's inner circle of friends. "But imagine being the daughter of a beautiful world object – even at 62, Jackie is one of the most desirable women in the world."

In fact, as many of Caroline's friends emphasise, mother and daughter enjoy an extremely close friendship. They see each other a couple of times a week, and often go shopping, to lunch, to the theatre or art galleries together.

Caroline is also on the board of the John F. Kennedy Library and is active in the Kennedy Foundation, and this involves her with her mother as well.

Above all, Jackie seems determined not to spoil her two grand-daughters. She has said repeatedly that the same disciplined upbringing that worked so well for her children needs to be given also to the next generation.

It is a lesson that Caroline and Edwin scarcely need reminding of. Both are acutely aware that Caroline will inherit a very large fortune – and that Rose and Tatiani are very privileged girls.

Friends say that one of the nicest things about Caroline and Ed is that while they respect their wealth, they do not flaunt it.

That wealth was added to by a second event – this time in February 1991 – which also meant much media attention for Caroline.

It was the publication of her first book, a book which for many recalled her father's Pulitzer Prize-winning *Profiles in Courage*.

But even at the launch of *In Our Defense: The Bill of Rights in Action*, Caroline tried to stay aloof, not wanting to get dragged into any controversy.

The book dramatises legal dilemmas involving such matters as freedom of religion, the death penalty, gun control, freedom of the press, the right to privacy, the right to face your accuser, and the right to an impartial jury.

It soon became a bestseller, with *The New York Times* saying that the late President's daughter was "helping people to care about the Constitution".

To care and to understand, and thus to make the world a better place.

Other Kennedys have chosen to do this by and through politics. Caroline has chosen to do it through the law and jurisprudence.

"We really had a general audience in mind when we thought up the book idea," she says. "We were surprised when we got to law school that the law wasn't as dry as we thought. In the stories we tell in the book, majestic principles of liberty and justice are played out in the lives of ordinary Americans, some heroic and some malevolent.

"The stories were chosen for many reasons. Some illustrate why the Founding Fathers protected individual rights against the power of the government, and why we still need them today. Others show how far we have come in 200 years. Still others raise difficult questions for the future."

For Caroline Kennedy that future promises to be fruitful, as she continues in her own way to serve the public, just as her illustrious father did.

Whether the lawyerly mask she has donned always stays in place is a moot point.

Up to now, as one reporter has pointed out, "There was always the sense about her that she both feared and loathed the spotlight".

No one can blame her for this, given the public spectacle that the Kennedys' lives have become.

But there remains the hope, voiced to me by Theodore Sorensen, that her contribution in the public domain may yet prove significant and enduring.

How proud John F. Kennedy would be of that, were he alive.

30

Kathleen

It is Friday, 13 November 1992. The 6.20 a.m. Amtrak Mainliner from Penn Station in Manhattan stops in Philadelphia. The last time I was in this city was in 1976 – the year of the American Bicentennial.

Then as now I have the Kennedys on my mind.

Back then I met a bright student on the Penn State campus, and over beers in Carney's Bar on Chestnut Street we talked about the powers of the US Presidency, and about how we might rate the holders of that august office in the 20th century.

The train is moving on: the stop in Philadelphia lasts only a few minutes.

My thoughts move on with it.

On the tray in front of me is a magazine with an article on the transition headed: MR CLINTON GOES TO WASHINGTON.

I know that soon I will be discussing the shape and priorities of a Clinton Presidency.

My destination is 200 West Baltimore Street, Baltimore, where Kathleen Kennedy Townsend works for the Maryland Board of Education.

After the elevated skyline of Manhattan dominated by the Empire State building and the twin towers of the World Trade Centre, Baltimore is more like an Irish city.

On the 7th floor, wearing a plastic "visitor" badge, I sit in an open-plan room while a dozen women answer phones or work at computer terminals.

What will Bobby Kennedy's eldest child be like?

Even as I ponder the question, she appears.

"Hi – I'm Kathleen Townsend."

She's 42 now, and smaller and less glamorous than her photographs. And bookish-looking. Her face – I can detect no trace of make-up – framed by large, thick spectacles reminds me more of her father than her mother, Ethel. She has the broad, easy smile that is so much a Kennedy stock-in-trade.

Kathleen is wearing a dark brown cardigan, black skirt, black stockings and black flat shoes. Her straight brown hair, showing little touches of grey, is cut severely at the chin.

Later I learn that Kathleen has never been interested in fashion. She wears what is appropriate and practical. And she is a workaholic. Her job involves carrying out a 1985 mandate written into the State Board of Education's bye-laws which requires every high school to introduce some form of public service into the curriculum.

We sit at a small conference table in an annex and she fetches a cup of coffee. I switch on my cassette recorder, and I'm asking myself – could this be the first woman President of the United States?

A definite yes.

The voice is firm, strong, assertive. It rings with confidence and authority.

This is not a woman to be trifled with.

People go by, moving between offices as we talk. She seems not to notice.

Clinton, politics and Washington absorb her.

She makes it clear that outside of Clinton's own circle, his victory over George Bush is nowhere more enthusiastically celebrated than among the Kennedys.

"Is this great – or is this great!" she yelps when I ask her how she feels about having a Democrat back in The White House.

"Yeah, special times are ahead."

She predicts that the agenda will change, that the economy, education, medical care, health and crime in the cities will start getting the attention they deserve under Clinton.

But not all at once. She is a political insider; she knows that it takes time for any new president to assert himself. And she knows something about the limits of power, and how obstructive the special interest groups can be.

"He won't just be able to wave a magic wand," she says, in words that carry more force today.

If she ever wields that magic wand, the role and status of women in society will be high on her agenda.

She is proud to be known as a feminist because for her it is something positive, liberating and enriching.

"I don't think I would ever have got really involved in politics or gone to law school if it hadn't been for the feminist movement."

Yet, although regarded as a superwoman of the nineties, she has struck a successful balance between family and career.

"It's important that I care for my children – that's an important function of my marriage – and at the same time that I can go and make a contribution to society. I can combine the two. It's difficult but possible. I just do it at different times.

"There were times when I didn't work, times when I worked part-time, and times when I worked full-time.

"That kind of flexibility is wonderful for me, who obviously has some means. But I think it is important that society provide those opportunities for lots of women so they don't feel that they're stuck."

That's now very much part of her political credo.

Kathleen Hartington Kennedy is the first child of Robert and Ethel Skakel Kennedy. She was born on 4 July, 1951, in Hyannis, Massachusetts and named after her father's sister, the Marchioness of Hartington, who died in a plane crash in 1948. However, Robert Kennedy placed a condition on the naming of his first child – he stipulated that she should never be called "Kick", his sister's nickname.

He had revered his fun-loving, strong-willed sister until she defied their father and married outside her Catholic faith.

He did not want to see his daughter treading the same rebellious path.

Kathleen had other ideas. Friends say she spent her life fighting for her independence.

Kathleen attended the Sacred Heart Country Day School in Bethesda, Maryland, but then persuaded her father to send her to the non-Catholic co-educational Putney School in Vermont.

It was the first indication of a questioning, critical attitude towards her Catholicism. At one stage, she even stopped going to Mass regularly, something which hurt her mother deeply.

During her high school years, she rebelled against the constraints of the Church, protesting that she wanted to experience a wider outlook on life.

However, she never abandoned her religion. Today she believes the Catholic Church is progressing, though not quickly enough.

After Putney, she went to the exclusive and expensive Radcliffe College. It marked a turning point in her life.

During her years at Radcliffe she fell in love with David Townsend, her six-foot four red-bearded tutor, who was four years her senior.

Like her, he was a Catholic. They both shared an interest in ecology, and during her sophomore year she studied southern United States literature with him.

In 1972 the pair planned a three-week trip down the Mississippi River on a raft called the Snopes to honour Mark Twain's *Huckleberry Finn*. The trip proved to be more of an adventure than they had expected. David ended up with a hairline skull fracture.

Kathleen surprised herself when, angered after a two-hour wait, she resorted to using her family name at the hospital to get David treated.

The following September they became engaged. And on 17 November 1973 they were married at the Holy Trinity Church in Washington. Uncle Ted gave his brother's daughter away.

The Townsends, who now live in an old Victorian house in Baltimore, have three daughters – Meaghan, born in 1977, Maeve, born in 1979, and Rose Katherine, called Kate, born in 1984.

When JFK was elected President in 1960, Kathleen's father became Attorney-General and their home, Hickory Hill in McLean, became the venue for regular seminars involving politicians, journalists and intellectuals.

It was an exciting, magical time.

Kathleen was twelve when her uncle Jack was assassinated in Dallas.

The effect on her father was devastating. He withdrew from the Justice Department.

In 1964 he decided to run for the US Senate from New York, and had an easy win. In time he was prevailed upon to challenge President Lyndon B. Johnson for The White House. Once again politicians, journalists and intellectuals filled the McLean mansion.

But in mid-1968, with Bobby on the crest of an electoral wave, the family's excitement over their probable return to The White House was tragically shattered.

One of Kathleen's secret fears, perhaps the deepest, since the assassination of her uncle five years previously had become a horrifying reality.

She was told that her father had been shot, after being awakened from a peaceful sleep in her school dormitory. She flew to Los Angeles and just managed to see Bobby before he died.

Although only 16 years old, she maintained a stoical exterior and determined after the funeral to continue her father's work for peace, justice, equality and an end to racial and other forms of discrimination.

The horror of Los Angeles changed her. Those who knew her well said that up to then the serious side of her personality was balanced by a fun-loving, mischievous side. Henceforth, the sober-minded, intense side of her personality prevailed.

Both to escape public attention and to fulfill a promise she had made to her father, Kathleen spent the following summer working with a Navajo tribe in Arizona. That experience, and a profound desire to live out her father's dream, led her in the direction of public service.

"I think he would have made a great President," she told me when we spoke in Baltimore.

Understandably, she will not be drawn into comparisons between her father and her uncle. "I don't like to look back, though I have my own special memories."

Does she pay any attention to conspiracy theories surrounding her father's death?

"I don't pay any attention to them. What's past is past. You can't recreate it. You can't revive the dead. Let's go on. I'm very future-orientated."

Strong-willed and determined, Kathleen was the first Kennedy woman ever to consider running for public office. She was – and remains – convinced she could break into national politics.

A feminist and an environmentalist, she has been associated with political causes almost from the day of her father's assassination.

Money has never been her motive, but having it helps and she has never been embarrassed to admit this.

"A lot of my brothers and sisters can make a lot more money too. They understand that you do get some satisfaction by trying to make a difference. The crowning joy of life is public service. And I think that's really a strong part of my family, and there's a great deal of satisfaction in that. Thomas Jefferson wrote about life, liberty and the pursuit of happiness. If you read Hannah Arendt, she talks about what Jefferson means by happiness . . . in her book on revolution. And of course I go along with her on this – she says that what he was referring to was the happiness of participating in public affairs. I think this is what we should teach children as well."

It was a lesson she, like other Kennedys, learned early on.

Her entry into politics (she made an unsuccessful bid for Congress in 1986) prompted some commentators to talk of her combination of naivety and guts.

Others felt her message was too general and goody-goody – let's help the poor and all that.

She learned fast, and has since been emphasising her independence, working to ensure that she is not pigeon-holed or dismissed as a "Kennedy liberal".

Kathleen Townsend is interested in ideas, and her test is whether an idea is good or not – not where it came from.

"I talk about ideas," she says. "When I advocate a police corps or a teacher corps, I do it because I just think it's a good idea."

She explains that under police and teacher corps plans, students have their tuition paid in exchange for working several years in these fields after graduation.

Nobody doubts that she will continue to be a force to be reckoned with in politics.

Indeed, some observers maintain that if there is a potential president among the younger generation of Kennedys, it will be the eldest of Bobby's 11 children.

When the time comes for America's first woman President – and that time may not be too far off – Kathleen Townsend could make it to The White House.

The idea neither surprises nor alarms her.

"Me for President – sure. Why not?"

Would past circumstances cause her to reconsider.

A broad smile and a firm shake of the head. "No."

Looking at her, you just know she isn't kidding. This very able, very tough lady would go for it. Correction – will go for it. That's my bet. She embodies her father's competitiveness and love of a challenge.

Women and family values are high on her agenda. She sees the need for parents to create a stronger sense of morality in their children.

I ask her what the big problems are for America in the Clinton era.

"Unemployment and violence in our cities. We hear about the violence in Northern Ireland, but it doesn't compare at all, in numbers of people killed by violent acts, to what is going on in our cities.

"You can't create a culture where there is no family, where people are being killed every day, where people are afraid to walk down the street. You have to look at our value-systems. The children have no sense of right and wrong."

She says this is also why there is so much drug abuse, and you remember that her brother David died of a drug overdose in 1984.

She has no problem with drug testing of federal employees, and says flatly: "Using drugs is wrong – period."

Like other members of her family, Kathleen has made several visits to Ireland and has a keen interest in developments in Northern Ireland.

In September 1992, at the invitation of SDLP leader, John Hume, she attended an international "Beyond Hate" conference in Derry.

We talked about the furore over reports that President Clinton might yet send a peace envoy to the North.

"Why anybody should object to a peace initiative from Washington, given all that has happened in the North, is something I just don't understand."

Like many others, she hopes to see a political settlement before the year 2000.

That will also be the year when Bill Clinton's stint in The White House comes to an end, assuming he is elected for a second term in 1996.

So will she be a contender then? Will she pick up the Kennedy torch?

The smile is warm and wary.

"We'll see. That's a long way off, and who knows what may happen in between?"

She knows that much is expected of the Kennedys. More importantly, she expects much of herself.

"Compared to most people, we really are lucky. And I really do think that caring for others is important. And clearly it's easier if you have the means. We should be able to do it, to achieve whatever task is at hand."

How would she like the public to see her?

"I am very proud of my family and of what my mother and father have done for this country. But the people have to judge me on my own."

One thing is sure where Kathleen Kennedy Townsend is concerned – she will continue to lead the kind of superwoman career-cum-mother life she has established for herself – wherever that leads, even if it's all the way to The White House.

31

Kerry

Kerry Kennedy Cuomo is very pretty, very bright, very passionate, and very, very determined.

Perhaps more than any other of the Kennedys, she embodies the will to affect change, the thirst for social reform.

On the wall leading to her 7th floor office on East 33rd Street in New York, the following extract from a speech made by her father, Robert F. Kennedy, is painted in large blue letters: "Each time a man stands up for an ideal or acts to improve the lot of others or strikes out against injustice, he sends forth a tiny ripple of hope, and crossing each other from a million different centres of energy and daring, those ripples build a current that can sweep down the mightiest walls of oppression and resistance."

That speech was made in South Africa in 1966, and the extract is the key to the personality of an extraordinary woman.

Five minutes in her presence was enough to convince me of that.

We sat on leather-covered chairs across from the desk in her small office, and talked about a framed photograph on a shelf. Her description of it is part of her credo.

The photo shows a young man standing in front of a tank in Tiananmen Square in Beijing.

"I think that is one of the great images of our time," she said. "In some ways, that man was blessed because he believed in something so strongly that he was willing to confront a tank for it. One of the things that was so fantastic about it was that it was not a still photo. It was a video. So you could see the tank manoeuvring, and the guy manoeuvring in front of the tank so that he could stay facing the gun."

What had prompted her to talk about the photo was a question I asked about another Kennedy Presidency.

Would it bother her, in view of what had happened to her uncle and her father, if another Kennedy contested The White House?

The answer came unhesitatingly.

"If you start thinking about the possibility of personal harm, it can stop you from doing anything.

"I would hope that whoever is running for President – whether in my family or otherwise – would believe in that cause so much, would believe in the policies that they are trying to get adopted by the American people, that they would risk anything.

"I work in the area of international human rights. I work every day with people from all over the world who believe so strongly in what they are doing that they are willing to stand in front of the military, they are willing to risk imprisonment and torture. God, when you know that people like that exist, and if you are able to help them, then thinking about your own safety becomes a very small matter . . . "

I was reminded of the line from her uncle's famous Inaugural Address of 1961: "Bear any burden, pay any price."

Kerry smiled and shook her head: "I don't know if I would put it like that."

But what if circumstances opened up the possibility of another Kennedy Presidency?

"I think that would be great. Our family has very good, very strong values, and a tremendous commitment to serve the country. It's hard to talk about it in the abstract, but I think another Kennedy Presidency would be very good for the country."

We started to discuss RFK's legacy.

"His sense of justice and his compassion for those who were deprived and struggling, both at home and abroad – these are two very strong qualities which manifested themselves throughout his lifetime."

So would he have been a better President than JFK?

Kerry smiled and shrugged.

"I'm not going to compare my father and his brother. I come from a family of 10 brothers and sisters, and I was constantly being compared to the others. Sometimes that hurt.

"They had different qualities and different strengths as men. But my father would have made a great President."

What about the circumstances of her father's death, especially the persistence of conspiracy theories?

I knew it was painful for her to have to consider this. Haltingly, I explained that while I didn't wish to press her on this, it was something I had to ask.

"I don't dwell on that at all. And I don't pay any attention to talk about a conspiracy. I think it's a kind of sick obsession."

In 1968 she was just three months short of her ninth birthday when her father was shot.

Thinking of that, I waited, giving her space, not knowing what thoughts were running through her mind.

"I like to think about his life, not his death," she said quietly.

She can be touchingly straightforward about very personal things.

"The difference between us and people not in the spotlight is that sometimes when something private happens, a lot of people know about it and you would like it to be more private. When they find out I'm Bobby Kennedy's daughter, so many people tell me where they were when he died. What do most people want to remember about their father? Not what happened when he died."

Yet the sense of loss will never vanish.

On 20 November 1990, the day on which RFK would have turned 65, Kerry saw a preview of a film entitled *Bobby Kennedy: In His Own Words*. Much of the footage came from private archives and Kennedy home movies, shots of Bobby dancing and then shots of him in Mississippi, in South Africa, and in Vietnam.

With trembling voice, Kerry spoke about it: "When I saw this film I was filled with . . . I was overwhelmed with a mix of emotions, of pride in RFK the politician. But then I thought of Robert Kennedy, my father. And of his love. And of his laugh. And of his touch. And then I missed him, and thought of the tremendous loss that we won't see him again . . . "

Kerry Kennedy Cuomo, the seventh child of Ethel Skakel and Robert Francis Kennedy, was born on 8 September 1959 in Boston, Massachusetts.

Ethel and her children had been spending the summer at Hyannis Port, and Robert, who was in Washington working to finish his first book *The Enemy Within*, flew up to greet his third daughter.

According to her godmother, Kerry, from early infancy, was "delightful, full of energy, and bubbling with enthusiasm".

Kerry always seemed more independent than her older sisters, and even as a small child had very definite ideas about what she wanted to do and how she would do it.

"With dark eyes and blond hair, she had a joie de vivre that made her beautiful."

While religion is very important to all the Kennedys, some are more observant than others. Kerry has always been among the most deeply religious and friends have testified that she considers her faith a source of strength and guidance.

She graduated from Brown University in 1982 with a Bachelor of Arts degree and from Boston College Law School in 1987. She worked in the Middlesex County Prosecutor's office, and later she worked in the Norfolk County District Attorney's office trying criminal cases.

In April 1988 Kerry founded the Robert F. Kennedy Memorial Centre for Human Rights and serves today as its executive director.

Her father was her inspiration.

"On Saturday afternoons my father would pile all the kids into the station wagon and take us to the Justice Department. It was a formal building with a lot of pomp, tradition, and old portraits.

"But the walls in the largest room of all, my father's office, were covered with paintings and drawings by his children. It was his way of telling himself and visitors what was important in his life.

"In many ways his philosophy was that of Mary Baker Eddy – 'Comfort the afflicted and afflict the comfortable'. One day, when I was seven, we were all running around, screaming and making a mess as usual, when suddenly the door opened and my father walked in. He'd been visiting homes of poor people in the Mississippi Delta. 'I've just been to a house where three families live in a room this size,' he said quietly. 'I hope you do something for those children. You've got to do something for them.'

"Those words and his involvement with the Civil Rights movement helped show us that life is larger than oneself. That's why I became interested in working for human rights."

That work has taken her all over the world, to some of the neediest, bloodiest, most neglected places on earth.

She has led or taken part in human rights delegations to: Chile, 1988; Czechoslovakia, 1991; El Salvador, 1989; Haiti, 1991; Hungary, 1987 and 1991; Kenya 1989; The Philippines, 1992; Poland, 1987 and 1991; South Korea 1988, 1990 and 1992, and Venezuela in 1989.

She has lectured extensively throughout the United States about human rights, and has published articles in *The Boston Globe*, *The Chicago Sun-Times* and *The New York Times*.

She is also a special correspondent for the environmental magazine television programme *Network Watch* and reports on human rights and the environment.

The Memorial Centre is a small organisation compared to Amnesty International – there are a couple of staffers and some interns, and its funding comes from the Memorial's small total endowment of $3.5 million.

The centre gives a human rights award each year "to a person who stood up to government repression at great personal risk".

It has gone to the mothers of the disappeared in El Salvador, to leaders of the Solidarity Movement in Poland, and to Gibson Kamau Kuria, a lawyer from Kenya who risked his life and was tortured for taking the cases of dissidents. When the Kenyan Government refused to allow Kuria out to accept the award, Kerry went to Kenya to give it to him. Parliament stayed in session in order to condemn her trip.

She says she never thought about doing anything else. "Never, ever, did my mother say, 'Look, you have to do this, you have to go into public service.' Personally, I just feel fulfilled. I don't feel it's a burden, because I love it. I think there are certain moral values Robert Kennedy stood for and his life was a testament to. To the extent that I share those values and to the extent that I can carry on those values or give a hand to those who share them, I'd like to."

Her eyes are shining now, the voice stronger.

"When I think of my father I think of a courageous man who tried to use the law to empower people who were disadvantaged, who were rejected or passed over by society. And that's what I think about the day he went to help Cesar Chavez and all his aides said, 'Don't go'. It was the day before he announced his Presidential candidacy. Why would somebody do that? There was no political gain; in fact, there was political loss. Because it was the right thing to do. That's the way I think about him, you know."

The voice is still impassioned, but very soft now.

"He said moral courage is a rarer commodity than bravery in battle or rare intelligence, yet it is the one essential, vital quality for those who seek to change a world that yields most painfully to change. If there's something I can do to help those people who show moral courage, then I want to do that."

One of the places where she wants to see change is Ireland.

Ireland has always had a special appeal for her. "I feel a special closeness to Ireland. This is the place my ancestors came from. This is the land they loved, and for which they named me Kerry."

As part of a delegation, she visited the North in 1988 and 1989.

On 9 June 1990 Kerry married Andrew Mark Cuomo, the son of New York Governor Mario Cuomo, in St Matthew's Church in Washington.

In the media, there was much talk of a "political union" involving two families so much in the private eye.

Kerry offered a more conventional explanation. She simply said: "He's the man I love."

Her husband's father dealt with the rumours that the marriage had been engineered to merge two political dynasties in a more blunt fashion: "That's really a lot of baloney!"

Family friend and adviser Gerard Doherty, a Boston lawyer, calls her "the real superstar", the one to watch.

On one occasion her four-minute appeal for funds for the Memorial Centre turned into a passionate speech on behalf of the disadvantaged and the downtrodden.

Some watching were deeply moved.

Close your eyes and it's another decade, another Kennedy.

Says her friend Bryan Carey, son of former New York Governor, Hugh Carey: "She really believes that stuff."

RFK would smile at that and no doubt say: "That's my girl!"

32

The Once and Future King

He is often referred to by admiring ladies as "the incredible hunk". And little wonder since, at 31, John F. Kennedy Jr is one of the world's most eligible bachelors, a status that could soon change if he marries the actress Daryl Hannah.

Like his famous father, JFK Jr is handsome, dashing and intelligent.

His colleagues describe him as a genuinely nice guy who attracts incredible loyalty from his friends.

Polished and poised, JFK Jr is regarded by some as more of a Bouvier than a Kennedy.

While he likes to go out and have a good time, the pressure is on from his mother and his sister, Caroline – to keep his "clean cut" image, to maintain an untarnished reputation.

Media interest in his love-life and in his romantic escapades is, of course, insatiable.

His comings and goings are a staple of the gossip columns.

And like his father, the world of show business has a special fascination for him.

Apart from Daryl Hannah, his name has been linked to Madonna, Molly Ringwald, Princess Stephanie of Monaco, and Brooke Shields.

He lives – alone – in a sophisticated part of New York's Greenwich Village, near his favourite night-spots.

And most days he cycles to work in the DA's office in uptown Manhattan.

Once known as "John-John", it was impossible not to notice the raw excitement when he addressed the Democratic National Convention in 1988.

Here was a living connection to a lost icon.

It was his debut as a political performer, and he got rave reviews.

"In a very real sense, because of you, he is still with us," he told the convention, speaking of his father.

That sentence, of course, could have been spoken the other way around. In a real sense, because of John Jr, his father, the martyred President, is still with us.

John Jr is the once and future President – or so many would like to believe.

In him, for many, lives on the promise of another Kennedy sitting in the Oval Office.

He has looks, charm and charisma.

In the past John Jr had tended to make the news more for his dates than his political views.

These days his interest in politics is growing. So will he run for elective office?

The question has not yet been answered, a political future has not been ruled out.

The boy who saluted his father's coffin on a gun carriage might not have the full say in his destiny.

The man who was one of his father's closest aides, Theodore Sorensen, believes John Jr has changed.

"He is more interested in politics now than he was five years ago. And five years from now he could be more interested still. Who knows?"

Sorensen may well be right.

If there is to be a second coming for the Kennedys in terms of the Presidency, John Jr may be the member of the family to do it.

During a rare interview on national television, Kennedy was asked to explain his career aspirations.

"Listen, my father was in politics. My uncles were in politics. My cousins are in politics. We grew up amidst political life."

But will he follow in his father's footsteps?

He demurred. "The answer is a big 'I don't know yet', and when I do you'll probably find out."

A beguilingly honest response, yet others, like Sorensen, believe he is closer now to a career in politics than ever before.

It wasn't always so.

He could have the political world at his feet, yet for a time he didn't seem to want it.

And nor is it yet clear that he does.

Many of the young Kennedys appear to have the same driving ambition as the previous two generations. Some of Robert and Ted Kennedy's have gone for elective office.

Already the latest crop of the world's most visible American-Irish family can boast a couple of congressmen and a few close electoral misses.

But Jack's son, whom pundits say has the best chance of being the next Kennedy in The White House, has, until recently, expressed little or no interest.

Relative after relative has sat down with him and told him he can do it. So far, his attitude has been: "No way."

Is that changing?

That's a question American Democrats would love to have the answer to.

For a long time the son that Jack left had ideas about what he wanted to do with his life which had no direct connection with politics.

Perhaps influenced by the fact that he was brought up almost exclusively by his mother – the only other father-figure he knew was the ageing Greek shipping tycoon Aristotle Onassis, to whom Jackie was married for a mere six years – he seemed the very opposite of a true Kennedy.

Despite his JFK jaw, he's not pushy. And he's not ambitious. The settlement his mother negotaited for him when Onassis died guaranteed he'd be a millionaire for life. So he doesn't need an income.

Then there was the theatre.

For a time it seemed that his burning passions were reserved, not for politics, but for acting.

And the thought that he might become a committed actor alarmed his family, especially his mother.

He acted regularly throughout his undergraduate university days. Many friends still recall his gifted turns on the stage. The productions he appeared in included Woody Allen's satire *God*, and in the summer of 1985 he starred in a revival of a Brian Friel play called *Winners*, which was put on in the 75-seater Manhattan Irish Arts Centre. He played the part of a Northerner who meets a tragic end. The play ran for six performances, and was invitation only.

But what was noted by all the gossip columnists was that his normally supportive mother never turned up for a single show.

Friends said Jackie had no time for "this acting business", and has been more encouraging in telling John to become a lawyer, like his sister.

The acting rumours kept cropping up, however. There were even reports that he was to appear in a new television soap opera. But the news was no sooner confirmed by the show's director than it was immediately withdrawn.

Then he was asked by Robert Stigwood, the producer of the box-office hit *Fame*, to play his father in a feature film based on the President's early years.

John Jr was all set to head to Hollywood when Jackie issued an authoritative "No – never!"

And that was that.

According to classmate, John Jr had "incredible" stage presence. "He could have had a brilliant stage or screen career."

John and his mother argued long and bitterly about his stage aspirations. To the former First Lady, an acting career was entirely unsuitable for her son.

And she prevailed.

At present his career is in law; tomorrow it could be politics.

Who knows?

At 32, he is the scion of the most charismatic American family, heir to its vast fortune and bearer of its most famous name.

Against the odds – given the unparalleled tragedies which have befallen the Kennedys – John Jr has turned out to be a healthy, productive and sensible young man.

Much of the credit for this must go to his mother.

Despite all the fame that attaches to his name, the public acclaim, the attention and sometimes paternalistic admonitions from the media, the most remarkable thing about him, as his friends and colleagues like to point out, is his ability to remain a "regular guy".

This regular guy also happens to be one of the most eligible bachelors in America – no, make that the world.

One of America's favourite news and celebrity magazines, *People*, named him "The Sexiest Man Alive", and ran a full-colour shirtless picture of him on the cover.

Known as a fitness freak, he works out five days a week.

The gym is one of his favourite haunts, and he takes enormous pride in his physical appearance.

He bicycles around Manhattan, and is an excellent water-skier, tennis player, swimmer and soccer player.

His admirers insist that he has a brain to match his brawn.

While at Brown University, in addition to his regular scholastic chores, he also got down to the serious work of learning as much as he could about his father.

He even took a seminar on the war in Vietnam to explore Jack Kennedy's role in the decision-making processes which took America down that tragic path.

His fame brings its burdens as well as its benefits and privileges.

He has to live with his father's legacy, though there is no sign that he finds this burdensome.

"A lot of people admired what my father did and I am grateful to be part of that wonderful legacy."

Sometimes, however, the fame closes in around him, and he craves anonymity.

When he went out with top model Christie Brinkley he got annoyed when the paparazzi followed him all over Manhattan. And he tried, without success, to go incognito to a Guns 'n' Roses concert.

Throughout all of this, he has made conscious efforts not to be bowled over by the fame, by all the media attention.

One of his close friends, Jann Wenner, the founder and editor of *Rolling Stone* magazine, says: "He is a good egg. A real regular guy. If you took away the Kennedy name, he would be perfectly normal."

The name, of course, is part of the legacy, part of the reason why many still regard him as the crown prince, waiting to reclaim the lost throne.

That may never happen. He may never be president, though we'll always be hearing about him because he is, after all, a Kennedy.

Some Kennedy-watchers insist the genetic fire of ambition burns strongly within him.

That remains to be seen.

But few doubt that if he wishes to become the new white knight of America, JFK Jr will take precedence over all other Kennedys when it comes to political advancement.

It has not gone unnoticed that as the crown prince of the Camelot myth, he has dutifully – if apparently reluctantly – put himself on the traditional political preparatory path.

Some say this has been done largely to please his mother.

She, more than anyone, could determine whether his future is to be within politics, or outside of it.

And if it is the former, it is hardly likely, given his pedigree and the Kennedy track record, that he would come into politics and not try for the top prize – the Presidency itself.

Not for nothing is the son that Jack left sometimes referred to as the one for whom there will be a second coming.

33

The Restoration

It is possible to date precisely the beginning of the Kennedy Restoration.

It happened in the fall of 1979 – 21 October 1979 to be exact – when a select group came to Boston for the dedication of the JFK Memorial Library at Columbia Point.

It was a windy day, good for sailing, and JFK's boat *Victura*, flapped its sails impatiently, even though it would never go to sea again.

Fittingly, Dr Martin Luther King's widow, Coretta, was there.

So was Jimmy Carter, the second President since the Civil War (1862-65) to come from the Deep South.

Jackie was there, of course, and Edward, the surviving brother. And other familiar faces from Camelot, memories of which were lovingly evoked especially when John F. Kennedy Jr, the son of the slain President, rose and read Stephen Spender's poem "The Truly Great", as the sun flitted in and out of the clouds.

Born of the sun, they travelled a short while toward the sun,
And left the vivid air signed with their honour.

It was a day of sorrow, a day of remembrance, and a day also of celebration.

Above all, it was a day of re-dedication by and on behalf of America's most famous family.

It was also a poignant reminder that for half a century the Kennedys have almost personally held the hopes and aspirations of liberal America in their hands.

Indeed, there have been no more exciting moments in twentieth century politics than when John F. Kennedy, at the age of 43, was swept into The White House on a wave of enthusiasm and idealism in 1960.

The tragedies of 1963 and 1968 that were to follow, and the rise of the New Right, meant that for a time the Kennedy star waned.

But the dream remained intact, and the idealism never died.

And that October day in 1979 was both a reaffirmation of the past and a pointer to the future.

Ever since, the recovery of JFK's political reputation has steadily gathered momentum.

In addition, a new generation of Kennedys has added a second strand to the restoration process by holding out the hope of another Kennedy Presidency.

Whether that will ever actually happen is something that none of us can forecast.

It is in the lap of the gods.

Back in March 1962 when Teddy Kennedy, 20 days after his 30th birthday, announced his candidacy for the Senate, the *Chicago Tribune* prophesied for The White House: "President John F. (1961-69), President Robert F. (1969-77), President Edward M. (1977-), and before you know it we are in 1984 with Caroline coming up fast and John F. Jr just behind her . . . "

It may have seemed like that at the time, and nobody could be blamed for attributing dynastic ambitions to the family.

Whether JFK ever seriously contemplated a Kennedy dynasty in The White House is a moot point.

Some say he did. We know he joked about it.

He certainly must have felt that his brother Bobby would have made an excellent President.

He admired Bobby and respected his qualities.

As for Teddy, he worried about his immaturity, but that too would change in time.

Time, however, is something JFK didn't have. And Bobby didn't fare much better. In this year of 1993 we mark the 30th anniversary of the death of JFK, and the 25th anniversary of the death of RFK.

I don't know about you, but 30 years after Dallas, and notwithstanding all that has happened in between, I'm still very much a John Fitzgerald Kennedy fan.

I can't look at a photograph of him without thinking that he was handsome and witty and intelligent, but that he might also have been a great president.

These days that's not the in-thing anymore. It's 30 years since Dallas, and in-between, the image of the golden boy of American politics has been tarnished quite a bit.

We have been told over and over again that JFK was a womaniser, that his father, old Joseph Kennedy, bought the 1960 election for him, and that he consorted with people who had Mafia connections.

It all adds up to a pretty bad picture. But is it the whole picture?

To judge by some of the stuff in the British press in recent months, you would be convinced that it is the whole picture.

What you have to remember is that the British never liked Kennedy, partly due to his Irish connections.

They could never be sure about what he was thinking. What might his attitude be on the North, for instance, or on the ending of Partition?

We now know from official government papers that the Unionists were very worried at the prospect of a Kennedy Presidency in 1960.

The Kennedy reputation hasn't been helped, of course, by other events, such as the tragedy at Chappaquiddick in 1969, when Teddy Kennedy drove off a bridge and the woman in the car with him, Mary Jo Kopechne, lost her life.

Then, just recently, we were all spectators at one of the most publicised trials in modern history – the William Kennedy Smith rape case.

It was confidently predicted by various media types that this trial would mark the end of the line for the Kennedys – America's Royal Family. Camelot, it was said, would finally be disgraced, leaving the Kennedy Dynasty in ruins.

Remember Camelot? According to legend, it was the place where King Arthur and his knights held court.

When Kennedy defeated Nixon for the Presidency he brought to Washington with him a whole new generation of young "knights" – the brightest and the best – and a new Camelot was born.

It was a time of great pride, great idealism, great hopes and great dreams. And, suddenly, everything seemed possible. Here was this young, dashing, elegant President telling Americans that they should not ask what their country could do for them, but what they could do for their country.

The torch had indeed passed to a new generation. And at its head was a man not just of style, but of substance.

I thought of that again the other day as I watched footage of the Kennedy visit to Ireland on RTE television.

This was part of the day-long programme screened on Network 2 to mark the 30th anniversary of the founding of what was originally called Telefis Eireann.

I watched Kennedy in Cork, speaking in the City Hall, and remembered how I had run through the city streets to get a second glimpse of him.

And I listened to him later in Dáil Eireann, and felt a surge of pride as he extoled the contribution made on the world stage by such a small nation as Ireland.

Many years later I visited his grave in Arlington Cemetary, and for hours afterwards in a pub in Washington, I talked to local journalists about him, and what he might have achieved – if he had lived.

Camelot has been revisited many times since. Many questions have been asked.

Many judgements made.

Yet the Kennedy myth refuses to die.

From Dallas to Los Angeles (where Bobby Kennedy was assassinated) to Chappaquiddick to Palm Beach – there have been many tragedies and much scandal.

Yet the image of Camelot, and the hope which it signified, refuses to recede into history.

And after all the muck-raking and the mud-slinging, the pendulum is swinging back.

A new appreciation of what President Kennedy stood for is emerging, along with a new sense of loss at what he might have achieved.

Despite the sensationalism of the William Kennedy Smith trial, and the attempt by a succession of authors to rubbish JFK, the Kennedy political legacy endures.

Even now, 30 years after his death, four million people visit JFK's grave at Arlington cemetery each year, remembering, praying, reciting words from the great speeches.

Other, younger Kennedys – John Junior, Caroline, Joseph Kennedy III, Bobby Junior and Patrick Kennedy – are preparing to carry the torch into a new century.

A future Kennedy Presidency cannot be ruled out. The urge to serve is deeply embedded in the clan – and great credit is due to the family for that, given the awful price they have paid.

The actress Shirley MacLaine is right. When asked once about Kennedy's womanising, she replied: "So what? We elected a man to The White House, not a saint. A saint wouldn't survive there anyway. And remember, Jack Kennedy gave us the most precious thing of all – he gave us hope!"

As for the present generation of Kennedys, the possibilities and permutations are endless where they are concerned.

That is why predictions that the House of Kennedy is crumbling are premature.

Indeed, rising from the ashes is a Kennedy tradition.

Bibliography

Alderman, Ellen, and Kennedy, Caroline, *In Our Defense: The Bill of Rights in Action* (Avon Books), New York, 1992

Baritz, Loren, *Backfire: A History of How American Culture Led Us into Vietnam* (Ballantine Books), New York, 1985

Bradlee, Benjamin C., *Conversations With Kennedy* (W.W. Norton & Company), New York, 1975

Brandon, Henry, *Special Relationships* (Macmillan), London, 1988

Burns, McGregor James, *Edward Kennedy and the Camelot Legacy* (W.W. Norton & Company), New York, 1976

Chellis, Marcia, *The Joan Kennedy Story* (Simon and Schuster), New York, 1985

Collier, Peter, and Horowitz, David, *The Kennedys: An American Drama* (Pan Books), London, 1984

Cross, Robin, *JFK: A Hidden Life* (Bloomsbury), London, 1992

Davis, John H., *The Kennedys: Dynasty and Disaster* (S.P.I. Books), New York, 1992

Exner, Judith, *My Story* (Grove Press), New York, 1977

Galbraith, John Kenneth, *Ambassador's Journal: A Personal Account of the Kennedy Years* (Signet), New York, 1970

Gardner, Ava, *Ava: My Story* (Bantam), New York, 1992

Garrison, Jim, *On the Trail of the Assassins* (Penguin Books), London, 1992

Giglio, James N., *The Presidency of John F. Kennedy* (University Press of Kansas), Lawrence, Kansas, 1991

Halberstam, David, *The Making of a Quagmire* (Ballantine Books), New York, 1965; *The Best and the Brightest* (Fawcett Crest), New York, 1972

Heymann, C. David, *A Woman Named Jackie* (Mandarin), London, 1990

Jellinek, George, *Callas: Portrait of a Prima Donna* (Panther), London, 1961

Karnow, Stanley, *Vietnam: A History* (Penguin), London, 1984

Kelley, Kitty, *Jackie Oh!* (Ballantine Books), New York, 1978

Kennedy, Robert F., *Thirteen Days: A Memoir of the Cuban Missile Crisis* (W.W. Norton & Company), New York, 1971

Kunhardt Jr, Philip B., *Life in Camelot: The Kennedy Years* (Little, Brown & Company,) Boston, 1988

Maclear, Michael, *Vietnam: The Ten Thousand Day War* (Thames/Methuen), London, 1981

Mailer, Norman, *The Presidential Papers* (Panther), London, 1964; *Marilyn; A Biography* (Coronet Books), London, 1974

Manchester, William, *The Death of a President* (Pan), London, 1967; *One Brief Shining Moment: Remembering Kennedy* (Little, Brown & Company), Boston, 1983

Marrs, Jim, *Crossfire: The Plot That Killed Kennedy* (Carroll & Graf), New York, 1989

Martin, Ralph G., *A Hero For Our Time: An Intimate Story of the Kennedy Years* (Fawcett Crest), New York, 1983

Miller, Arthur, *Timebends: A Life* (Methuen), London, 1987

Menendez, Albert J., *John F Kennedy: Catholic and Humanist* (Prometheus Books), Buffalo, 1971

Murray, Levin, and Repak, T.A., *Edward Kennedy: The Myth of Leadership* (Houghton Mifflin Company), Boston, 1980

Newfield, Jack, *Robert Kennedy: A Memoir* (Jonathan Cape), London, 1970

Newman, John M., *JFK and Vietnam* (Warner Books), New York, 1992

Noguchi, Thomas T., *Coroner To The Stars* (Corgi Books), London, 1983

Noonan, Peggy, *What I Saw at the Revolution: a Political Life in the Reagan Era* (Ivy books), New York, 1990

O'Donnell, Kenneth P., and Powers, David F., *Johnny, We Hardly Knew Ye* (Little, Brown & Company), Boston, 1972

Oglesby, Carl, *The JFK Assassination: The Facts and the Theories* (Signet), New York 1992

Reeves, Thomas C., *A Question of Character* (Arrow Bookws), London, 1991

Reston Jr, James *The Lone Star: The Life of John Connally* (Harper & Row), New York, 1989; *Report of the Warren Commission* (Bantam), New York, 1964

Rollyson Jr, Carl E., *Marilyn Monroe: A Life of the Actress* (New English Library), London, 1990

Schlesinger Jr, Arthur M., *The Cycles of American History* (Penguin Books), London, 1986; *A Thousand Days: John F. Kennedy in The White House* (Fawcett Premier), New York, 1965; *Robert Kennedy and His Times* (Futura Publications), London, 1978

Sciacca, Tony, *Who Killed Marilyn?* (Manor Books), New York, 1976

Sheehan, Neil, *A Bright Shining Lie* (Jonathan Cape), London, 1989

Shevey, Sandra, *The Marilyn Scandal: The True Story* (Arrow Books), London, 1987

Sidey, Hugh, *John F. Kennedy: Portrait of a President* (Penguin), London, 1964

Slatzer, Robert F., *The Marilyn Files* (S.P.I. Books), New York, 1992

Slevin, Jonathan, and Spagholo, Maureen, *Kennedys: The Next Generation* (St Martin's Paperbacks), New York, 1992

Sorensen, Theodore C., *Kennedy* (Hodder and Stoughton), London, 1965; *The Kennedy Legacy* (Macmillan), New York, 1969

Spoto, Donald, *Marilyn Monroe: The Biography* (Chatto & Windus), London, 1993

Stassinopoulos, Arianna, *Maria Callas* (Arrow Books), London, 1980

Steinem, Gloria, *Marilyn* (Penguin), London, 1987

Summers, Anthony, *The Kennedy Conspiracy* (Sphere Books), London, 1989

Tierney, Gene, *Self-Portrait* (Bantam), New York, 1978

Truman, Margaret, *Murder in Georgetown* (Fawcett Crest), New York, 1986

Vankin, Jonathan, *Conspiracies, Cover-Ups and Crimes: From JFK to the CIA Terrorist Connection* (Dell), New York, 1992

White, Theodore H., *The Making of the President 1960* (Jonathan Cape, London, 1964

Wills, Garry, *The Kennedys: A Shattered Illusion* (Orbis), London, 1983

Wofford, Harris, *Of Kennedys and Kings* (Farrar, Straus, Giroux), New York, 1980

Periodicals and Newspapers

The Washington Post

The New York Times

The Boston Globe

The Guardian

The Observer

The Sunday Times

The Cork Examiner

The Irish Times

The Irish Press

The Sunday Press

The Sunday Tribune

New Times

Hot Press

Mirabella

Vanity Fair

Time

Newsweek

Playboy

Ramparts

Rolling Stone

Documentation on the Cuban Missile Crisis is contained in files from the Department of the Taoiseach for 1962 – especially File No: S 17061/62 – in the National Archives in Dublin.